FOUR TEXTS ON SOCRATES

Plato and Aristophanes

FOUR TEXTS
ON SOCRATES

Plato's *Euthyphro, Apology,* and *Crito*
and Aristophanes' *Clouds*

Revised Edition

TRANSLATED WITH NOTES BY

Thomas G. West AND
Grace Starry West

INTRODUCTION BY
Thomas G. West

Cornell University Press

ITHACA AND LONDON

First published 1984 by Cornell University Press
Revised Edition first published 1998 by Cornell University Press
First printing, Cornell Paperbacks, 1998

Printed in the United States of America

Library of Congress Cataloging in Publication Data

Four texts on Socrates, revised edition.

   Bibliograpy: p.
   1. Socrates.   I. Plato.   II. West, Thomas G., 1945–   .   III. West, Grace
Starry, 1946–   .   IV. Aristophanes. Clouds. 1984.
B316.F68   1984   183'.2   84-7657
ISBN-13: 978-0-8014-8574-9
(pbk.: alk. paper)

Cornell University Press strives to use environmentally responsible suppliers and ma-terials to the fullest extent possible in the publishing of its books. Such materials in-clude vegetable-based, low-VOC inks and acid-free papers that are recycled, totally chlorine-free, or partly composed of nonwood fibers. For further information, visit our website at www.cornellpress.cornell.edu.

Paperback printing   10   9   8   7   6   5

Contents

Translators' Note

We have striven for the most accurate possible English rendition of the Greek. In spite of the wide gulf between modern English and ancient Greek, this collection offers reliable translations that can be studied with profit by Greekless readers. Currently available versions of these works are unnecessarily loose. In the case of the *Clouds*, particularly, most translators forgo precision in their concern for style and humor. Our versions may seem strange at first, but with greater familiarity the reader will appreciate the simplicity and vigor of the straightforward Greek diction.

A perfectly literal translation from the Greek is impossible. The Greek words have connotations whose resonances are rarely caught with lexicon equivalents, and many Greek idioms would be unintelligible if translated literally. Furthermore, Plato and Aristophanes often use traditional terms in novel ways, and their deliberate play with the meanings of such terms is integral to the meanings of their works. If the translator tries to capture the particular shade of meaning intended on each occasion a given word appears, the reader remains ignorant that the word recurs at all. But if the word is rendered by a consistent English expression, distortions and awkwardness inevitably mar the translation. Our inelegant and incomplete solution has been to use, wherever possible, consistent translations of important words and phrases supplemented by explanatory notes.

The four works were translated from John Burnet's edition of *Plato's Euthyphro, Apology of Socrates, and Crito* and K. J. Dover's edition of Aristophanes' *Clouds* by permission of Oxford University Press. The translation of the *Apology of Socrates* was previously published; the present version incorporates a number of mostly minor changes. Occasionally we have departed from Burnet's and Dover's

texts in favor of the original manuscript reading or a manuscript different from the one followed by them. In the notes to the translations, we have mentioned these departures when they make a difference in the interpretation.

The notes also explain translations that may not be immediately clear and identify persons and events referred to in the texts. These notes often rely on the editions of other scholars, notably Burnet and Dover.

We have used paragraph divisions and quotation marks in the translations. There were no such divisions or devices in the original Greek. Long sentences have sometimes been broken up for the sake of clarity.

We wish to thank the Earhart Foundation for the generous grants that enabled us to undertake this project.

Additional Note, Revised Edition

In this 1998 edition, we have updated the Bibliography to include writings published since 1984. We thank John Grant for his help in tracking down the recent secondary literature.

Pages 9 to 12 of the Introduction were rewritten for the 1998 printing.

We would like to take this occasion to describe the division of labor between the authors.

Introduction and other front matter: Written by TGW.

Euthyphro and *Crito*: TGW and GSW each did a draft translation; they then combined their efforts by talking through their differences.

Apology of Socrates: Translated by TGW, in consultation with GSW.

Clouds: GSW prepared the first draft of the translation; TGW worked from there to produce the final version.

The footnotes to the *Apology* were written by TGW; the rest by TGW and GSW.

TGW selected the items in the Bibliography and wrote the comments.

THOMAS G. WEST
GRACE STARRY WEST

Irving, Texas

Introduction

This collection contains four well-known works that present the thought and way of life of Socrates as they come to sight in confrontation with his political community.

The Platonic dialogue *Euthyphro* takes place just before Socrates' trial on a charge of impiety and corrupting the young. The theme of the *Euthyphro* is a question—"What is piety?"—that is crucial to understanding the charge against him.

In the *Apology of Socrates*, we are given Plato's version of Socrates' defense speech at that trial.

The *Crito* shows us Socrates, now in prison awaiting the death penalty, persuading his oldest friend that it is better for him to stay in Athens and die, rather than to escape to another country and live in exile.

Aristophanes' *Clouds* puts forward in comic form a profound critique of Socrates by a leading poet of the day—a critique that appears to lend support to the much later prosecution presented in Plato's *Apology*. Socrates mentions the play in his defense speech. It is a leading cause, he says, of the prejudice against him that led to his trial.

To understand these seemingly simple but actually very rich writings, there is no substitute for close study and meditation on the texts themselves. This Introduction and the works in the Selected Bibliography at the end of this book may be consulted as aids to that study.

The Modern Rejection of Reason

The modern image of Socrates on trial is of a defiant philosopher standing alone against his city and daring to repudiate its narrow-minded superstitions. Socrates is often hailed as a forerunner of modern liberalism, but he did not assert against Athens a right to individual self-expression. He did not believe in "the right to define one's own concept of existence, of meaning, of the universe, and of the mystery of human life."[1]

[1]U.S. Supreme Court, opinion by Justices O'Connor, Kennedy, and Souter, *Planned Parenthood v. Casey*, 112 S. Ct. 2791 (1992), 2807.

Instead, Socrates insisted that life, both public and private, ought to be guided by knowledge of what is right. But knowledge is not the same as opinion. Socrates refused to defer to opinions for which no reasoned account could be given. It did not matter whether those opinions were grounded in venerable tradition, poetic inspiration, or sincere personal convictions about "one's own concept of existence." Socrates' standard was the truth about right and wrong. He did not think that truth was easy to come by. He sometimes wondered if it could be discovered at all. But he never gave up trying. He never stopped "conversing and examining both myself and others" on the topic of human excellence or virtue (*Apology* 38a).

In our time, the idea that reason can discover permanent truths about right and wrong is ridiculed or denounced by many academic elites. Richard Rorty, for example, a Stanford philosophy professor, argues that "there is nothing deep down inside us except what we have put there ourselves, . . . no rigorous argumentation that is not obedience to our own conventions."[2] In other words, to use a Socratic metaphor from Plato's *Republic*, there is no possibility of escape from the cave, of transcending the limits of our own time and its prejudices.

A group of prominent humanities professors has echoed Rorty in these words: "All thought inevitably derives from particular standpoints, perspectives, and interests." Scholars should, therefore, abandon the "ideal of objectivity and disinterest" that has been the aspiration of Western science and philosophy at least since Socrates. These professors reject out of hand the Socratic attempt to discover the truth about how we should live.[3]

There are some who half-heartedly try to deny the relativism that obviously flows from these claims. Gordon Wood, a highly reputed historian, insists that he too is "looking for truth—truth that may not be eternal, but that at least cuts across a decade or two or across several cultures at the same time." Does Wood mean that if it is wrong to commit murder today, that in "a decade or two" it might be quite all right? That is exactly what Richard Rorty, quoting the existentialist Jean-Paul Sartre, asserts: If Hitler had won World War II, it would have established "fascism [as] the truth of man, and so much the worse for us."[4]

One might wonder why any of this matters. Perhaps it is all empty academic talk, and life will go on fine with or without it. Unfortunately, what people believe sooner or later affects how they act. If people become convinced by these relativistic doctrines, they will eventually realize that nothing but blind habit holds them back from indulgence in the most predatory passions. We already see such passions celebrated in rap music

[2]Rorty, "The Fate of Philosophy," *The New Republic*, October 18, 1982, quoted in Sanford Levinson, *Constitutional Faith* (Princeton: Princeton University Press, 1988), p. 176.
[3]"Speaking for the Humanities," a report of the American Council of Learned Societies, *The Chronicle of Higher Education*, January 11, 1989, p. A14.
[4]Gordon S. Wood, "The Fundamentalists and the Constitution," *New York Review*, February 18, 1988, p. 34. Rorty, quoted in Levinson, p. 176.

and the nastier varieties of rock. We see a growing coarseness in the relations between men and women. At the same time, relativism is taught ever more routinely in high schools and universities. As economist John Maynard Keynes once wrote, "the ideas of economists and political philosophers, both when they are right and when they are wrong, are more powerful than is commonly understood. Indeed, the world is ruled by little else."[5]

At the beginning of the twenty-first century, we can look back on the twentieth as a time of great achievement and invention—but also a time of tremendous brutality and moral disarray. The most murderous tyrannies of world history thrived in Hitler's Germany, in Stalin's Soviet Union, and in Mao's China. The men who ruled these three empires all rejected the idea of permanent moral truth—Stalin and Mao because they embraced Marx's historical dialectic, Hitler because he turned to the triumph of the will over reason. These tyrannies are gone for now, but the abandonment of reason that helped to bring them about is now everywhere.

There is an ominous tribalism growing throughout the Western world. There are dark hints from people of one ethnic group or another that race is what matters, not our common humanity or citizenship. Principles like "all men are created equal," once regarded as self-evident to every rational person who understands what it means to be human, are now often dismissed as the quaint ideology of eighteenth-century America.

The Socratic Alternative

In light of the obvious dangers spawned by the modern rejection of reason, it is worth reexamining the case for reason. Socrates was the first in a long Western tradition of philosophic rationalists. He looked to reason as a guide to life. He relentlessly refused to accept answers untested in conversation and debate.

In the *Apology*, Socrates tells us that when he examined the opinions of the Athenians, he discovered that they did not know what they presumed to know. He pointed out their errors. They were annoyed. To his fellow citizens, he seemed to be questioning the authority of the city's gods and its laws. He was, of course. But Socrates also appeared to be unable to provide the Athenians with a satisfactory alternative account of the ends of human life. He insisted that he was as ignorant as they in regard to "the greatest things" (*Apology* 22d).

By undercutting the laws and the tradition, he seemed to be justifying the self-indulgent pursuit of pleasure—the argument of Unjust Speech in Aristophanes' *Clouds*. From this point of view, Socrates' quarrel with the city and its traditions, carried on in daily conversations and listened to by

[5]*General Theory of Employment, Interest, and Money* (1935; repr. New York: Harcourt, Brace, 1965), p. 383.

many impressionable young men, was bound to appear irresponsible. This difficulty, presented in comic form in the *Clouds*, is a leading part of Aristophanes' case against Socrates.

But the Socrates of Plato's dialogues does not oppose Athens without offering a substitute for its defective opinions and institutions. Knowledge of ignorance is not ignorance. Socrates knows that he does not know, and, we may add, he knows *what* he does not know, namely, "the greatest things."

Therefore, he knows enough to establish for himself a way of life devoted to asking and thinking about those most important matters. He calls that way of life "philosophy." Tentatively, but for practical purposes finally, virtue is defined as the philosophic life. The conditions for that life include qualities of soul and political institutions conducive to supporting the philosophic life. This is the Socratic answer.

Thus Socrates' thought is characterized by an uncompromising dedication to knowledge, but also by a moderation that stems from his awareness of his own ignorance. Socrates' achievement, which deserves our careful consideration, was to combine rigor with skepticism without giving in to the temptation of absolutism on the one extreme or relativism on the other.

This Socratic insight, applied to our own time, may offer a basis for defending a healthy constitutionalism—one that secures political liberty on the basis of the consent of the governed, without hesitating to check the licentious conduct that would destroy freedom as well as the philosophic way of life. Freedom secures the philosopher's ability to inquire. Democracy and limited government are a reasonable response to the boastfulness of those who claim on the basis of expertise that they alone should rule—the same boastfulness exposed by Socrates when he examined the intellectuals and politicians of his day. And finally, morality secures the conditions of freedom by teaching citizens to stand up against those who would oppress them, to restrain their destructive passions, and to respect each other's rights.[6]

Plato's *Euthyphro*

This dialogue, like the *Crito*, portrays a private conversation between Socrates and an acquaintance, in this case Euthyphro. They meet in the marketplace at a government building where each has court business. Each tells the other about his case: Socrates is being prosecuted for impiety, while Euthyphro is prosecuting his own father for an alleged murder that allegedly involves impiety. Then Socrates asks the self-confident Euthyphro to teach him what "the

---

[6]For a fuller account, see Thomas G. West, *Vindicating the Founders: Race, Sex, Class, and Justice in the Origins of America* (Lanham, Md.: Rowman & Littlefield, 1997), chs. 4 and 7.

pious" is. Euthyphro's several attempts to do so are thwarted by Socrates' refutations, and Euthyphro finally puts an end to the discussion by claiming business elsewhere.

At the beginning of the dialogue Euthyphro looks upon Socrates as a kindred spirit. Both men make unusual claims to close association with the divine—Socrates because of the daimonic voice which comes to him on occasion (*Euthyphro* 3b, *Apology* 31c–d), Euthyphro because of his claim to possess intimate knowledge of divine things, including prophetic knowledge of the future. Both men are at odds with the Athenian multitude, although with this difference: Euthyphro's pretensions arouse laughter, while Socrates' teaching arouses anger, so much so that Meletus in all seriousness is prosecuting him for impiety.

But it quickly becomes clear that Socrates and Euthyphro are not very similar at all. Euthyphro takes his bearings from the stories told by poets and others about Zeus and the gods, while Socrates does not accept the truth of those stories (6a). So when Euthyphro is asked what the pious is, his first answer is prosecuting wrongdoers, and his proof is the story that Zeus bound his father Kronos. Just as Zeus attacked Kronos, so Euthyphro is prosecuting his own father for murder. In other words, we may infer, piety as Euthyphro understands it is imitating the gods.

Euthyphro is perhaps not quite aware of this implication, for when Socrates presses him for a formal definition of the pious, he responds that it is "what is dear to the gods." Socrates first points out that if the traditional stories are true and the gods quarrel about justice among themselves, then what some gods love, others must hate. Euthyphro then amends his definition, saying that the pious is what *all* the gods love. Socrates gets Euthyphro to agree that a loved thing is loved because something loves it. Therefore, "Not because [the thing loved] is something loved, is it loved by those by whom it is loved, but because it is loved, it is something loved" (10c). So the fact that the gods love something does not define it as pious, but only as loved.

This abstruse argument evidently confuses Euthyphro, as it also confuses readers of the *Euthyphro*. The validity of Socrates' refutation has been successfully challenged on logical grounds. But the substantial point behind Socrates' dry logic-chopping seems to be that the gods' love or will must be directed by that which really is good, noble, and just, or else the meaning of human life must be dependent on the arbitrary will of mysterious beings who may not even be friendly to men, and—given the multitude of willful authorities (the many gods)—the life of men and gods alike must be a tale of ignorant armies clashing by night on a darkling plain. Further, if the gods *are* guided by knowledge and do not give merely willful commandments, the guidance provided to men by divine law must be superfluous for one who is wise enough to discover for himself the truth of the good, noble, and just. The wise man has no need of gods. (The question of whether God is to be understood primarily as willful or reasonable became a central concern of the later Western theological tradition. See, for example, Thomas Aquinas' *Summa Theologiae* and Maimonides' *Guide of the Perplexed*.)

Finally, in response to a suggestion of Socrates, Euthyphro proposes that the pious is the "tendance of gods," which he explains as skillful service to the gods. In return for prayer and sacrifice, he says, the gods preserve families and cities. Socrates interprets this piety as "a certain art of commerce" which knows how to acquire things from the gods by knowing what to give them. However, Euthyphro denies that the gods have any need for the gifts that men can provide, although they do *love* the honors that men pay them. Socrates then accuses Euthyphro of returning to his earlier contention, already refuted, that the pious is what the gods love, and Euthyphro breaks off the conversation.

At the beginning of the dialogue Euthyphro came to sight as a likeness (or caricature) of Socrates: his single-minded pursuit of piety even at the expense of his own father and his extravagant claim to know more than all other men remind one of some of Socrates' claims in the *Apology of Socrates*. Both men claim to transcend common opinion. But by the end we see that Euthyphro has more in common with the traditional piety of Socrates' accuser Meletus than with Socrates himself. Euthyphro may be viewed as a buffo exaggeration, with a bit of the fanatic in him, of the law-abiding, pious citizen. Why, we may wonder, did Plato choose such a fool as Euthyphro for Socrates' interlocutor in *the* dialogue on piety? Perhaps the Euthyphro type embodies more clearly than the decent citizen an extreme tendency of civic piety, a tendency which is blunted or concealed in most men by a deference to other generally accepted opinions and practices. Like the good citizen, Euthyphro accepts the authority of the stories told by the poets and depicted by the painters in temples (6b), but unlike most people, he abstracts his piety from the proper objects of its care. Although Euthyphro himself is somehow aware (when prodded by Socrates) that the purpose of piety is to "preserve private families as well as the communities of cities" (14b), he forgets that end in his straight-minded concern for the pious. He is attacking his own father.

Understandably, Euthyphro's family is entirely opposed to this prosecution. They believe it to be impious (4d–e). In the person of Euthyphro we see the foolishness and danger of a simple piety which, forgetting its roots in the traditions handed down by family and city, assumes a position of imperious independence from which it presumes to contend against the family.

It should be noted that one part of the action of the dialogue consists of Socrates' attempt to tame Euthyphro. He moves Euthyphro from the outlandish and arrogant view that piety is imitation of God to the safely conventional view that piety is praying and sacrificing for the sake of preserving one's family and city. Socrates perhaps also curbs Euthyphro's ardent wish to prosecute his father in a very dubious case by making Euthyphro see how difficult it will be for him to convince a jury of his father's guilt (see 9b, for example). One might argue that Socrates displays his own piety by leading back to the fold a lost sheep who strayed because he too zealously followed "Zeus" or the publicly declared principle of the herd. Yet the principle by which Socrates' piety—if that is what it is—is governed is not "Zeus" or traditional customs, but reason. Socrates' view of piety is in its external manifestation more conservative, but in its internal thought more radical, than is Euthyphro's convention-based extremism.

The *Euthyphro* appears to end without any clarity about the pious, yet the dialogue allows us glimpses of Socrates' own view. Above all Socrates affirms the primacy of reasonable judgment of what is right against any merely willful or arbitrary authority. This means that Socrates implicitly agrees with Euthyphro's denial of the most ordinary meaning of piety: deference to one's father, or, more generally stated, to the ancestral. (Socrates denigrates the wisdom of his own ancestor Daedalus [11c].) Yet although he doubts the traditional stories, Socrates asserts that all good things come from the gods (15a; compare the account of the gods at the end of *Republic* Book II). Furthermore, he argues that the pious is part of the just (12d). He may mean that the terms of man's obligations to gods flow from a consideration of the altogether human virtue of justice, which, according to Socrates in the *Republic*, is concerned with the right order of the political community and of the human soul. The example of Euthyphro himself shows why political or philosophic control of religious enthusiasm is necessary: ungoverned piety may easily turn into "pious cruelty," to use Machiavelli's expression (*Prince*, ch. 21). The piety of the citizen is doubtless politically preferable to Euthyphro's holy passion, even if such civic piety is indistinguishable from a calculating commercial transaction between men and gods.

Different from both is the "service to the god" of which Socrates speaks in the *Apology of Socrates* (29c–30a): the philosophic way of life.[4]

Plato's *Apology of Socrates*

Plato regarded the trial and death of his teacher Socrates as the turning point in his life (*Seventh Letter*). In Socrates' fate Plato discovered the heart of the problem of man and politics. He portrayed that problem succinctly and unforgettably in the *Apology* ("Defense Speech") *of Socrates*.

Life's most urgent question is "How should I live?" It is answered, at least in part, by the answer to another question, "What are the highest beings?" For in both private and public life, men are guided by what they most look up to or respect. The life of a political community is grounded in shared convictions about what truly matters. The Athenians regard the gods of the city as the highest beings, and believe that one should live by obeying the laws sanctioned by the gods.

Socrates, however, cannot accept the city's answers to these questions, for he has examined conventional opinion and found it incoherent or otherwise wanting. And he knows that he himself does not possess adequate knowledge about the most important things. Socratic skepticism challenges civic dogmatism. In light of Socrates' lifelong search for knowledge about these highest questions, the city's supposed certitudes come to sight as obstacles standing in the way of genuine education. Convictions that citizens hold to be final are merely beginning points for Socratic inquiry. (Consider Socrates' conversation with Cephalus about justice at the beginning of the *Republic*.) On first reading, the *Apology of Socrates* appears not merely to endorse but to celebrate this Socratic way of life. We see the noble seeker of truth beset by the envious, narrow-minded ignorance of his fellow citizens. Yet a closer reading belies that first impression, at least in part.

The *Apology* consists of three speeches, of which the first and longest is Socrates' formal defense before the jury. The first speech has five parts:

1. Preface on his manner of speech
2. Response to charge of the "first accusers"

[4]For this account of the *Euthyphro* I am indebted to an unpublished lecture by Leo Strauss on the dialogue.

1. *Preface (17a–18a)*. Socrates begins by contrasting his own disorderly, unattractive, but truthful speech with his accusers' beautiful, well-ordered, persuasive, but false speech. Socrates seems to suggest that truthful speech cannot be persuasive speech, or, in other words, that what is true can never be shared by many men because it cannot be presented convincingly to them. Socrates implies that he is doomed from the start because of this unbridgeable gulf between the philosopher and his community—between the one who knows the truth and the many who follow beautiful and persuasive falsehoods. This is the human predicament of which the trial is an exemplary instance: the truth-telling philosopher will inevitably be hated by the many, while the ignorant many will inevitably be misled by untrue imaginings.

2. *Response to the "first accusers" (18a–24b)*. This predicament is elaborated in the body of the speech. First Socrates recalls the old slanders told about him, now widely believed, according to which Socrates is a busybody who investigates the things in the heavens and under the earth, who makes the weaker argument the stronger, and who teaches others these same things. This "first charge" against him has long been spread about, he says, especially by "the comedy of Aristophanes" (he means the *Clouds*). Socrates simply denies that he has any share in such celestial or subterranean inquiry (we would call it physics and astronomy). He does not deny that he pursued such studies when he was younger; on the day of his death he confesses that he did (*Phaedo* 99). (He admits later in his speech that he is familiar with the astronomical theories in the books of the philosopher Anaxagoras.) Socrates notes that people who engage in such inquiry are reputed to be atheists. (Aristophanes shows why in the *Clouds*. The investigation of thunder and lightning, for example, stems from the doubt that Zeus causes them. Nature, the permanent and necessary order of things accessible to reason, replaces the willful and mysterious Zeus [*Clouds* 365–411].) As to the rest of the "first charge," Socrates is silent except to deny that he teaches for pay. These denials are obviously not convincing to the jury.

Why, then, if Socrates is innocent, do people say these things about him? Socrates answers this objection by telling a story about the Delphic oracle, a story that seems to be new to the jury. In answer to a question put by Socrates' companion Chaerephon (who is Socrates' chief associate in the *Clouds*), the oracle once declared that no one was wiser than Socrates. At first Socrates thought it likely that the oracle was wrong, so he began to converse with those reputed to be wise in order to gather evidence to refute the oracle. He examined the politicians, poets, and artisans and found that they were almost completely ignorant (except for the artisans, who at least knew well their own areas of expertise), and that all thought they knew things, especially "the greatest things," but in fact they did not know them. Since Socrates was at least aware of his own ignorance, he ranked himself above them in wisdom. Socrates thus moved from being almost in opposition to the god's oracle to being its firm supporter. One should note, however, that Socrates' support of the city's god in this instance is based entirely on his reasoned testing of his oracle. Socrates accepts "revelation" not on divine authority and not because it is supported by the laws but only insofar as it passes the test of reason.

As a result of his frequent and embarrassing refutations of Athenians who make any claim to wisdom, Socrates has incurred hatred and envy. Further, the youth who follow him also imitate him, and they make their elders look foolish by showing up their ignorance. In this way, says Socrates, arose the charge of corrupting the young, to which was added the impiety charge, ready at hand against all who philosophize.

The oracle story implies that Socrates already had a reputation for wisdom—even if only among Chaerephon and other admirers—before he began his examinations of the opinions of his fellow Athenians. The oracle therefore represents a turning point in Socrates' life, from one kind of inquiry to another—perhaps away from his youthful astronomical and physical studies, certainly toward the distinctively Socratic concern with moral and political opinions. This turn to the examination of opinions brought Socrates into conflict with the city as such, for his doubt of the worth of generally accepted opinions was also a challenge to the most authoritative opinions, those which concern the city's gods and the city's laws ("laws" in the broad sense of the Greek term *nomoi*, including customs and traditions). Socrates made thematic the political and moral questions that were to some extent implicit, as Aristophanes' *Clouds* suggests, in his investigations of nature. By virtue of this "turn," philosophy became political.

Socrates' challenge was rightly perceived by the fathers of his young followers as an attack on their paternal and political authority. This attack touched not merely their vanity—that was painful enough—but their most deeply cherished convictions about the meaning and conduct of human life. By what right did this ugly old man, this pied piper and "wise guy," presume to question those beliefs on which the family and the city depended—indeed, which constituted their very reason for being?

3. *Response to the present accusers (24b–28b)*. Socrates now responds to the charge of the present accusers, the charge for which he is on trial. He conducts his defense here by showing that Meletus, his accuser, cannot offer a consistent account of the charge against him; Socrates does not however establish his own innocence. To the charge of corrupting the young, he gives two answers. First, he elicits from Meletus the assertion that the laws, or rather the multitude of citizens who know the laws, are the best educators of the young, while Socrates alone corrupts them. Socrates responds that one or few are more likely than many to be expert educators, just as few are competent in the art of horsemanship. (Socrates does not claim to be more of an expert on education than the laws or even than the many. If he is not, then his argument proves nothing about his own innocence.) Second, Socrates argues that he could not intentionally corrupt, that is, harm the young, because he is well aware that harming someone is likely to lead to harm in retaliation. And if he harms the young unintentionally, out of ignorance, then he deserves instruction, not punishment. (Here too Socrates' argument is weak. Someone harmed will seek revenge only if he is aware that he is harmed; if he is deceived into thinking that moral corruption is not so much harmful as liberating, then there will be no danger to the corrupter.)

Socrates' response to the impiety charge is no more convincing: it amounts simply to a proof that Meletus contradicts himself (not even that the charge contradicts itself!). Socrates is completely silent about whether he believes in any gods at all, let alone the gods of the city. Yet, as he admits, this is the heart of Meletus' charge against him (26b).

In view of the weakness of this defense, and considering the admissions Socrates has already made in the defense against the "first accusers," it is safe to say that he is guilty of the formal charges against him. He does not believe in the gods in which the city believes, for he knows that he does not know the truth about them. He corrupts the young (in the legal sense of "corruption"), for he teaches them to disbelieve in the authority of gods and laws by insisting that firm knowledge replace mere opinion about them.

4. *Digression on his way of life (28b–34b)*. But Socrates' defense does not end here. He continues to speak at considerable length, opening up the whole question of his way of life. This apparent digression constitutes the heart of his defense, for if Socrates' way of life is good,

then the city's understanding of impiety and corruption must be judged deficient. This part of his speech is divided into two parts, each introduced by anticipating an objection that might be raised against Socrates' conduct. The first part shows Socrates in his role as public man, the savior of Athens; the second explains why Socrates remains a private man who stays out of politics.

In the *first part* (28b–31c), Socrates compares himself to Achilles, the warrior hero of Homer's *Iliad*. Like Achilles, Socrates defies death on behalf of what is right and just. But here the resemblance ends. In fact Socrates implicitly proposes himself as a *successor* of the Homeric hero. The "real man" must give way to the genuine human being. Socrates' quiet conversations and exhortations to care for prudence, truth, and the good of the soul replace Achilles' bloody deeds of war. By promoting himself as a new Achilles, Socrates challenges the young men's attachment to a tradition that endorses the life of manly self-assertion and political ambition (see Callicles in Plato's *Gorgias*). But Socrates fails in this attempt to legislate, so to speak, a new way of life for Athens by teaching the jurors to become admirers of Socrates and philosophy. He is no Homer, whose poetry was said to have taught all Greece its gods and manner of life. When the Athenian jury shouts out its protest against Socrates' claims, he implicitly concedes his defeat by revising the heroic comparison of himself to the demigod Achilles: now he is a mere subhuman gadfly, an irritating pest, who bites the horse which is Athens, serving it ceaselessly by waking it up from its lethargic slumber.

In the *second part* of his account of his way of life (31c–34b), Socrates says that he stays out of politics because of the warning of a daimonic voice which has come to him from childhood on. He obeys this voice because he has always found it to be correct in its warnings. (Again, "divine revelation" must meet the test of reason. However, the *daimonion* is probably no revelation but rather the name Socrates assigns to the promptings of his heroic-erotic nature, ever situated, like a daimon, between the divine perfection it seeks and the all-too-human self-complacency it escapes. See West, *Plato's Apology of Socrates*, pp. 151–155, 181–187.) He says he would long ago have been killed if he had actively participated in political life, since those who publicly fight for justice always perish. Socrates recalls the trouble he got into by opposing unjust measures of the democracy and later of the Thirty. As for his supposed students, he claims he never taught anyone anything, and he is willing to converse openly with everyone, without pay. Such conversation is "not unpleasant," especially when it exposes the pretentious ignorance of those who claim to be wise.

5. *Conclusion on his nobility and justice (34b–35d).* Socrates concludes his defense by refusing to appeal for pity. He will not bring his family into court, weeping and lamenting, as others do. He calls this custom womanly and unjust. He implies that his own standards of justice and manly nobility are superior to those of Athenian custom. Thus he closes by denigrating the generally accepted opinions of the many, as he has done throughout his speech. The jury, composed of members of "the many" in question, votes him guilty.

We may summarize Socrates' strategy in the latter part of his defense speech as follows. Turning away from the formal charge against him, which he cannot escape, Socrates proposes a novel standard of justice by setting himself up as the exemplar of civic excellence. He presents his own philosophic care for virtue as superior to that of the traditional laws, for the laws are informed by a defective, "Achillean" conception of human excellence. What is admittedly corruption of the young by the standard of the prevailing laws, now comes to sight as education or at least as an ingredient of education (since Socrates professes not to *know* what virtue is). In addition to this new approach to education, Socrates introduces a new view of the divine. Obedience to the god turns out to require a life of philosophy. Socrates himself as gadfly is a "gift of the god" to the city, and his *daimonion*, his daimonic voice, like a private Delphic oracle, elevates him to a stature greater than human. Socrates, then, redefines education and piety so as to render himself innocent of corruption and impiety. But if Socrates is to be held innocent in deed, he must succeed in "refounding" Athens by persuading the jury to accept the Socratic "legislation." The verdict of "guilty" testifies to the failure of Socrates' political project. And since that project was intended only half seriously, Socrates' fall is not the tragedy it appears to be, but rather something more like a farcical satyr-drama.

Second speech: the counterproposal (35e–38b). After announcement of the verdict, Socrates' accuser Meletus proposes the death penalty. Socrates must offer a counterproposal, and the jury will then vote for one or the other of the two proposed penalties. Socrates first proposes that he be given free meals for life in the Prytaneum, the ancient and sacred hearth of the city. This privilege is reserved for Olympic victors, outstanding generals and other public benefactors, and representatives of families whose ancestors had performed great deeds for the city. Socrates claims to be such a benefactor because he makes the city not to seem but to *be* happy. Socrates' friends, however, call on him to withdraw this proposal, and they offer to be guarantors of a fine. Socrates proposes this fine, but the jury, perhaps angered by the blithe arrogance of his first counterproposal, votes for the death penalty.

Socrates' proposal that he be publicly honored with a seat at the city's hearth is the appropriate culmination of the extravagant claims of his first speech. In light of his earlier failure to persuade the jury of his innocence, that proposal cannot but appear hubristic and boastful. The effrontery of this second speech is heightened by the fact that Socrates here drops his claim to divine authority for his way of life. The *daimonion* is not even mentioned. In the second speech frank *logos* supersedes the mythic pretensions of the first speech. Socrates now openly argues on a basis that only reasonable men can understand: he deserves honor because he makes the city happy. But he knows well that if he maintains that "it is a very great good for a human being to make speeches every day about virtue," the Athenians will not be persuaded by him at all (38a). By this remark Socrates indicates that he knows the limits of reason even while he is making the very speech wherein he asserts most bluntly his right to public honor because of his superior rational understanding of human life. Although he is aware that it is unreasonable to expect reason to be honored by the city, he demands it none the less. Thus he deliberately brings on his condemnation to death.

Third speech: parting words to the jury (38c–42a). In his third speech, delivered before he is taken away to prison to await execution, Socrates speaks first to those who voted to condemn him. He predicts that his followers, who are much harsher than himself, will avenge his death by taxing the Athenians with Socratic reproaches even more than he did while alive. (Socrates' prediction was borne out by the success of Plato's and Xenophon's defenses of their teacher. There are also stories from antiquity, although not well attested, that the Athenians soon regretted their condemnation of Socrates and visited harsh treatment on his accusers.) Then, to those who voted to acquit him, Socrates says he will tell stories or "myths" (39e). As a sign that the trial's outcome is nothing bad, he mentions that the *daimonion* did not oppose him as he spoke. He then presents two arguments that death is good. First, it is good because it is like sleep. (But we remember that Socrates earlier compared himself to a gadfly who wakes up the horse that is Athens by his irritating stings. Thought and sleep are enemies.) Second, if death does lead to an afterlife, as people say, Socrates will simply continue the way of life he has led on earth, conversing with and questioning those whom he meets there, especially those with great reputations. (Socrates indicates his reservations about this prospect by peopling his Hades with poets and figures familiar to the Athenians primarily from poetry. He also opens and closes his account of Hades with the expression "if the things that are said are true." We may wonder whether in Socrates' mind such an afterlife exists only in the realm of poetic fiction.)

Socrates takes leave of his acquitters by exhorting them to believe that the gods always take care of good men. Socrates does not say whether *he* believes this. As for himself, he says that it is *now* best for him to be released from troubles. This remark implies that Socrates' defense, which in a certain light appears to be a choice for death, was not governed by the sort of abstract considerations about the nature of death which he just rehearsed, but rather by weighing the particulars of the situation he was facing. Perhaps, as Xenophon suggests (*Apology of Socrates to the Jury* 5–9), he chose to escape the burdens of incipient old age. More likely, Socrates sought to demonstrate through the event of his trial and death the truth of man's relation to the city, and to this end he seized the occasion of Meletus' indictment of himself when he was an old man. (Apparently the trial could have been avoided entirely: *Crito* 45e.)

On first reading, the *Apology of Socrates* appears to present a critique of political life from the point of view of philosophy. The citizens and their politicians are necessarily boasters, for they claim to know things about which they hold only opinions, not knowledge. But Socrates and Plato also allow us to see philosophy from the city's standpoint. Socrates appears to disrupt prevailing opinion without providing a satisfactorily sound opinion to replace it. Exhorting the citizens to embrace virtue is not enough, for Socrates denies that the generally accepted understanding of virtue is adequate. His ironic solution—that he replace Achilles and Homer as the hero and poet of a new moral dispensation—instead turns out to be a profound posing of the problem.

As Plato portrays it, Socrates' defense speech was a failure, but a deliberate failure. Plato's published *Apology of Socrates* turns that failure into enduring success. Ever since, Socrates has served as the model of the nobility and justice of philosophy. The rhetorical achievement of Plato may lead one to doubt Socrates' apparent assertion that there is a necessary opposition between truth and persuasion, justice and practical politics, reason and beauty. Plato's statesmanlike writing on behalf of Socrates undoubtedly went far to legitimate the philosophic life within the Greek cities and later throughout the West. Philosophy was now tolerated. In this respect Plato attained the poetic and political eminence to which Socrates aspired, if only playfully, in his defense speech. Still, the example of Plato's satyr-hero never allows us to forget that any reconciliation between the city and man is always bought at the price of clarity about the divergence between man's highest longings and the necessities of political life.[5]

Plato's *Crito*

At the very center of the *Apology* Socrates proclaims that he will never stop philosophizing, no matter what the Athenians might order him to do. The *Crito* culminates in Socrates' apparent total submission to the laws of Athens. We seem, then, to be facing a massive contradiction between a Socrates who in the name of philosophy defies Athens and its laws in the former dialogue and a Socrates who restores the laws' authority in the latter.

In large measure the differences between the two dialogues may be attributed to the differences between their audiences and circumstances. To see why this is so, let us briefly review the action of the *Crito*.

The *Crito* portrays a private conversation between two old friends in the dark interior of the prison where Socrates is being held until his execution. (In its extreme privacy the *Crito* stands at one pole of the cosmos of Platonic dialogues; at the other extreme is the *Apology of Socrates*, a speech delivered in broad daylight before a large audience.) Crito tries to persuade Socrates to escape and go into exile. Everything has been arranged; all that is needed is Socrates' agreement to proceed. Crito has not been moved at all by the noble rhetoric of Socrates' defense speech. In fact, he is ashamed of Socrates' conduct at his trial, which he regards as unmanly (45e). Crito even accuses him of injustice and cowardice on the ground that Socrates is not a courageous defender of his own (himself, his family, his companions) (45c–46a). Crito's is precisely the perspective of the city—of the many—that Socrates attacked in the *Apology* and will attack again here. (It is noteworthy that Crito, like the lethargic Athenians of whom he is one, is a great admirer of the pleasures of sleep. Cf. *Apology* 31a with *Crito* 43b.)

[5]This account of the *Apology of Socrates* is based on West, *Plato's Apology of Socrates*.

Socrates responds by trying to persuade Crito that it is preferable for him to obey the laws and suffer the death penalty. To persuade Crito, Socrates must speak on Crito's level. Socrates cannot repeat the appeal to philosophy and the good of the soul that he used in his defense speech, for Crito did not respect that speech. (The words "philosophy" and "soul" do not occur at all in the *Crito* or *Euthyphro*; in neither dialogue does the perspective rise to the level of the *Apology of Socrates*.) Evidently Crito particularly respects the opinion of the many (44b–d). He is preoccupied with the harm that his own reputation will suffer among the many if he fails to rescue Socrates.

So Socrates uses the laws of Athens as a lever against that opinion of the many which guides Crito, the opinion that calls for loyalty to and defense of one's own. The many, and Crito along with them, respect the laws above all else, at least whenever the full majesty and power of the laws are vividly present to their imaginations. The god-like "epiphany" of the laws conjured up by Socrates may be explained as Socrates' attempt to overwhelm Crito's care for his own (for his companion Socrates and his own reputation) by means of an awe-inspiring vision of the laws as the supreme authority on earth. Socrates thereby reconciles Crito, the good citizen who admires him, to Socrates' execution and at the same time to the city that condemned him.

Our suggestion that Socrates appeals to the laws in order to persuade Crito raises the question of whether Socrates believes his own appeal. This question is all the more pressing in light of the seeming conflict between the *Apology of Socrates* and the *Crito* regarding the authority of the laws. Would Socrates lie to Crito? It is surely safer to assume that Socrates always tells the truth. In any event we must take a close look at what he says.

Socrates' response to Crito's plea for him to escape falls into two distinct parts. First occurs a dialogue between Socrates and Crito in which Socrates elicits Crito's acceptance of certain principles of conduct (46b–50a). Then Socrates presents a long speech such as the laws of Athens might deliver if they were to appear before them and address them (50a–54d).

This latter rhetorical set piece, in which the laws allow scarcely any opportunity for response, and in which they assert their authority in a despotic tone, contrasts strikingly with the gentle conversation between the two old companions which precedes it. In that conversation Socrates first secures Crito's agreement to the view that one should not follow the opinion of the many but rather that of the expert—of "the one, and truth itself" (48a). The expert is to be obeyed because he knows what is best for whoever or whatever is under his supervision. Second, Socrates argues that doing injustice is to be avoided because it injures "whatever it is of the things that belong to us which both injustice and justice concern" (48a). Finally, the two men agree that it is always wrong to return evil for evil in retaliation for a wrong done, and that there can be no common counsel or deliberation between those who affirm this opinion and those who deny it (49d).

The speech that Socrates then puts into the mouth of the laws departs surprisingly from these three dialogical results. Let us make explicit these differences which Socrates leaves only implicit. First, the laws assert their authority not on the ground that they prescribe what is best but rather on the ground that they beget, nourish, and educate the citizens. Without the laws the citizen would be nothing; this absolute dependence on the laws gives rise to his absolute subordination to them. Being the laws' "offspring and slave," the citizen has a duty to obey as limitless as a son's duty to his father or a slave's to his master. Not excellence but paternity and convention are the criteria of just rule. Second, injustice (or disobedience to the laws) is to be avoided not because it injures one's own soul (about which the laws are silent) but because it injures and tends to destroy the laws. Third, the laws return evil for evil as a matter of course in their assignment of punishments for disobedience.

From here we may draw several inferences concerning the character of laws in general. Most important, the laws conceal the place of nature in human life. They exaggerate when they claim that they, rather than the parents, beget the city's children, just as their claim to educate them hardly accounts for the higher education of a Socrates. The laws' insistence on unconditional obedience reminds one of those gods alluded to in the *Euthyphro* whose might (arbitrary will) alone makes right. Neither such gods nor the *Crito*'s laws admit the existence of a natural order of right and wrong beyond themselves (although they perhaps imply it at 51c), an order in light of which the laws' commands ought ultimately to be fashioned (cf. *Republic*, beginning of Book VI).

Further, when the laws claim to be identical to city and fatherland (51a–c), they forget the primacy of the political regime, the way of life of the community as established by its most powerful group. The laws and customs of a democracy are different from those of an aristocracy, as ideological tyranny differs from traditional monarchy. The Soviet communist regime, for example, is extirpating the manners, morals, language, and religion that were formed under the Russian regime of centuries past, as Solzhenitsyn shows so well. One might well doubt whether a regime with bad laws has the same right to claim obedience as one with good or at least decent laws. Besides, laws are presumably made by the human beings who predominate in the political order. Yet Socrates' laws in the *Crito* speak as though they possess a divine pedigree from time immemorial. Perhaps laws as such wish to claim divinity and to identify themselves with the fatherland in order to conceal their human and to some extent arbitrary origin.

The laws seem to retreat somewhat with the "contract argument" that follows. Since the citizen is permitted to emigrate at any time, "keeping his own things" (51d), it follows, say the laws, that remaining in the city is tantamount to approval of the laws and hence to an implicit contract to obey them. For why else would one remain if not for the laws? (51c–53a). Yet there are many reasons why a man might choose to remain in a city with bad laws. Here again Solzhenitsyn provides an example. Although he hated the Soviet regime, he refused to emigrate voluntarily because he could not take with him the land, the buildings, or the old prerevolutionary Russian traditions, not to mention his fellow Russians. "One's own things" are never completely portable.

The laws conclude their speech with arguments that it is *good* for Socrates to remain in Athens (53a–54c). This final appeal to self-interest is of course incidental to the laws' main claim, that Socrates owes them his obedience out of duty, but it does appear to soften the harshness of that claim. The arguments that the laws present are somewhat plausible but hardly convincing. Typical is their statement that exile amounts to a choice between a well-governed city nearby, where Socrates would be reproached for his lawlessness, and an ill-governed city far away, where the manner of life is hostile to virtue (53b–54a). The laws omit to discuss the possibility of escape to a well-governed place far away, where no one would have heard of Socrates, like Crete (mentioned at 52e). Plato's *Laws*, which takes place in Crete and whose central character is an old Athenian philosopher-stranger who reminds us of Socrates, would seem to show the feasibility of exile there.

The above considerations and others lead one to conclude that Socrates does not accept the laws' arguments. He certainly does not affirm them himself. At the end he says that the booming echo of the laws' speeches, like that of the passionate music used to cure nervous disorders, drowns out all other arguments.

Why then did Socrates stay in prison? He followed "the one, and truth itself," so far as he was able. The "argument that appears best to [him] upon reasoning" (46b) is stated in the dialogical part of the *Crito* and in the *Apology of Socrates*.

Still, the laws' speech is not quite false either. For the laws do provide a practical man's equivalent of philosophy (or of the good of the soul, or of God) as a guide to life. They point to the standard of "the one, and truth itself" to which Socrates seeks to ascend on his own but which lies beyond the simpler Crito's ken. Reverence for the laws instills the proper human awareness that not everything is permitted. Respect for laws imitates and prepares the way for respect for truth.

Furthermore, the laws' authority shines brighter so long as the philosophic quest remains unfinished, as Socrates admits it is. He himself indicates that the expert on the human soul may not be available ("if there is such an expert"—47d). The failure of Socrates' educational-legislative project to replace the Athenian laws in the *Apology of Socrates* is appropriately acknowledged by his bow to the laws in the *Crito*.

Finally, we must distinguish between Socrates' self-presentation to the public and Plato's presentation of Socrates to the public. By "publishing" (or inventing) the *Crito*, a most private conversation that would otherwise never have seen the light of day, Plato mitigates and to some extent conceals the effect of Socrates' defense speech. Plato's Socrates will be remembered by posterity not only as a man willing to die on behalf of a way of life that his city opposed, but also as a law-abiding citizen of his country. Plato took more care than did Socrates that this latter memory would be preserved.[6]

---

[6]For this account of the *Crito* I am indebted to Leo Strauss, "On Plato's *Apology of Socrates* and *Crito*," in Strauss, *Studies in Platonic Political Philosophy* (Chicago: University of Chicago Press, 1984).

The three Platonic dialogues translated here belong to a group of seven dialogues whose dramatic dates place them at the time of Socrates' trial and death. The clue to their dramatic order comes at the end of the *Theaetetus,* where Socrates arranges to meet Theodorus the next day (see *Sophist* beginning) and then says he must go to the Porch of the King, the very place where the *Euthyphro* begins. The sequence, then, runs as follows: *Theaetetus, Euthyphro, Sophist, Statesman, Apology of Socrates, Crito, Phaedo.* Of these seven, the first three are theoretical, dealing respectively with the questions: What is knowledge? What is piety? and What is a sophist? The final three are practical, portraying the *deed* of Socrates' trial and death. The central *Statesman* provides the transition, being a theoretical inquiry into the practical man, the *politikos* or statesman. It should be noted that at the beginning of the *Sophist* Socrates proposed a discussion of sophist, statesman, and philosopher. *Sophist* and *Statesman* were written, but *Philosopher* was not. In the sequence of seven dialogues the *Apology of Socrates* takes the place of the *Philosopher*.

Aristophanes' *Clouds*

1. *Socrates' guilt.* The Socrates of Aristophanes' *Clouds* denies the existence of Zeus, introduces novel Cloud-goddesses into Athens, and teaches a young man that incest and father-beating are permissible. In short, Socrates disbelieves in the gods of the city, introduces novel *daimonia,* and corrupts the young—the very charges on which he was convicted twenty-four years after the *Clouds* was first produced. It appears that Aristophanes takes the side of Athens against Socrates. This is true in part, but there are other and deeper differences between the poet and the philosopher—as there are also differences between the poet and Athens.

2. *The plot.* The *Clouds* tells the story of Socrates' disastrous encounter with Strepsiades, an old man whose son's extravagance is about to ruin him. Strepsiades goes to Socrates' "thinkery" to learn how to make the weaker speech the stronger (111–115; cf. *Apology* 19b), that is, how to twist his way out of the grasp of his creditors' lawsuits. He quickly discovers that the Socratic course of instruction goes far beyond training in courtroom oratory. It is concerned with the truth about the nature of all things, including the things in the heavens and under the earth (187–194; cf. *Apology* 19b), and especially with the truth about the gods. Zeus does not even exist, says Socrates; the true gods are the Clouds, those airy forms in the sky that imitate all beings.

Strepsiades, being old and somewhat literal-minded, finds out that his intellect is too meager to complete the rigorous program of Socratic theology, grammar and meter, and dialectical problem-solving. When Socrates refuses to have any further dealings with such stupidity, Strepsiades compels his unwilling son Pheidippides to go in his place. Pheidippides turns out to be a star pupil. The old man is overjoyed to see that his son's newly acquired rhetorical skills will free him from financial ruin. When the creditors come to collect their debts, Strepsiades drives them away with contempt.

Strepsiades feasts his son at a banquet celebrating their reconciliation, which is quickly disrupted, however, by a quarrel over poetry. Pheidippides refuses to have anything to do with the old-fashioned songs and insists on reciting a tale of incest from the modern poet Euripides. When Strepsiades objects, Pheidippides beats him. The son justifies his outrageous conduct by appealing to nature, according to which it is just for the wise to punish the foolish for their own good. The father reluctantly concedes the point. However, when Pheidippides proposes to beat his mother as well, Strepsiades is shocked and refuses to hear another word. Probably the father suddenly realizes that the matter on which his son has just instructed him so violently—the permissibility of incest—could have real, practical consequences within his own family.[7] Strepsiades immediately reasserts his belief in Zeus, and he angrily burns down Socrates' thinkery, urged on by the god Hermes himself. Strepsiades' flirtation with Socratic atheism ends when he sees that he needs Zeus to maintain the integrity of his family.

3. *Is this the Socrates we know from Plato?* It is tempting to assume, and many scholars do assume, that Aristophanes' play is not really about Socrates, and that the poet attaches to the philosopher's name "the characteristics that belonged to the sophists in general but did not belong to Socrates."[8] This assumption is convenient because it allows one to avoid taking the *Clouds* seriously as a critique of Socrates. But the resemblances between Aristophanes' and Plato's Socrates are numerous and inescapable.

First, unlike the sophists, Socrates in the *Clouds* lives in utmost poverty and charges no fee for his instruction (see *Clouds* n. 48). Further, Socrates sometimes proceeds in his teaching in the manner familiar to us from Plato, beginning from the opinions held by the man he is talking to and drawing out their implications. For example, Socrates' proof that Zeus does not exist begins from Strepsiades' own experience with digestive disorders (385). (Consider also Strepsiades' Socratic cross-examination of the creditor at 1279–1295.) In the *Clouds* as in Plato, Socrates leads one to self-knowledge, which at least in the first instance is knowledge of one's own ignorance (842). His instruction is in the form of short speeches, as in Plato, and not set-piece orations. The comparison of education to initiation into secret religious rites ("Mysteries") is found in Plato (see *Clouds* n. 32). Aristophanes even takes care that features peculiar to Socrates are mentioned: his barefootedness, his casting his eyes from side to side, his capacity to endure pain (362–363).

To be sure, there are differences between the Socrates of Aristophanes and Plato. The question is whether these differences are decisive. It is true that the Aristophanic Socrates is an avid student of nature—of "the things under the earth and the heavenly things" (*Apology* 19b)—while the Platonic Socrates shows little in-

---

[7]This is the persuasive suggestion of Leo Strauss, *Socrates and Aristophanes* (New York: Basic Books, 1966), p. 43. Strauss's book is the basis for much of the present statement on the *Clouds*.

[8]K. J. Dover, ed., Aristophanes, *Clouds*, p. xlix. On "sophists" see *Apology of Socrates* 19e.

terest in such matters. Yet in Plato's *Phaedo* Socrates admits that he did pursue such inquiries when he was younger. Could Aristophanes be writing about the young Socrates? Possibly so, but Socrates was already forty-six at the time the *Clouds* was first produced. Aristophanes may have seen that although Socrates had abandoned the experimental physical science of his youth, he continued in other ways his quest to know *all* the things that are. Plato's Socrates certainly affirms such a comprehensive concern (*Phaedo* 99e, *Charmides* 166d; see also Xenophon, *Memorabilia* IV.6.1). Aristophanes may have chosen to caricature that philosophic quest by portraying it in the trappings of natural science.

Other differences between Plato's and Aristophanes' accounts of Socrates might be mentioned. Plato's Socrates does not teach people how to "make the weaker speech the stronger." Still, anyone was free to listen to Socrates talking and refuting others, and his example obviously enabled some of his followers to learn how to speak cleverly (*Apology* 23c, 33a–b). Further, the Platonic Socrates is a great defender of justice and piety, unlike the debunking Socrates of the *Clouds*. Nevertheless, Plato's Socrates departs radically from the traditional understanding of these virtues, denying in particular Zeus's authority as their sanction. Finally, Socrates in the *Clouds* never discusses the soul, a prominent theme for the Platonic Socrates. We will return to this point in our discussion of Aristophanes' critique of Socrates.

4. *The Aristophanic Socrates*. In order to grasp Aristophanes' conception of Socrates let us consider further the several points just mentioned. First, Aristophanes traces the root of Socrates' distinctive perspective to his study of nature, from which Socrates believes he has learned that not Zeus but "Vortex" is the first principle of all things (380). In order to demonstrate the nonexistence of Zeus, a being whose governance of the cosmos involves will and choice, Socrates must examine everything from the intestines of gnats to the courses of the moon in order to demonstrate that all things proceed from necessity rather than will (see 376 and n. 70 there). His way of life is therefore wholly devoted to knowing the truth about the whole. He cares nothing for money and reputation. He is a philosopher.

But does Socrates not believe the Clouds to be Zeus-like deities? He does tell Strepsiades to regard the Clouds as gods. They are heavenly beings that imitate the forms of all things. (In this respect there is a certain comic resemblance to Plato's ideas; see *Euthyphro* 5d and note.) Yet after Strepsiades is taken indoors for instruction (during the parabasis, 510–626), Socrates never again refers to the Clouds as gods. Instead, he speaks mostly of "air" and equivalents (627), as does Strepsiades (667). Apparently the teaching that the Clouds are gods is part of Socrates' exoteric introduction for beginners, a teaching which is modified or dropped during the indoor or esoteric instruction. As Socrates already implies in his discussion of rain and thunder, the truth is that the Clouds are mere mist, subordinate to air or "Vortex," by which they are governed "by necessity" (376–380). Strepsiades later swears "by the Mist," an expression he must have learned from Socrates during his indoor instruction (814).

Second, Socrates gives considerable attention to speech and language. He instructs Strepsiades in poetic meters and in correct grammatical usage (658–693), and he teaches Pheidippides persuasive speaking. Socrates is especially concerned, for example, that words with masculine gender be applied to masculine beings. He seeks to reform language so that it will be as precise as possible in portraying the things it names. We may sum up Socrates' linguistic interests as twofold: correctly describing the natures of things and teaching or persuading others to accept one's own opinions.

Third, Socrates' indifference to justice and piety in the play might lead one to think that he gives no thought to moral matters. It is true that he does not speak of them explicitly, but we see the effects of his opinions about them. Socrates keeps Just and Unjust Speech on the premises of the thinkery (886). This means that he is aware of and examines the various arguments for and against conventional or legal justice. Further, we may assume that Strepsiades learned from Socrates the arguments he uses against his creditors: that the wise have no obligations to the ignorant (1248–1251, 1279–1284), and that taking interest is unjust because contrary to nature, since money, like the sea, does not naturally increase in size (1286–1295). Beyond this, from Strepsiades' quarrel with his son we see that Socrates taught Pheidippides to respect the wisdom of Euripides, *the* anti-traditional poet, who appears not to regard incest as wrong (1377). Most revealing, Pheidippides proposes that relations between son and father, and son and mother, be based not on traditional family roles but on nature. If the son is wiser than the father, then he may justly beat him for his own good, just as the father beat the son when he was a child (1377, 1409–1414). And it is hinted that the son may likewise take the father's place even in the matter of conjugal rights (1443–1446). Pheidippides regards the shocking crimes of Oedipus as perfectly acceptable conduct. The sacred prohibitions of the traditional laws, and ultimately of Zeus, have no relevance whatever (1420–1431, 1470).

In sum, the Socrates of the *Clouds* holds that conventional laws and customs must be judged in light of nature, and that the cosmos is governed by a natural principle or being, not by a willful god. On earth, wisdom is the natural title to rule, and there is nothing sacred about family relations. The purpose of life is to pursue knowledge of all things—to philosophize.

When due allowance is made for the comic caricature of these notions, they are hardly unfamiliar to a reader of Plato. They may be found in part, stated less bluntly and offensively to be sure, in the dialogues translated in this collection. Socrates develops them most fully in the *Republic*.

5. *Is Unjust Speech a spokesman for Socrates?* So far we have not had occasion to discuss the public contest between Just and Unjust Speech which Socrates stages for Pheidippides' sake (889–1104). In this perhaps most memorable scene of the comedy, Just Speech, the spokesman for the old-fashioned, traditional way of life in Athens, is defeated in argument by Unjust Speech, who shamelessly celebrates immoderate self-indulgence.

Just Speech defends justice by appealing to the gods, about whom he has learned from the poets, and to the ancestral ways. He describes the education in moderation, manly strength, and respect for the old that enabled the former Athenians to defeat the Persians at the battle of Marathon. Just Speech is no enemy of sexual pleasure, but he insists that it be pursued with decency and restraint (973–980). Unjust Speech refutes Just Speech by pointing out the contradictions in the very authorities that his opponent cites: the poets approve of spending time in the marketplace (1055), Heracles indulges in luxury (1050), and Zeus himself practices adultery and father-beating (1080, 905). Moreover, all the prominent Athenians are known passive homosexuals (1083–1102). Just Speech's position, which rests entirely on convention—that is, on the authoritative opinions of the poets and respectable men—turns out to be opposed by those very authorities. The argument of Just Speech therefore self-destructs.

Many scholars suppose that Unjust Speech is a spokesman for Aristophanes' Socrates,[9] but in fact there are decisive differences between them. Unjust Speech is popular in Athens (920), while Socrates is ignored or despised by all (102–104). Unjust Speech praises indulgence in pleasures, but Socrates teaches extreme self-denial. Although Unjust Speech claims to appeal to nature, he follows the same standards—poetry and public opinion—as Just Speech. Unjust Speech endorses openly the homosexual pleasures covertly preferred

[9]Dover, *Clouds*, p. xxxv.

by Just Speech. Unjust Speech despises conventionality, but only for the sake of conventionality's secret convictions about the good. In short, neither Just nor Unjust Speech transcends the plane of received opinion; unlike both, Socrates in the *Clouds* resolutely pursues knowledge of nature by learning.

The contest between Just and Unjust Speech explores—and explodes—the premises of ordinary law-abidingness and ordinary lawlessness. It may therefore be understood as Socrates' way of introducing Pheidippides to the problem of justice, a problem that will be adequately treated only in the young man's indoor instruction, which takes place during the second parabasis (1115–1130). We see the results of that indoor instruction in Pheidippides' conduct during the remainder of the play.

6. *Aristophanes' criticism of Socrates.* The *Clouds* is the most outstanding surviving example of the "ancient quarrel between philosophy and poetry" for the title of wisdom (*Republic* 607b). Aristophanes' bantering mockery of Socrates harbors a serious critique. We may sum this up under three heads.

First, Socrates is ignorant of, or at least pays no attention to, the fundamental requirements of political life. This is especially evident in his attack on the foundations of the family: the prohibition of incest and of father-beating, and the belief in the city's justice-enforcing gods. Socrates needs the city for his students and his food, but he speaks and acts as though he had no such dependence. By keeping his head in the clouds and being self-forgetting, Socrates becomes not only self-destructive but also dangerous to the community. Aristophanes is careful not to make the same mistake. Although he is as skeptical as Socrates about the conventional foundations of the community (as may be seen especially in his *Birds*, whose plot involves the successful overthrow of Zeus), Aristophanes praises justice, gives sensible advice to Athens, and defends the family.

Second, Aristophanes portrays Socrates as a man ignorant of the human soul. Socrates overestimates the ability of men to think rationally, as is shown by his willingness to reveal his secret teachings to the ignoramus Strepsiades. Socrates also forgets the power of human love, especially of that love of one's own which centers upon wife and children. As a consequence of these two misjudgments Socrates never grasps men's need for gods—that is, the primacy of the sacred in human life—for the gods are at once the preservers of what one loves and the common man's substitute for rational inquiry. Socrates strips Strepsiades of his belief in Zeus without giving him anything in Zeus's place but empty air. Aristophanes, on the other hand, never denies the existence of Zeus, even when he attempts, by means of this play, to introduce novel *daimonia* (the Clouds themselves) into the city. The Clouds too always speak as though Zeus exists (564). They praise Socrates for his endurance and his respect for them- selves, but never for his wisdom or judgment (358–363).

Third, Socrates is ignorant of the truth about the gods. He misun- derstands the Clouds. As gods, they perform a double role: they are images of everything that exists and they are indiscriminate patrons of all those who are talkers, such as poets, philosophers, sophists, and even oracle-mongers (316, 331–355). Their main appeal for Soc- rates is likewise twofold. As imitators of all beings, the Clouds point to *nature*, Socrates' ultimate guide for knowledge and life. And as lovers of speeches, the Clouds point to correct (philosophic) *speech*, which represents or imitates accurately the nature of all things. (Soc- rates' belief that speech can correctly imitate being may be seen in his rather tedious instruction on the correct use of language at 658–692.) Aristophanes' own understanding of the Clouds is very different. In the parabasis, at least, the leading Cloud turns out to be the poet himself (518–562). It would seem, then, that Aristophanes endorses the Clouds' affirmation of all speech whether true or false, so long as it be clever, sophisticated, or powerful. Such an attitude would not be altogether surprising in a poet who in a certain respect "nothing affirmeth." Speech does not reveal nature: it is pure puffery, mist, smoke. Furthermore, the suggestion that the Clouds' leader is a poet- god may mean that the doctrine of nature and reason that Socrates teaches is in fact a creation, intended to become authoritative, of innovating poets like Aristophanes and Euripides. The Clouds, at any rate, are eager to become recognized as deities by the Athenians (575– 579), as they already are by poets and sophists. As was mentioned, Socrates pays attention to the Clouds only insofar as they are images of something real. He believes that he does not believe in them as gods, that is, as willful, personal authorities. (He is of course glad to pretend that they are gods for the sake of beginning students like Strepsiades who are willing to give up their belief in Zeus but are not yet ready for the total atheism of the indoor instruction.) But if the Clouds are poets or creations of poets, then the authoritative nature and rational speech that Socrates follows may be an illusion that he has come to believe in as a result of poetic teachings. He may not be the atheist that he thinks he is (nor, to be sure, is Aristophanes the theist he appears to be). Does the philosopher's endless quest for knowledge rest according to Aristophanes on a non-rational convic- tion learned from poets? Is the philosopher's chief error the belief that nature can be known through rational speech and that it can provide an adequate guide to life? Does the only source of human meaning, then, spring from the authoritative gods created by the wisest poets? For answers to these questions, one would have to investigate the other ten surviving plays of Aristophanes.[10]

7. *Plato's defense of Socrates.* It is probably impossible to say how much of the Platonic Socrates is a deliberate "poetic creation" of Plato in response to Aristophanes' attack. Plato himself raises the question when he says in his *Second Letter* (314c) that his dialogues are those of a Socrates become "young and beautiful" (or "new and noble"). (It should be noted that Plato was only about twenty at the time of Socrates' death, so his dialogues were written many years after the *Clouds*.) In any event, let us consider Plato's implicit responses to the three Aristophanic criticisms of Socrates just mentioned.

First, does Plato's Socrates support the foundations of the city? We saw in our discussion of the *Apology of Socrates* and *Crito* that the Socrates of these works appears to be more of a supporter of ordinary law-abidingness than he really is. But we also noted that the surface impression gathered by the reader is more appealing and less shocking than the surface impression created by Socrates on his audience within the *Apology of Socrates*. Plato's readers think Socrates noble, but Socrates' jurors condemned him to death. It seems that even the Platonic Socrates has some trouble concealing from the many the convention-assaulting implications of his private views.

Second, as for Socrates' alleged misunderstanding of the human soul, his dealings with Euthyphro and Crito suggest a man far more perceptive of human character than the Socrates of the *Clouds*. In each case the interlocutor is left with his conventional convictions more or less intact and perhaps improved. And this pattern would seem to be true of Plato's other Socratic dialogues as well. Some questions might be raised, however. Does Socrates' stripping away of conventional opinions from young Charmides have the effect of liberating that vain young man from a certain habitual decency (see the *Charmides*)? Does Socrates' conversation with young Lysis cut him off from the conventional trust that renders most friendships—and most families—possible (see the *Lysis*)? Does Socrates know his man in each case before he undertakes with him his unsettling inquiries? A persuasive defense of Socrates is probably possible in these and other instances, but the *Clouds* makes us wonder whether these defenses could be entirely

---

[10]On this theme, see the provocative essay by Harry Neumann, "Civic Piety and Socratic Atheism: An Interpretation of Strauss' *Socrates and Aristophanes*," *Independent Journal of Philosophy* 2 (1978), 33–37.

successful. Certainly the Platonic Socrates' theoretical grasp of the soul is far-reaching; one need only think of the impressive psychology of the *Republic*. Still, even Plato makes us wonder how adequately Socrates applied his insights in his dealings with ordinary men. One might contrast the Athenian stranger of Plato's *Laws*, from whose words the gods are rarely absent, with Socrates, whose allusions to the divine are usually taken by his listeners to be ironic.

Finally, on the principal question of whether poetic creativity is superior to philosophic knowledge of nature, it appears that Plato entirely endorses Socrates' view. To be sure, in Plato one does encounter the hesitation appropriate to the unfinished character of the philosophic quest for wisdom. Consequently, the Platonic philosopher is attentive to the claims of his adversaries, whether Zeus and traditional Athens or poetic wisdom, and not contemptuous of them as is the Socrates of the *Clouds*. Consider, for example, Plato's willingness to give pious old Cephalus a hearing (*Republic* Book I) and his examinations of the case for poetry (in Books II–III and X, and in the *Ion*).

We may conclude that Plato's defense of Socrates succeeds in rescuing philosophy from the poet's condemnation. Although his defense partly concedes the validity of Aristophanes' charges, it goes on to show that there is no necessary conflict between the philosophic life on the one hand, and knowledge of the human soul and public responsibility on the other. Characteristic of Plato's teaching in this respect is his turning away from Socrates' city of virtue whose public hero is the philosopher (this is Socrates' ironic proposal in the *Apology of Socrates*, elaborated in the *Republic*). Instead, Plato put forward in his *Laws* a regime in which authority was to be shared, under the rule of law, by moneyed men (oligarchs) and commoners (democrats). In such a regime philosophers could live and teach, and the public opinion of that regime could be formed by philosophic-poetic writings, like those of Plato himself, addressed to a wide audience.

FOUR TEXTS ON SOCRATES

Plato's *Euthyphro*

[*Or, On the Pious*]¹

EUTHYPHRO.² What is new, Socrates, that you have left the places   2a³
in Lyceum where you usually spend your time and are now spending time here around the Porch of the King?⁴ For surely you don't
also happen to have some lawsuit before the King, as I do.

SOCRATES. In fact, Euthyphro, the Athenians don't call it a lawsuit, but an indictment.⁵

EUTHYPHRO. What are you saying? Someone, as is likely, has   b
brought an indictment against you. For I won't charge you with
doing so against another.

---

¹"Or, On the Pious" may be Plato's subtitle or, more likely, may have been added by a later
Greek editor.

²About the man Euthyphro nothing is known besides what appears in this dialogue, except
that the inspired and "wise" etymologist named Euthyphro, mentioned with (ironic?) praise
by Socrates in the *Cratylus* (396d and elsewhere), may be the same man. (In the notes to these
translations works mentioned without an author are by Plato.) The name Euthyphro is composed of elements that mean "straight" (*euthy*) and "thought" (*phrōn*).

³The marginal numbers and letters (2a, 2b, etc.) are from Stephanus' Renaissance edition of
Plato; they are used today as standard pagination in most editions and translations.

⁴Socrates frequented the gymnasium at Lyceum, a suburb of Athens, where he would
converse with the young men who came there to exercise and socialize (*Symposium* 223d, *Lysis*
203a, *Euthydemus* 271a). The "King," a public official or archon selected annually by lot, had
jurisdiction over the "preliminary inquiry" in judicial cases involving matters concerning the
gods, such as impiety. His office, being a remote descendant of the kingship of Athens'
distant past, retained vestiges of the ancient kings' authority in the city over sacred things. He
performed "the most venerable and ancestral of the ancient sacrifices" (*Statesman* 290e). The
Porch (Stoa) of the King was a public building in the marketplace.

⁵"Lawsuit" (*dikē*) and "indictment" (*graphē*) are technical judicial terms. *Dikē* was the general term for "case," whether public or private, although sometimes (as in Euthyphro's case
here) *dikē* refers specifically to private injury. (Murder was viewed as an injury not to the city
but to the family of the victim.) A *graphē*, on the other hand, is a case in which injury to the
public is alleged, as in the present case of Socrates. The literal meaning of *dikē* is "justice"; of
graphē, "writing."

SOCRATES. Certainly not.   2b

EUTHYPHRO. But someone else against you?

SOCRATES. Quite so.

EUTHYPHRO. Who is he?

SOCRATES. I myself don't even recognize the man at all, Euthyphro. He is apparently someone young and unknown. But they
say his name is Meletus, as I suppose. He is from the deme Pit-
theus,[6] if you can think of some Pitthean Meletus with long
straight hair, not quite full-bearded, but somewhat hook-nosed.

EUTHYPHRO. I can't think of him, Socrates. But what indictment
has he brought against you?

SOCRATES. What indictment? Not an ignoble[7] one, it seems to me   c
at least. For it is no paltry thing for one who is so young to have
become cognizant of so great a matter. For as he asserts, he knows
in what way the young are corrupted and who their corrupters are.
And he is probably someone wise, and having discerned my ignorance, he is going before the city, as if before his mother, to accuse
me of corrupting those of his own age. And he alone of the
politicians[8] appears to me to begin correctly. For it is correct to take   d
care of the young first, so that they will be the best possible, just as
a good farmer properly takes care of the young plants first, and
after this of the others as well. And so Meletus is perhaps first
cleaning us out, the corrupters of the young sprouts, as he asserts.   3a
Then, after this, it is clear that when he has taken care of the older
ones, he will become the cause of the most and greatest good
things for the city. At least that is the likely outcome for someone
beginning from such a beginning.

EUTHYPHRO. So I would wish, Socrates, but I am afraid that the
opposite will happen. For he seems to me simply to be doing evil to
the city, beginning from the hearth, by attempting to do injustice
to you. Tell me, what does he assert that you do[9] to corrupt the
young?

SOCRATES. Strange things, you wondrous man, at least on first   b
hearing. For he asserts that I am a maker of gods, and on this
account—that I make novel gods and don't believe in the ancient
ones—he has indicted me, as he asserts.

---

[6]A *deme* is a political subdivision of Athens.

[7]"Ignoble" translates *agennes*, literally, "not well born." This term is to be distinguished
from *kalon*, always translated "noble" in the *Euthyphro*. See *Apology* n. 16.

[8]The term *politikoi* is not pejorative; it might also be translated "statesmen."

[9]The word translated "do" is *poiein*, the same word translated "make" in Socrates' reply.
The word "maker" is *poiētēs*: Socrates is accused of being a "poet" of gods.

EUTHYPHRO. I understand, Socrates; it's because you assert that   3b
the *daimonion*[10] comes to you on occasion. So he has brought this
indictment, claiming that you are making innovations concerning
the divine things, and he is going into the law court to slander you,
knowing that such things are easy to make slander about before
the many. And me too—whenever I say something in the Assem-   c
bly concerning the divine things, predicting for them what will be,
they laugh at me as if I were mad. And yet, of the things I have
foretold, I have spoken nothing that is not true. Nevertheless, they
envy us all who are of this sort. But one should not give any
thought to them, but should confront them.

SOCRATES. My dear Euthyphro, being laughed at is perhaps no
matter. For in fact the Athenians, as it seems to me, do not much
care about someone whom they suppose to be clever, unless he is a
skillful teacher of his own wisdom. But their spiritedness is
aroused against anyone who they suppose makes others like him-   d
self, either from envy, as you say, or because of something else.

EUTHYPHRO. That's why I do not at all desire to try out how they
are disposed toward me in this regard.

SOCRATES. Perhaps *you* seem to make yourself available only
infrequently and not to be willing to teach your own wisdom. But I
fear that *I*, because of my philanthropy, seem to them to say pro-
fusely whatever I possess to every man, not only without pay, but
even paying with pleasure if anyone is willing to listen to me. So if,
as I was saying just now, they were going to laugh at me, as you
say they do at you, it would not be unpleasant to pass the time in   e
the law court joking and laughing. But if they are going to be
serious, then how this will turn out now is unclear except to you
diviners.[11]

EUTHYPHRO. Perhaps it will be no matter, Socrates, and your
contesting of the lawsuit will proceed as you have a mind for it to
do, as I suppose mine will too.

SOCRATES. And your lawsuit, Euthyphro, what is it? Are you
defending or prosecuting?

EUTHYPHRO. Prosecuting.

SOCRATES. Whom?

EUTHYPHRO. Someone whom in prosecuting I again seem mad.   4a

---

[10]Socrates explains his *daimonion*, his daimonic or divine sign, in *Apology* 31c–d. The actual
impiety charge against him was: "He does not believe in the gods in whom the city believes,
and he brings in other *daimonia* [divine or daimonic things] that are new." See *Apology* nn. 37,
38, 56.

[11]A "diviner" is a *mantis*, a seer or prophet. See *Apology* n. 30 on "divination."

SOCRATES. What then? Are you prosecuting someone who   4a
flies?[12]

EUTHYPHRO. He is far from flying; in fact, he happens to be quite
old.

SOCRATES. Who is he?

EUTHYPHRO. My father.

SOCRATES. Your father, best of men?

EUTHYPHRO. Certainly.

SOCRATES. What is the charge, and what is the lawsuit about?

EUTHYPHRO. Murder, Socrates.

SOCRATES. Heracles! Surely the many, Euthyphro, are ignorant
of what way is correct. For I don't suppose that it is the part of just
anyone to do this correctly, but of one who is no doubt already far   b
advanced in wisdom.[13]

EUTHYPHRO. Far indeed, by Zeus, Socrates.

SOCRATES. Is the man who was killed by your father one of your
family? Or isn't it clear? For surely you wouldn't proceed against
him for murder on behalf of an outsider.

EUTHYPHRO. It's laughable, Socrates, that you suppose that it
makes any difference whether the dead man is an outsider or of the
family, rather than that one should be on guard only for whether
the killer killed with justice or not; and if it was with justice, to let it
go, but if not, to proceed against him—if, that is, the killer shares
your hearth and table. For the pollution turns out to be equal if you   c
knowingly associate with such a man and do not purify[14] yourself,
as well as him, by proceeding against him in a lawsuit.

Now the man who died was a laborer of mine, and when we
were farming on Naxos,[15] he was serving us there for hire. So in a
drunken fit he gets angry with one of the family servants and cuts
his throat. So my father, binding his feet and hands together and
throwing him into a ditch, sends a man here to ask the exegete[16]

[12]Socrates plays on the word prosecute, *diōkein*, which literally means "pursue." Euthyphro's suit is likened to a wild-goose chase.

[13]Socrates is surprised, and Euthyphro seems (is reputed to be) mad, because murder
prosecutions were ordinarily brought by a member of the family of the victim, certainly not by
someone from the family of the alleged murderer.

[14]The crime of homicide was thought to be a personal injury to the dead man's family and
to create a religious pollution for those who consorted with the murderer. The word "purify"
is *aphosioun*, related to *hosion*, "pious" (n. 17). The "King" (n. 4) had jurisdiction over homicide cases because of the pollution created by murder.

[15]Naxos was a colony of Athens until she lost the Peloponnesian War with Sparta in 404,
five years before the time of this dialogue. Euthyphro does not explain the long delay between
the alleged crime, which presumably occurred in 404 or even earlier, and his prosecution of
his father.

[16]Athens had several officials called "exegetes" (interpreters), who expounded the sacred
and ancestral laws of the city. In this sentence "here" means "to Athens."

what he should do. During this time he paid little attention to the   4d
man he had bound and was careless of him, on the ground that he
was a murderer and it was no matter even if he should die, which
is just what happened to him. For because of hunger and cold and
the bonds, he dies before the messenger returns from the exegete.

This, then, is just why my father and the rest of my family are
indignant: because on behalf of the murderer I am proceeding
against my father for murder, although he didn't kill him, as they
assert, and besides, even if he did kill him, since the man who died
was a murderer anyway, they say that one needn't give any
thought to someone of that sort—for it is impious for a son to   e
proceed against his father for murder—they knowing badly, Socrates, how the divine is disposed concerning the pious and the
impious.[17]

SOCRATES. But before Zeus, do you, Euthyphro, suppose you
have such precise knowledge about how the divine things are
disposed, and the pious and impious things, that, assuming that
these things were done just as you say, you don't fear that by
pursuing a lawsuit against your father, you in turn may happen to
be doing an impious act?

EUTHYPHRO. No, there would be no benefit for me, Socrates, nor
would Euthyphro be any different from the many human beings, if   5a
I didn't know all such things precisely.

SOCRATES. Then, wondrous Euthyphro, wouldn't it be best for
me to become your student and, before Meletus' indictment comes
to trial, to challenge him on these very things? I would say that
even in time past I regarded it as important to know the divine
things, and now, since he asserts that I am doing wrong by acting
unadvisedly and making innovations concerning the divine things,
I have become your student. "And, Meletus," I would say, "if you
agree that Euthyphro is wise in such things, then hold that I too   b
believe correctly and drop the lawsuit. But if not, then bring a
lawsuit against him, my teacher, instead of me, on the ground that
he is corrupting the old, me and his own father, by teaching me
and by admonishing and punishing him." And if he isn't persuaded by me and doesn't give up the lawsuit or indict you instead

---

[17]The "pious" (*hosion*) refers in the traditional usage of the Greek language to that which is
allocated by the gods to men. This may be thought of in two aspects: (1) that which is
prescribed by the gods to men, both concerning men's proper dealings with one another (in
contrast to merely human law and justice) and also concerning men's proper conduct toward
the gods; (2) that which is permitted or given by the gods to men, in contrast to the sacred
(*hieron*), which the gods reserve to themselves. Priests and temples are *hieron*, sacred, while
the rest of the city, given over to men, is *hosion*, pious or (in contrast to sacred) profane.

of me, shouldn't I say in the law court these very things on which I   5b
challenged him?

EUTHYPHRO. Yes, by Zeus, Socrates, if he should then attempt to
indict me, I would discover, as I suppose, where he is rotten, and   c
our speech in the law court would turn out to be much more about
him than about me.

SOCRATES. And since I am cognizant of these things, my dear
comrade, I do desire to become your student, knowing that neither
this Meletus nor, no doubt, anyone else even seems to see you; but
me he discerns so sharply and easily that he has indicted me for
impiety.[18] So tell me now, before Zeus, what you just now strongly affirmed that you know plainly: what sort of things do you say
the pious and the impious[19] are, concerning murder and concern-   d
ing other things? Or isn't the pious itself the same as itself in every
action, and again, isn't the impious opposite to everything pious,
while it itself is similar to itself and has one certain *idea*[20] in accordance with impiety—everything, that is, that is going to be
impious?

EUTHYPHRO. Entirely so, doubtless, Socrates.

SOCRATES. Speak, then, what do you say the pious is, and what
the impious?

EUTHYPHRO. I say, then, that the pious is just what I am doing
now: to proceed against whoever does injustice regarding murders
or thefts of sacred things, or is doing wrong in any other such
thing, whether he happens to be a father or mother or anyone else   e
at all; and not to proceed against him is impious. Now contemplate, Socrates, how great a proof I will tell you that the law is so
disposed—a proof, which I have already told to others as well, that
these things would be correctly done if they take place in this
way—that one is not to give way to the impious[21] one, whoever he

---

[18]The term is *asebeia*, the name of the legal crime of impiety. *Asebeia* is closely related to
asebes, "impious" or "irreverent," and is the opposite of *eusebes*, "pious" or "reverent."
(However, the words "reverent" and "irreverent" are not quite strong enough as translations.) *Eusebes* is similar in meaning to *hosion* ("pious"), but *eusebes* emphasizes the reverence
and respect, even fear, which one feels or ought to feel toward the gods. To distinguish it
from *hosion* and cognates (always translated "pious," etc.), we will note all instances of *eusebes*
and cognates.

[19]In this sentence "pious" and "impious" translate *eusebes* and *asebes*.

[20]The Greek word *idea*, here left untranslated, literally means "look." The word *eidos*, of
similar meaning, is also left untranslated at 6d below. These are the terms used by Plato in his
so-called doctrine of ideas (e.g. "the idea of the good," *Republic* 505a). The *idea* or *eidos* of a
thing may be thought of as the look it has, in the mind's eye, when it is truly seen for what it
is.

[21]The term is *asebes* (n. 18).

happens to be. Human beings themselves believe that Zeus is the   5e
best and most just of the gods, at the same time that they agree that
he bound his own father because he gulped down his sons without   6a
justice, and that the latter, in turn, castrated his own father because of other such things.[22] Yet they are angry at me because I am
proceeding against my father when he has done injustice, and so
they contradict themselves both concerning the gods and concerning me.

SOCRATES. Is this, Euthyphro, why I am a defendant against the
indictment: that whenever someone says such things about the
gods, I receive them somehow with annoyance? Because of this, as
is likely, someone will assert that I am a wrongdoer. So now, if
these things seem so to you too, who know well about such things,   b
it is certainly necessary, as is likely, for us to concede them as well.
For what else shall we say, since we ourselves also agree that we
know nothing about them? But tell me, before the god of friendship,[23] do you truly hold that these things have happened in this
way?

EUTHYPHRO. Yes, and things even more wondrous than these,
Socrates, which the many do not know.

SOCRATES. And do you hold that there really is war among the
gods against one another, and terrible enmities and battles, and
many other such things, as are spoken of by the poets and with
which our sacred things have been adorned by the good painters,   c
particularly the robe filled with such adornments which is brought
up to the Acropolis in the Great Panathenaea?[24] Shall we assert
that these things are true, Euthyphro?

---

[22]Hesiod and later Greek poets report that Kronos castrated his father Ouranos (Heaven) at
the urging of his mother Gaia (Earth). She had sought vengeance against Ouranos because he
hid away their children within the earth as soon as they were born. Kronos in turn swallowed
his own children at birth because of a prophecy that one of his sons would overthrow him.
But Kronos' wife concealed baby Zeus from Kronos, and Zeus eventually led the Olympian
gods in a successful war against Kronos and the other Titans (Giants) at the end of which
Kronos and the Titans were imprisoned. (Hesiod, *Theogony* 132–182, 453–506, 617–819.) In the
poem, Gaia explains Kronos' castration of Ouranos as a punishment for evil-doing, but Zeus
claims no such justification for his violent overthrow of Kronos. Euthyphro, however, sees in
both actions a concern for justice.

[23]The oath refers to Zeus, the god and protector of friendship. In the previous sentence
(and elsewhere in these dialogues) Socrates employs the common Greek practice of using
"we" and "us" as a modest way of referring to himself.

[24]The Athenians held an annual festival in honor of their patron goddess Athena with
games, sacrifices, and a procession which carried the robe of Athena up to her temple on the
Acropolis. The robe, which was embroidered by Athenian girls, depicted among other things
the battle between the Olympian gods and the Titans. Every fourth year the festival was
celebrated with particular magnificence and was called the "Great" Panathenaea. The word in
this sentence translated as "sacred things" (*hiera*) may also mean "temples" (see n. 17).

EUTHYPHRO. Not only these, Socrates, but as I said just now, I   6c
will also explain many other things to you, if you wish, about the
divine things; and when you hear them, I know well that you will
be astounded.

SOCRATES. I shouldn't wonder. But you will explain these things
to me some other time, at leisure. Now, however, try to say more
plainly what I was asking you just now. For you did not teach me   d
sufficiently earlier, comrade, when I asked what ever the pious is.
Instead, you told me that what you are now doing, proceeding
against your father for murder, happens to be pious.

EUTHYPHRO. Yes, and what I was saying is true, Socrates.

SOCRATES. Perhaps. But in fact, Euthyphro, you also say that
many other things are pious.

EUTHYPHRO. Yes, and so they are.

SOCRATES. Do you remember that I didn't bid you to teach me
some one or two of the many pious things, but that *eidos* itself by
which all the pious things are pious? For surely you were saying
that it is by one *idea* that the impious things are impious and the   e
pious things pious. Or don't you remember?

EUTHYPHRO. I do.

SOCRATES. Then teach me what ever this *idea* itself is, so that by
gazing at it and using it as a pattern, I may declare that whatever is
like it, among the things you or anyone else may do, is pious, and
that whatever is not like it is not.

EUTHYPHRO. If this is the way that you wish, Socrates, I'll tell you
in this way too.

SOCRATES. Yes, that's just what I wish.

EUTHYPHRO. Then what is dear to the gods is pious, and what is
not dear is impious.   7a

SOCRATES. Altogether noble, Euthyphro. You have now answered just as I was seeking for you to answer. Whether it is true,
however, I don't yet know. But clearly you will go on to teach me
that what you say is true.

EUTHYPHRO. Certainly.

SOCRATES. Come then, let us consider what we are saying. The
thing dear-to-the-gods and human being dear-to-the-gods are
pious, while the thing hateful-to-the-gods and he who is hateful-
to-the-gods are impious.[25] The pious is not the same as the impious, but most opposite. Isn't this so?

[25]The expression "dear-to-the-gods" translates the single Greek word *theophiles* ("god-
dear," "god-loved"). Without the hyphens, "dear to the gods" translates *prosphiles tois theois*.
Likewise with "hateful-to-the-gods." The *phil-* root, here rendered "dear," is translated "to
love" when it occurs in its verb form, *philein*. The noun *philos* is "friend."

EUTHYPHRO. This is so.   7a

SOCRATES. And it appears to have been well said?

EUTHYPHRO. It seems so to me, Socrates, for that is what was   b
said.

SOCRATES. But wasn't it also said that the gods quarrel, Euthyphro, and differ with each other, and that there are enmities
among them toward each other?

EUTHYPHRO. Yes, that is what was said.

SOCRATES. What is the difference *about*, best of men, that makes
for enmity and anger? Let's consider as follows. If you and I should
differ about number—which of two groups of things is greater—
would our difference about these things make us enemies and
angry at each other? Or would we go to calculation and quickly
settle it, at least about such things as these?

EUTHYPHRO. Quite so.   c

SOCRATES. And if we should differ about the greater and less,
wouldn't we go to measuring and quickly put a stop to our
difference?

EUTHYPHRO. That is so.

SOCRATES. And would we go to weighing, as I suppose, to come
to a decision about the heavier and lighter?

EUTHYPHRO. Of course.

SOCRATES. Then what would we differ about and what decision
would we be unable to reach, that we would be enemies and angry
at each other? Perhaps you have nothing ready to hand, but consider while I speak whether it is these things: the just and the   d
unjust, and noble and shameful, and good and bad. Isn't it because
we differ about these things and can't come to a sufficient decision
about them that we become enemies to each other, whenever we
do, both I and you and all other human beings?

EUTHYPHRO. Yes, this is the difference, Socrates, and about these
things.

SOCRATES. What about the gods, Euthyphro? If they do differ at
all, wouldn't they differ because of these same things?

EUTHYPHRO. Most necessarily.

SOCRATES. Then among the gods too, well-born Euthyphro,   e
some believe some things just, others believe others, according to
your argument, and noble and shameful and good and bad. For
surely they wouldn't quarrel with each other unless they differed
about these things, would they?

EUTHYPHRO. What you say is correct.

SOCRATES. And don't they each also love whatever they believe
noble and good and just, and hate the opposites of these?

EUTHYPHRO. Quite so.   7e

SOCRATES. But the same things, as you assert, some believe just, and others unjust; and in disputing about these things they quarrel   8a
and war with each other. Isn't this so?

EUTHYPHRO. It is so.

SOCRATES. Then the same things, as is likely, are both hated and loved by the gods, and the same things would be hateful-to-the-gods as well as dear-to-the-gods.

EUTHYPHRO. It's likely.

SOCRATES. Then the same things would be both pious and impious, Euthyphro, by this argument.

EUTHYPHRO. Probably.

SOCRATES. Then you didn't answer what I asked, you wondrous man. For I wasn't asking what same thing is at once both pious and impious: whatever is dear-to-the-gods is also hateful-to-the-gods, as is likely. Consequently, Euthyphro, in doing what you are now   b
doing, punishing your father, it is nothing wondrous if you are doing something dear to Zeus but hateful to Kronos and Ouranos, and dear to Hephaestus but hateful to Hera.[26] And if there are other gods who differ with one another about it, it is so with them in the same way.

EUTHYPHRO. But I suppose, Socrates, that none of the gods differs one with another about this, at least: that whoever kills someone unjustly must pay the penalty.

SOCRATES. What, then? Have you ever heard any human being claim in a dispute that one who kills unjustly, or does anything else   c
at all unjustly, need not pay the penalty?

EUTHYPHRO. Certainly. They don't stop disputing in this way, especially in the law courts. For although they have done very many injustices, they will do and say anything at all to escape the penalty.

SOCRATES. Do they in fact agree, Euthyphro, that they have done injustice, and having agreed, do they nevertheless assert that they need not pay the penalty?

EUTHYPHRO. In no way, not this at least.

---

[26]For Kronos and Ouranos, see n. 22. Father-punishing is perhaps dear to Hephaestus because he was once cast down violently from heaven by his father Zeus (*Iliad* I.586–594). It may be hateful to Hera because it would mean the overthrow of her husband Zeus, through whom she holds prominence among the gods. Alternatively, Hera may fear that father-punishing could be a prelude to mother-punishing (as in Aristophanes, *Clouds* 1443). There is also a story that Hera once threw Hephaestus down from heaven, in retaliation for which Hephaestus sent Hera a throne which bound her with invisible bonds when she sat down. It should be noted that father-punishing is a persistent if subdued theme of the *Euthyphro*, as it is an explicit theme of the *Clouds*.

SOCRATES. Then they will not do and say anything at all. For I   8c
suppose they don't dare to dispute by saying that even if they have
done injustice they need not pay the penalty. Instead, I suppose   d
they assert that they haven't done injustice, don't they?

EUTHYPHRO. What you say is true.

SOCRATES. Then they don't dispute by claiming that the doer of
injustice need not pay the penalty; instead, they perhaps dispute
who the doer of injustice is, and what he did, and when.

EUTHYPHRO. What you say is true.

SOCRATES. Aren't the gods also affected in the same way, if they
do in fact quarrel about the just and unjust things, as your argument says? Don't some of them assert that others do injustice while
the others deny it? For surely, you wondrous man, no god or
human being dares to say that the doer of injustice ought not to   e
pay the penalty.

EUTHYPHRO. Yes, in this, Socrates, what you say is true, at least
in the main.

SOCRATES. But I suppose, Euthyphro, that the disputants dispute
about each of the particular things done, both human beings and
gods, if gods do dispute. They differ about a certain action, some
asserting that it was done justly, others unjustly. Isn't this so?

EUTHYPHRO. Quite so.

SOCRATES. Come then, my dear Euthyphro, teach me too, so that   9a
I may become wiser, what your proof is that all gods believe that
that man died unjustly who while serving for hire became a murderer, and then, bound by the master of the man who died, met his
end because of his bonds before the one who bound him found out
from the exegetes what he should do about him; and that it is
correct for a son to proceed against his father and denounce him
for murder on behalf of someone of this sort. Come, try to show
me in some way plainly about these things, that all gods believe   b
more than anything that this action is correct. And if you show me
sufficiently, I will never stop extolling you for wisdom.

EUTHYPHRO. But perhaps it is no small work, Socrates, although I
could display it to you quite plainly.

SOCRATES. I understand. It's because I seem to you to be poorer
at learning than the judges, since clearly you will show *them* that
such things are unjust and that all the gods hate them.

EUTHYPHRO. Quite plainly, Socrates, at least if they do listen to
me when I speak.

SOCRATES. They will listen, if you do seem to speak well. But   c
while you were speaking, I thought of the following and I am
considering it with regard to myself: "Even if Euthyphro should

teach me that all the gods believe that such a death is unjust, what   9c
more will I have learned from Euthyphro about what ever the
pious and the impious are? For although this deed would be hateful-to-the-gods, as is likely, it became apparent just now that the
pious and the not pious are not defined by this, for it became
apparent that the hateful-to-the-gods is also dear-to-the-gods."

So I will let you off from this, Euthyphro. If you wish, let all the
gods believe it unjust and let all hate it. But is this the correction   d
that we are now making in the argument: that whatever all the
gods hate is impious, and whatever they love is pious, but whatever some love and others hate is neither or both? Is this how you
now wish it to be defined by us concerning the pious and the
impious?

EUTHYPHRO. Yes, for what prevents it, Socrates?

SOCRATES. Nothing on my part, Euthyphro. But consider on
your part whether by positing[27] this you will most easily teach me
what you promised.

EUTHYPHRO. Well, I would say that the pious is whatever all the   e
gods love, and that the opposite, whatever all gods hate, is
impious.

SOCRATES. So shouldn't we consider again, Euthyphro, whether
this is said nobly?[28] Or should we let it go and just accept what we
ourselves and others say, conceding that something is so if only
someone asserts that it is? Or ought we to consider what the speaker says?

EUTHYPHRO. It ought to be considered. However, I suppose that
this is now said nobly.

SOCRATES. Soon, my good man, we will know better. Think   10a
about something like the following. Is the pious loved by the gods
because it is pious, or is it pious because it is loved?

EUTHYPHRO. I don't know what you are saying, Socrates.

SOCRATES. Then I will try to explain more plainly. We speak of
something carried and carrying, and of led and leading, and seen
and seeing. And do you understand that all such things are different from each other and how they are different?

EUTHYPHRO. It seems to me that I understand.

SOCRATES. And isn't there also something loved and, different
from this, the thing loving?

EUTHYPHRO. Of course.

[27]"Positing" translates *hypotithesthai*, "hypothesize," i.e., "set down as an underlying
basis." At 11c, "suppositions" translates *hypotheseis*.

[28]For the Greeks something is "nobly" (or "beautifully") said when it is spoken aptly and to
the point (though perhaps not in every case truly: see 7a). The word is *kalon*.

SOCRATES. Then tell me, is the thing carried something carried   10b
because it is carried, or because of something else?[29]

EUTHYPHRO. No, it is because of this.

SOCRATES. And the thing led because it is led, and the thing seen
because it is seen?

EUTHYPHRO. Quite so.

SOCRATES. Then it isn't because it is something seen that it is
seen, but the opposite: because it is seen, it is something seen. Nor
is it because it is something led that it is led; rather, because it is
led, it is something led. Nor because it is something carried is it
carried; rather, because it is carried, it is something carried. Isn't it
quite clear, Euthyphro, what I wish to say? I wish to say that if   c
something comes to be something or is affected, it isn't because it is
something coming to be that it comes to be, but because it comes to
be, it is something coming to be. Nor because it is something
affected, is it affected; rather, because it is affected, it is something
affected. Or don't you concede that this is so?

EUTHYPHRO. I do.

SOCRATES. And isn't the thing loved either something coming to
be or something affected by something?

EUTHYPHRO. Quite so.

SOCRATES. Then this too is just like the previous ones. Not because it is something loved, is it loved by those by whom it is
loved, but because it is loved, it is something loved.

EUTHYPHRO. Necessarily.

SOCRATES. Now what are we saying about the pious, Euthyphro?   d
Isn't it loved by all gods, as your argument says?

EUTHYPHRO. Yes.

SOCRATES. Because it is pious, or because of something else?

EUTHYPHRO. No, it's because of this.

SOCRATES. Then is it loved because it is pious, rather than pious
because it is loved?

EUTHYPHRO. It's likely.

SOCRATES. But in fact, just because it is loved by gods, it is something loved and dear-to-the-gods.[30]

EUTHYPHRO. Of course.

SOCRATES. Then the dear-to-the-gods is not pious, Euthyphro,
nor is the pious dear-to-the-gods, as you say, but the one is different from the other.

---

[29]In the following discussion Socrates makes use of passive participles (e.g., *pheromenon*,
"something carried") and the passive form of the verb (e.g., *pheretai*, "it is carried").

[30]"It is loved" is *phileitai*; "something loved" is *philoumenon*; "dear-to-the-gods" is *theophiles*
(see n. 25).

EUTHYPHRO. How so, Socrates?   10e

SOCRATES. Because we agree that the pious is loved because it is pious, not that it is pious because it is loved, don't we?

EUTHYPHRO. Yes.

SOCRATES. And further, that the dear-to-the-gods, because it is loved by gods, is dear-to-the-gods by this very fact of being loved, and not that it is loved because it is dear-to-the-gods.

EUTHYPHRO. What you say is true.

SOCRATES. But if the dear-to-the-gods and the pious were the same, my dear Euthyphro, then, on the one hand, if the pious were loved because of being pious, the dear-to-the-gods would   11a
also be loved because of being dear-to-the-gods; and on the other hand, if the dear-to-the-gods were dear-to-the-gods because of being loved by gods, the pious would also be pious because of being loved. But as it is now, you see that the two are opposite, since they are entirely different from each other. For the one, because it is loved, is the sort of thing to be loved; the other, because it is the sort of thing to be loved, is loved.

And probably, Euthyphro, when you are asked what ever the pious is, you don't wish to make clear to me its substance, but rather to speak of a certain affection[31] concerning it: that the pious is affected in being loved by all gods. But what it is, you haven't yet   b
said. So if you please,[32] don't hide it from me, but say again from the beginning what ever the pious is, whether it is loved by gods or however it is affected—for we won't differ about this—but tell me eagerly, what are the pious and the impious?

EUTHYPHRO. But Socrates, I have no way of telling you what I have in mind. For whatever we put forward somehow always keeps going around for us and isn't willing to stay where we place it.

SOCRATES. The things said by you, Euthyphro, are likely to belong to our ancestor Daedalus. And if I were saying them and   c
setting them down, perhaps you would make fun of me by saying that after all it's because of my kinship with him that my works in speech run away and aren't willing to stay where someone sets them down.[33] But as it is now, the suppositions are yours, and

---

[31]"Substance" is *ousia*, "beinghood"; "affection" is *pathos*, "that which happens to something when it is affected." These two terms became important parts of Aristotle's "technical" vocabulary.

[32]"If you please" is *ei soi philon*, literally, "if [it is] dear to you."

[33]Socrates perhaps playfully alleges a relationship between his father, who was said by later authors to have been a statuary, and Daedalus, a legendary Athenian master craftsman and

some other gibe is needed. For they aren't willing to stay still for   11c
you, as it seems to you yourself as well.

EUTHYPHRO. It seems to me, Socrates, that the things said are in
need of nearly the same gibe. For as to their going around and not
staying in the same place, *I* didn't put them up to it. Rather, *you*
seem to me the Daedalus, since, as far as I'm concerned, they   d
would stay as they were.

SOCRATES. Then probably, comrade, I have become more clever
at the art than that man, insofar as he made only his own things
not stay still, while I, besides my own things, also do this to those
of others, as is likely. And in particular, for me the most exquisite
part of the art is that I am involuntarily wise. For I would wish
rather for the speeches to stay still for me and to be placed un-
moved, than, in addition to the wisdom of Daedalus, to get the   e
money of Tantalus.[34]

But enough of this. Since you seem to me to be fastidious, I
myself will take an eager part in showing you how you may teach
me about the pious. And don't get tired out before the end. See if it
doesn't seem necessary to you that all the pious is just.

EUTHYPHRO. To me it does.

SOCRATES. And is all the just pious? Or is the pious all just, while   12a
the just is not all pious, but part of it is pious, part something else?

EUTHYPHRO. I don't follow, Socrates, what is being said.

SOCRATES. And yet you are no less younger than I am than you
are wiser. But as I say, you are being fastidious because of your
wealth of wisdom. Come, you blessed man, exert yourself, for it
isn't even hard to understand what I am saying. I am saying the
opposite of what the poet composed who said:

> Zeus, the one who enclosed and planted all these things,
> You are not willing to speak of; for where dread is, there too is   b
>   awe.[35]

---

inventor who was reputed to have constructed statues that could move about by themselves.
(See also *Alcibiades* I 121a and *Meno* 97d.) Socrates denies any connection with his father's (or
his father's ancestor's) art here, but he identifies himself closely with his mother's art of
midwifery in the *Theaetetus*, which immediately precedes the *Euthyphro* (see Introduction n.
6).

[34]Tantalus, by tradition a king and a son of Zeus, was proverbial for his wealth. Having
been admitted to the gods' company, he stole their food and gave it to his mortal acquaintances (Pindar, *Olympian* I.55–64). In another story he cut up his son Pelops and served him to
the gods, who had come to dine with him, in a gruesome stew. His punishment for these
crimes was to be eternally "tantalized" by the presence of food and drink that he could never
quite reach.

[35]According to a scholiast, these lines are from Stasinus, a post-Homeric poet who was the
supposed author of the lost *Cypria*, an epic poem describing the events of the Trojan war up to

Now I differ with the poet in this. Shall I tell you how?   12b

EUTHYPHRO. Quite.

SOCRATES. It doesn't seem to me that "where dread is, there too is awe." For many seem to me to dread when they dread diseases and poverty and many other such things, but to be in awe of none of these things that they dread. Doesn't it seem so to you too?

EUTHYPHRO. Quite so.

SOCRATES. But that "where awe is, there too is dread." For doesn't anyone who feels awe and shame in some matter also fear and dread a reputation for villainy?   c

EUTHYPHRO. Of course he dreads it.

SOCRATES. Then it is not correct to say, "where dread is, there too is awe," but rather "where awe is, there too is dread"—not, however, "wherever dread is, everywhere is awe." For I suppose that dread extends further than awe. For awe is part of dread, just as "odd" is part of "number." Hence not "wherever 'number' is, there too is 'odd,'" but "where 'odd' is, there too is 'number.'" Surely you follow me now?

EUTHYPHRO. Quite so.

SOCRATES. Now this is the sort of thing I was asking when I was speaking before: is it "where 'just' is, there too is 'pious'"? Or   d
"where 'pious' is, there too is 'just,'" but "where 'just' is, everywhere is not 'pious'"? Is the pious part of the just? Shall we say so, or does it seem otherwise to you?

EUTHYPHRO. No, but this is so. You appear to me to speak correctly.

SOCRATES. Then see what comes after this. If the pious is part of the just, then we need to discover, as is likely, what part of the just the pious would be. Now if you were asking me about one of the things mentioned just now, such as what part of number is the even and what this number happens to be, I would say "whatever is not scalene but rather isosceles."[36] Doesn't it seem so to you?

EUTHYPHRO. It does to me.

SOCRATES. You too, then, try to teach me what part of the just is   e

---

the point where the *Iliad* begins. (Another manuscript reads "showed affection for" instead of "enclosed." Burnet's Oxford text, departing from all the manuscripts, reads: "Even he who planted all these things is not willing to quarrel with Zeus, who wrought it.") Socrates calls particular attention to the poet's activity by the expression he uses to introduce this quotation: "what the poet composed who said," literally, "what the maker made who made" (*ho poiētēs epoiēsen ho poiēsas*). —The meaning of *aidōs*, here translated "awe," extends from "a sense of shame" to "respect" to "reverence."

[36] "Scalene" means "limping" or "unequal"; "isosceles" is "equal-legged." An even number is composed of two equal parts or "legs," while an odd number can only be divided into unequal parts.

pious, so that we may also tell Meletus not to do us injustice any   12e
longer and not to indict us for impiety,[37] on the ground that we
have already learned sufficiently from you the things both reverent
and pious and the things not.

EUTHYPHRO. Then it seems to me, Socrates, that that part of the
just is reverent as well as pious which concerns the tendance of the
gods, while that which concerns the tendance of human beings is
the remaining part of the just.

SOCRATES. And what you say appears noble to me, Euthyphro,
but I am still in need of a little something. For I don't yet com-   13a
prehend which tendance you are naming. Surely you aren't saying
that that concerning gods is of the same sort as the tendances
concerning other things—for surely we do speak of them? For
instance, we say that not everyone has knowledge of tending
horses, but rather the one skilled with horses, don't we?

EUTHYPHRO. Quite so.

SOCRATES. For surely skill with horses is a tendance of horses.

EUTHYPHRO. Yes.

SOCRATES. Nor does everyone have knowledge of tending dogs,
but rather the huntsman.[38]

EUTHYPHRO. Just so.

SOCRATES. For surely the huntsman's skill is a tendance of dogs.

EUTHYPHRO. Yes.   b

SOCRATES. And the herdsman's skill is a tendance of cattle?

EUTHYPHRO. Quite so.

SOCRATES. And piety and reverence[39] are a tendance of gods,
Euthyphro? Is this what you are saying?

EUTHYPHRO. I am.

SOCRATES. Doesn't every tendance bring about the same thing?
For instance, something like this: Is it for a certain good and benefit
of the one tended, just as you see that the horses tended by the
skill with horses are benefited and become better? Or don't they
seem so to you?

EUTHYPHRO. They do to me.

SOCRATES. And surely the same goes for the dogs tended by the
huntsman's skill, and the cattle by the herdsman's skill, and all the   c
others likewise? Or do you suppose the tendance is for the harm of
the one tended?

EUTHYPHRO. By Zeus, not I!

---

[37]The term is *asebeia*. "Reverent," later in this sentence and in the next sentence, is *eusebes*.
See n. 18.

[38]"Huntsman" is *kynēgetikos*, literally, "one skilled in leading dogs."

[39]"Reverence" is *eusebeia*. See n. 18.

SOCRATES. But for his benefit?   13c

EUTHYPHRO. Of course.

SOCRATES. So is piety too, being a tendance of gods, a benefit to the gods, and does it make the gods better? And would you concede that whenever you do something pious, you make one of the gods better by your work?

EUTHYPHRO. By Zeus, not I!

SOCRATES. No, and neither do I suppose, Euthyphro, that this is what you are saying. Far from it. Rather, I asked what tendance of the gods you were speaking of because I didn't believe that you   d
were saying that it is of this sort.

EUTHYPHRO. And you were correct, Socrates; for I am not saying it is of this sort.

SOCRATES. Well, then. But then what tendance of gods would piety be?

EUTHYPHRO. The one with which slaves tend their masters, Socrates.

SOCRATES. I understand. It would be a certain skillful service[40] to gods, as is likely.

EUTHYPHRO. Certainly.

SOCRATES. So could you tell me this: the skillful service to doctors happens to be a skillful service for producing what work? Don't you suppose it is for producing health?

EUTHYPHRO. I do.

SOCRATES. What about the skillful service to shipwrights? It is a   e
skillful service for producing what work?

EUTHYPHRO. Clearly, Socrates, for producing a ship.

SOCRATES. And surely that to housebuilders is for producing a house?

EUTHYPHRO. Yes.

SOCRATES. Then tell me, best of men: the skillful service to gods would be a skillful service for producing what work? It is clear that you know, since you assert that you know at least the divine things most nobly of human beings.

EUTHYPHRO. And what I say is true, Socrates.

SOCRATES. Then tell me, before Zeus, what is that altogether noble work which the gods produce, using us as servants?

EUTHYPHRO. Many noble things, Socrates.

SOCRATES. Yes, and so do the generals, my dear man. Neverthe-   14a

---

[40]"Skillful service" is *hypēretikē,* a term (its *-kē* ending indicating expertise) apparently coined by Socrates by analogy with the names of other arts and skills.

less, you could easily tell me their main one, that they produce   14a
victory in war. Or not?

EUTHYPHRO. Of course.

SOCRATES. The farmers too, I suppose, produce many noble
things. Nevertheless their main product is the food from the earth.

EUTHYPHRO. Quite so.

SOCRATES. What about the many noble things that the gods produce? What is their main product?

EUTHYPHRO. I also told you a little while ago, Socrates, that to
learn precisely how all these things are is a rather lengthy work.   b
However, I tell you simply that if someone has knowledge of how
to say and do things gratifying to the gods by praying and sacrificing, these are the pious things. And such things preserve private
families as well as the communities of cities. The opposites of the
things gratifying are impious,[41] and they overturn and destroy
everything.

SOCRATES. You could have told me much more briefly, Euthyphro, if you wished, the main point of what I was asking. But
you are not eager to teach me; that is clear. For you turned away   c
just now, when you were at the very point at which, if you had
answered, I would already have learned piety sufficiently from
you. But as it is—for it is necessary that the lover follow the
beloved[42] wherever he leads—again, what do you say the pious
and piety are? Isn't it a certain kind of knowledge of sacrificing and
praying?

EUTHYPHRO. Yes, I say so.

SOCRATES. Isn't sacrificing giving gifts to the gods, while praying
is making requests of the gods?

EUTHYPHRO. Very much so, Socrates.

SOCRATES. Then piety would be a knowledge of requesting from   d
and giving to gods, from this argument.

EUTHYPHRO. You have comprehended what I said, Socrates,
quite nobly.

SOCRATES. Yes, for I am desirous, my dear man, of your wisdom
and I am applying my mind to it, so that whatever you say won't
fall to the ground in vain. But tell me, what is this service to the
gods? Do you say that it requests from and gives to them?

EUTHYPHRO. I do.

---

[41]The word is *asebes* (see n. 18).

[42]The words for lover and beloved here are related to *erōs*, passionate sexual love, not *philia*,
the friendly love mentioned earlier in "what the gods love" (n. 25).

SOCRATES. Then wouldn't correct requesting be to request the   14d
things we need from them?

EUTHYPHRO. Certainly.

SOCRATES. And again, is correct giving to give them as gifts in   e
return the things they happen to need from us? For surely it
wouldn't be artful for a giver to bring someone gifts of which he
has no need.

EUTHYPHRO. What you say is true, Socrates.

SOCRATES. Then piety, Euthyphro, would be a certain art of commerce for gods and human beings with each other.

EUTHYPHRO. Yes, commerce, if it's more pleasing to you to give it
this name.

SOCRATES. But it's not at all more pleasing to me unless it happens to be true. Tell me, what benefit for the gods does there
happen to be from the gifts that they get from us? As to what they
give, it is clear to everyone, for there is no good for us that they do   15a
not give. But as to what they get from us, how are they benefited?
Or do we have so much of an advantage over them[43] in our commerce, that we get all the good things from them, while they get
nothing from us?

EUTHYPHRO. But do you suppose, Socrates, that the gods are
benefited from the things they get from us?

SOCRATES. Well, Euthyphro, what ever would these gifts from us
to the gods be?

EUTHYPHRO. What else do you suppose but honor and respect,
and, as I was just saying, gratitude?

SOCRATES. Is the pious then gratifying, Euthyphro, but not bene-   b
ficial or dear to the gods?

EUTHYPHRO. I for one suppose it is of all things most dear.

SOCRATES. Then this again, as is likely, is the pious: what is dear
to the gods.

EUTHYPHRO. Very much so.

SOCRATES. So in saying this, will you wonder if it is apparent that
your arguments don't stay still but walk about? And will you accuse me of being the Daedalus who is responsible for making them
walk about, when you yourself, being much more artful than
Daedalus, even make them go around in a circle? Or don't you
perceive that our argument has gone around and come back to the
same place? For surely you remember that it became apparent to us   c

---

[43]"To have an advantage over" or "to get the better of" is *pleonektein,* literally "to have
more." This "getting the better of others" is praised by Thrasymachus in his defense of
injustice (*Republic* 344a).

earlier that the pious and the dear-to-the-gods are not the same but   15c
different from each other. Or don't you remember?

EUTHYPHRO. I do.

SOCRATES. So aren't you aware now that you are asserting that
what is dear to the gods is pious? Does this turn out to be anything
else but dear-to-the-gods, or not?

EUTHYPHRO. Quite so.

SOCRATES. Therefore either we weren't agreeing nobly before,
or, if we did agree nobly then, we aren't setting it down correctly
now.

EUTHYPHRO. It's likely.

SOCRATES. Then we must consider again from the beginning
what the pious is, since I will not voluntarily give up out of cowardice until I learn it. Do not dishonor me, but apply your mind in   d
every way as much as possible and tell me the truth now. For if in
fact any human being knows, you do, and like Proteus,[44] you must
not be let go until you tell. For if you didn't know plainly the pious
and the impious, there is no way that you would ever have attempted to prosecute an elderly man, your father, for murder on
behalf of a hired man. Rather, as to the gods, you would have
dreaded the risk that you would not do it correctly, and as to
human beings, you would have been ashamed. But as it is now, I
know well that you suppose that you know plainly the pious and   e
the not pious. So tell me, Euthyphro, best of men, and don't hide
what you hold it to be.

EUTHYPHRO. Some other time, then, Socrates. For now I am in a
hurry to go somewhere, and it is time for me to go away.

SOCRATES. Such things you are doing, comrade! By leaving, you
are throwing me down from a great hope I had: that by learning
from you the things pious and the things not, I would be released
from Meletus' indictment. For I hoped to show him that I have   16a
now become wise in the divine things from Euthyphro, and that I
am no longer acting unadvisedly because of ignorance or making
innovations concerning them, and especially that I would live better for the rest of my life.

---

[44]Proteus, an immortal and unerring old man of the sea who serves the god Poseidon,
answers the questions of mortals if he can be caught and held fast, although he attempts to
escape by assuming the shapes of animals, water, and fire. Menelaus, instructed by the
goddess Eidotheia ("divine *eidos*"—see n. 20), with difficulty succeeds in catching Proteus and
learns what he must do to return home safely after the Trojan War from Egypt, where he has
been stranded by contrary winds: he must offer sacrifices to Zeus and the other gods. (*Odyssey*
IV. 351–569.)

Plato's
Apology of Socrates

How you, men of Athens, have been affected by my accusers, I do   17a
not know.[1] For my part, even I nearly forgot myself because of
them, so persuasively did they speak. And yet they have said, so to
speak, nothing true. I wondered most at one of the many falsehoods
they told, when they said that you should beware that you are not
deceived by me, since I am a clever speaker. They are not ashamed   b
that they will immediately be refuted by me in deed, as soon as it
becomes apparent that I am not a clever speaker at all; this seemed to
me to be most shameless of them—unless of course they call a clever
speaker the one who speaks the truth. For if this is what they are
saying, then I too would agree that I am an orator—but not of their
sort. So they, as I say, have said little or nothing true, while from me

Reprinted (with revisions) from Thomas G. West, *Plato's Apology of Socrates: An Interpretation, with a New Translation.* Copyright © 1979 by Cornell University, and published by Cornell
University Press.

[1]In the Athenian democracy of this time prosecutions could be initiated by any citizen or
group of citizens. The trial was conducted before a jury of probably five hundred citizens
(called "judges") selected by lot. There were officials to regulate the proceedings and to take
care of documents, but no "judge" in our sense. The trial proceeded in two stages: determination of innocence or guilt, then determination of penalty in case of guilt. In the first stage the
prosecutors or accusers (in this trial there were three) presented their arguments in separate
speeches, after which the accused gave his defense speech (*apologia*). Socrates' *apologia* concludes at 35d. The jury then voted on the defendant's innocence or guilt; Socrates was voted
guilty. There being no fixed penalty in Athenian law for Socrates' crimes, each party had to
propose a penalty for the jury to choose between. Socrates' accuser proposed the death
penalty; Socrates presents his counterproposal in the second speech of the *Apology* (35e–38b).
The jury voted to condemn him to death, probably by a larger margin than the vote for
"guilty" (Diogenes Laertius, *Lives of Eminent Philosophers* II.42). Socrates had time to make a
short third speech to the jurymen and bystanders while the officials were still busy with
matters pertaining to the trial (38c–end), after which he was taken away to jail to await
execution.

you will hear the whole truth—but by Zeus, men of Athens, not   17b
beautifully spoken speeches like theirs, adorned with phrases and   c
words; rather, what you hear will be spoken at random in the words
that I happen upon—for I trust that the things I say are just—and let
none of you expect otherwise. For surely it would not be becoming,
men, for someone of my age to come before you fabricating
speeches like a youth. And, men of Athens, I do very much beg and
beseech this of you: if you hear me speaking in my defense[2] with the
same speeches I am accustomed to speak both in the marketplace at
the money-tables, where many of you have heard me, and elsewhere, do not wonder or make a disturbance[3] because of this. For   d
this is how it is: now is the first time I have come before a law court,
at the age of seventy; hence I am simply[4] foreign to the manner of
speech here. So just as, if I really did happen to be a foreigner, you
would surely sympathize with me if I spoke in the dialect and way in
which I was raised, so also I do beg this of you now (and it is just, at   18a
least as it seems to me): leave aside the manner of my speech—for
perhaps it may be worse, but perhaps better—and instead consider
this very thing and apply your mind to this: whether the things I say
are just or not. For this is the virtue[5] of a judge, while that of an
orator is to speak the truth.

So first, men of Athens, it is just for me to speak in defense
against the first false charges against me and the first accusers, and
next against the later charges and the later accusers. For many have   b
accused me to you, even long ago, talking now for many years and
saying nothing true; and I fear them more than Anytus[6] and those
around him, although they too are dangerous. But the others are
more dangerous, men. They got hold of the many of you from
childhood, and they accused me and persuaded you—although it
is no more true than the present charge—that there is a certain

[2]To "speak in defense" is *apologeisthai*. In the title, "apology" (*apologia*) means "defense speech."

[3]The large Athenian juries often made known their approval or disapproval of a speaker by cheers, shouts of anger, or jeers.

[4]"Simply" in Greek is *atechnōs;* the word may be used as a pun on *atéchnōs,* "artlessly." On *technē* ("art") see 22d-e and n. 23.

[5]"Virtue" (*aretē*) is the specific excellence of a thing. That excellence may or may not involve what we call morality: Socrates speaks of the virtue of colts and cattle at 20b.

[6]Anytus was the most important of Socrates' three accusers, although he did not himself initiate the prosecution (Meletus did: *Euthyphro* 2b). Anytus appears in Plato's *Meno* (89e–95a), where he becomes angry with Socrates and threatens him in a discussion in which Socrates appears to praise the sophists and attack the politicians in their capacity as educators of the young. Anytus was said to be a tanner by trade.

Socrates, a wise man,[7] a thinker[8] on the things aloft, who has   18b
investigated all things under the earth, and who makes the weaker
speech the stronger.[9] Those, men of Athens, who have scattered   c
this report about, are my dangerous accusers. For their listeners
hold that investigators of these things also do not believe in gods.
Besides, there are many of these accusers, and they have been
accusing for a long time now. Moreover, they spoke to you at the
age when you were most trusting, when some of you were children and youths, and they accused me in a case that simply went
by default, for no one spoke in my defense. And the most unreasonable thing of all is that it is not even possible to know and to say   d
their names, unless a certain one happens to be a comic poet.[10]
Those who persuaded you by using envy and slander—and those
who persuaded others, after being convinced themselves—all of
these are most difficult to get at. For it is also not possible to have
any of them come forward here and to refute him, but it is necessary for me simply to speak in my defense as though fighting with
shadows and refuting with no one to answer. So you too must
deem it to be as I say: that there have been two groups of accusers,
the ones accusing me now, and the others long ago of whom I   e
speak: and you must also suppose that I should first speak in
defense against the latter, for you heard them accusing me earlier
and much more than these later ones here.

Well, then. A defense speech must be made, men of Athens, and
an attempt must be made in this short time to take away from you   19a
this slander, which you acquired over a long time. Now I would
wish that it may turn out like this, if it is in any way better both for
you and for me, and that I may accomplish something by making a
defense speech. But I suppose this is hard, and I am not at all
unaware of what sort of thing it is. Nevertheless, let this proceed in
whatever way is dear to the god, but the law must be obeyed and a
defense speech must be made.

---

[7]"Wisdom" (*sophia*), for the Greeks as for us, can denote the highest achievement of the
mind, but in this context the epithet "wise" (*sophos*)—like our "wise guy"—suggests a frivolous cleverness not consistent with a man's proper seriousness. ("Wisdom" may also indicate
technical skill in a manual or fine art, as at 22d–e.)

[8]Socrates is accused of being a *phrontistēs*, a "thinker" or "worrier." This term, which
implies excessive intellectuality, appears frequently in the *Clouds*. The related verb *phrontizein*
("think" or "worry") is consistently translated as "give thought to."

[9]"To make the weaker speech the stronger" is to use clever argument to accomplish an
unjust or improper purpose. See *Clouds* 112–118.

[10]The poet is Aristophanes, who portrayed Socrates in his *Clouds*, first produced in 423,
twenty-four years before the trial.

So let us take up from the beginning what the accusation is, from   19a
which has arisen the slander against me—which, in fact, is what   b
Meletus[11] trusted in when he brought this indictment against me.
Well, then. What did the slanderers say to slander me? Their
sworn statement, just as though they were accusers, must be read:
"Socrates does injustice[12] and is meddlesome, by investigating the
things under the earth and the heavenly things, and by making the
weaker speech the stronger, and by teaching others these same   c
things." It is something like this. For you yourselves also used to
see these things in the comedy of Aristophanes: a certain Socrates
was carried around there, claiming that he was treading on air and
spouting much other drivel about which I have no expertise, either
much or little.[13] And I do not say this to dishonor this sort of
knowledge,[14] if anyone is wise in such things (may I never be
prosecuted with such great lawsuits by Meletus!); but in fact I, men
of Athens, have no share in these things. Again, I offer the many[15]   d
of you as witnesses, and I maintain that you should teach and tell
each other, those of you who have ever heard me conversing—and
there are many such among you—tell each other, then, if any of
you ever heard me conversing about such things, either much or
little, and from this you will recognize that the same holds also for
the other things that the many say about me.

But in fact none of these things is so; and if you have heard from
anyone that I attempt to educate human beings and make money
from it, that is not true either. Though this too seems to me to be   e

---

[11]Meletus, who led the prosecution against Socrates, was "young and unknown" in Athens
(*Euthyphro* 2b). He or his father is thought to have been a poet, since Socrates says Meletus
indicted him "on behalf of the poets" (23e).

[12]The expression "to do injustice" in an indictment means "to commit a crime"; the specific
counts then follow.

[13]Socrates refers to *Clouds* 218–225, where he is suspended in a basket and utters his
"treading on air" line (225). That line is mockingly repeated by Strepsiades at the end of the
play during the burning of Socrates' "thinkery" (1503). The *Clouds* presents Socrates as an
investigator of the things aloft (171–173), as a teacher of how to make the weaker speech the
stronger (1148–1153), and as a disbeliever in Zeus and the traditional gods (365ff.). His
students in the play "investigate the things beneath the earth" (188). Cf. Socrates' account of
himself as a young man in *Phaedo* 96a–99d.

[14]We have consistently used "knowledge" to translate *epistēmē*, a word whose original
meaning is skill or know-how in doing or making. *Epistēmē* is derived from *epistasthai*, always
translated "to have knowledge." Other "know" verbs are *eidenai* (whose root sense is "to
have seen"), always translated "to know," and *gignōskein*, translated "recognize" or "be
cognizant."

[15]"The many" (*hoi polloi*), an expression referring here to the majority of the jurymen, also
suggests the "vulgar multitude" that we still hear in the words *hoi polloi*.

noble,[16] if one should be able to educate human beings, like   19e
Gorgias of Leontini, and Prodicus of Ceos, and Hippias of Elis.[17]
For each of them, men, is able, going into each of the cities, to
persuade the young—who can associate with whomever of their
own citizens they wish to for free—they persuade these young
men to leave off their associations with the latter, and to associate   20a
with themselves instead, and to give them money and acknowledge gratitude besides.

And as for that, there is another man here, from Paros, a wise
man, who I perceived was in town; for I happened to meet a man
who has paid more money to sophists than all the others, Callias,
the son of Hipponicus.[18] So I questioned him (for he has two sons):

"Callias," I said, "If your two sons had been born colts or calves,
we would have been able to get and hire an overseer for them who
could make the two of them noble and good[19] in their appropriate   b
virtue, and he would have been someone from among those skilled
with horses or skilled in farming. But as it is, since they are two
human beings, whom do you have in mind to get as an overseer[20]
for the two of them? Who is knowledgeable in such virtue, that of

[16]"Noble" is usually used to translate *kalon* in the *Apology*; it could also be rendered as
"beautiful" (as at 17c and frequently in the *Clouds*) or "fine." The word suggests the splendid
brilliance of something that shines forth, with the capacity for illumination and perhaps also
deception.

[17]These three men were known as "sophists" (the word is related to *sophos*, "wise": see n.
7), and all were foreigners, as Socrates emphasizes. The sophists were held in low esteem by
both the old-fashioned aristocratic gentlemen and the democratic politicians. Socrates' accuser
Anytus says in the *Meno*, "It is apparent that they maim and corrupt those who associate with
them" (91c). Gorgias (from Leontini, a Greek city in Sicily), a famous teacher of rhetoric,
taught that the art of persuasive speech is the chief part of education and that the possession
of that art enables one to accomplish anything one likes by ruling other men (*Gorgias* 449–452).
Prodicus (from Ceos, an Aegean island), a grammarian and philologist, stressed the need for
precision in the use of words (*Protagoras* 339e–341c). Hippias (from Elis, a city of southern
Greece) prided himself on the scope and diversity of his knowledge, which included that of
the heavenly things (*Hippias Major* 285c). The remarkable moneymaking abilities of these three
men are discussed at the beginning of the *Hippias Major*. Protagoras, the most famous sophist
of all, was dead by the time of Socrates' trial.

[18]Callias, a wealthy Athenian notorious for his dissolute and corrupt manner of life, was a
generous patron of sophists. In the *Protagoras* two of the three sophists mentioned above
appear as guests at his house. One of Callias' two sons reputedly was born of Callias' wife's
mother when she was a mistress of his (Andocides, *On the Mysteries* 124–132).

[19]In Greek, "noble and good" (*kalos kai agathos*) is the normal expression for a "perfect
gentleman." The term was often applied to the old aristocratic families. We have translated
the phrase literally to preserve the original force of the words, but the "perfect gentleman"
sense of the combination "noble and good" should also be remembered whenever it occurs.

[20]Socrates puns on the words *epistatēs* (overseer) and *epistēmon* (knowledgeable), implying
that the only suitable overseer is one who knows the art of education (20c).

human being and citizen?[21] For I suppose you have considered it,   20b
since you possess sons. Is there someone," I said, "or not?"

"Quite so," he said.

"Who," I said, "and where is he from, and for how much does
he teach?"

"Evenus," he said, "Socrates, from Paros: five minae."[22]

And I regarded Evenus as blessed if he should truly have this
art[23] and teaches at such a modest rate. As for myself, I would be   c
pluming[24] and priding myself on it if I had knowledge of these
things. But I do not have knowledge of them, men of Athens.

Perhaps, then, one of you might retort, "Well, Socrates, what is
your affair?[25] Where have these slanders against you come from?
For surely if you were in fact practicing nothing more uncommon
than others, such a report and account would not then have arisen,
unless you were doing something different from the many. So tell
us what it is, so that we do not deal unadvisedly with you."   d

In this, it seems to me, what the speaker says is just, and I will
try to demonstrate to you what ever it is that has brought me this
name and slander. So listen. Now perhaps I will seem to some of
you to be joking. Know well, however, that I will tell you the
whole truth. For I, men of Athens, have gotten this name through
nothing but a certain wisdom. Just what sort of wisdom is this?
That which is perhaps human wisdom; for probably I really am
wise in this. But those of whom I just spoke might perhaps be wise   e
in some wisdom greater than human, or else I cannot say what it
is. For I, at least, do not have knowledge of it, but whoever asserts
that I do lies and speaks in order to slander me.

Now please, men of Athens, do not make a disturbance, not
even if I seem to you to be boasting somewhat. For "not mine is the
story"[26] that I will tell; rather, I will refer it to a speaker trustwor-

---

[21]Alternative translation: "such virtue, human and political" (*anthrōpinon te kai politikon*).
On the meaning of "human being," see n. 49.

[22]Evenus (from the Aegean island of Paros), besides teaching for pay, wrote lyric poetry
and discussed rhetorical technique (*Phaedo* 60d–61c and *Phaedrus* 267a); a few fragments of his
poetry have survived. Five minae was not a large fee: Protagoras was said to have charged 100
minae. (See n. 72 on the value of a mina.)

[23]"Art" is *technē*, the specialized knowledge that guides the various human undertakings,
especially those involving production of something.

[24]"To plume oneself" (*kallynesthai*) contains the stem *kal-*, "noble" (n. 16).

[25]"Affair" is *pragma*, from *prattein*, "do" or "practice." Elsewhere, *pragma* is usually "matter" or "trouble."

[26]Socrates seems to quote part of a verse from the lost tragedy *Melanippe the Wise*, "not mine
is the tale, but from my mother"; however, he replaces Euripides' word for tale, *mythos*, with
logos (cf. *Symposium* 177a, where the word is quoted correctly). The verse occurs in a rationalis-

thy to you. Of my wisdom, if indeed it is wisdom of any kind, and   20e
what sort of thing it is, I will offer for you as witness the god in
Delphi. Now you know Chaerephon, no doubt. He was my comrade from youth as well as a comrade of your multitude, and he   21a
shared in your recent exile and returned with you. You do know
what sort of man Chaerephon was, how vehement he was in whatever he would set out to do.[27] And in particular he once even went
to Delphi and dared to consult the oracle about this—now as I say,
do not make disturbances, men—and he asked whether there was
anyone wiser than I. The Pythia[28] replied that no one was wiser.
And concerning these things his brother here will be a witness for
you, since he himself has met his end.

Now consider why I say these things: I am going to teach you   b
where the slander against me has come from. When I heard these
things, I pondered them like this: "What ever is the god saying,
and what riddle is he posing? For I am conscious that I am not at all
wise, either much or little. So what ever is he saying when he
claims that I am wisest? Surely he is not saying something false, at
least; for that is not sanctioned for him." And for a long time I was
at a loss about what ever he was saying, but then very reluctantly I
turned to something like the following investigation of it.

I went to one of those reputed[29] to be wise, on the ground that
there, if anywhere, I would refute the divination[30] and show the   c
oracle, "This man is wiser than I, but you declared that I was
wisest." So I considered him thoroughly—I need not speak of him
by name, but he was one of the politicians[31]—and when I consid-

---

tic account of the generation of the world that omits any mention of gods. Alternatively,
Socrates could be alluding to Euripides' *Helen*, in which Menelaus, shipwrecked and dressed
in rags, says, "[the] statement [*logos*] is not mine, but rather a word of wise men: 'nothing is
stronger than terrible necessity'" (513–514).

[27]Chaerephon, the principal companion of Socrates in the *Clouds*, shows his impetuosity at
the beginning of the *Charmides*, where Socrates calls him a "madman." According to
Aristophanes he was pale and withered (*Clouds* 504) and his nickname was "the bat" (*Birds*
1296). Chaerephon also appears at the beginning of the *Gorgias*.
"Your recent exile" refers to the supporters of democracy in Athens who were compelled to
escape the city during the brief but murderous reign of the oligarchy (the "Thirty Tyrants").
See 32c and n. 59 on the Thirty.

[28]"The Pythia" was the title of the priestess who delivered Apollo's oracles at Delphi.

[29]"Be reputed" and "seem" are the consistent translations of *dokein*, from which derives the
word *doxa*, "opinion" or "reputation." The realm of *doxa* proves to be a principal focus of
Socrates' investigation described here.

[30]"Divination" is *manteion*, which may also mean "prophecy." From the same root comes
mantis (diviner, seer, prophet).

[31]"Politician" is *politikos*, one who stands at the forefront of the public life of the *polis* (city).
The term *politikos* is not pejorative; it might also be translated "statesman."

ered him and conversed with him, men of Athens, I was affected   21c
something like this: it seemed to me that this man seemed to be
wise, both to many other human beings and most of all to himself,
but that he was not. And then I tried to show him that he supposed
he was wise, but was not. So from this I became hateful both to   d
him and to many of those present.

For my part, as I went away, I reasoned with regard to myself: "I
am wiser than this human being. For probably neither of us knows
anything noble and good, but he supposes he knows something
when he does not know, while I, just as I do not know, do not even
suppose that I do. I *am* likely to be a little bit wiser than he in this
very thing: that whatever I do not know, I do not even suppose I
know."

From there I went to someone else, to one of those reputed to be
wiser than he, and these things seemed to me to be the same. And   e
there I became hateful both to him and to many others.

After this, then, I kept going to one after another, all the while
perceiving with pain and fear that I was becoming hated. Nevertheless, it seemed to be necessary to regard the matter of the god
as most important. So I had to go, in considering what the oracle
was saying, to all those reputed to know something. And by the   22a
dog,[32] men of Athens—for it is necessary to speak the truth before
you—I swear I was affected something like this: those with the best
reputations seemed to me nearly the most deficient, in my investigation in accordance with the god, while others with more paltry
reputations seemed to be men more fit in regard to being prudent.[33]

Indeed, I must display my wandering to you as a performing of
certain labors[34] so that the divination would turn out to be unre-
futed. After the politicians I went to the poets, those of tragedies
and dithyrambs, and the others, in order that there I would catch   b
myself in the act of being more ignorant than they. So I would take
up those poems of theirs which it seemed to me they had worked
on the most, and I would ask them thoroughly what they meant,
so that I might also learn something from them at the same time. I

---

[32]"By the dog" is an oath apparently unique to Socrates. He swears "by the dog, the
Egyptians' god" at *Gorgias* 482b; "the dog" may be Anubis, the mediator between the upper
and lower world, whose Greek counterpart is Hermes.

[33]The Greek word *phronimos*, translated "prudent," ranges in meaning from merely "sensible" (as seems to apply here) to "wise."

[34]The expression "certain labors" recalls the famous labors of Heracles, the traditional
Greek hero; less obviously, Socrates' "wandering" may allude to the wise Odysseus' long
voyage from Troy back to his home in Ithaca, described in Homer's *Odyssey*.

am ashamed to tell you the truth, men; nevertheless, it must be   22b
said. Almost everyone present, so to speak, would have spoken
better than the poets did about the poetry that they themselves had
made. So again, also concerning the poets, I soon recognized that
they do not make what they make by wisdom, but by some sort of   c
nature and while inspired, like the diviners and those who deliver
oracles.[35] For they too say many noble things, but they know nothing of what they speak. It was apparent to me that the poets are
also affected in the same sort of way. At the same time, I perceived
that they supposed, on account of their poetry, that they were the
wisest of human beings also in the other things, in which they
were not. So I went away from there too supposing that I had
turned out to be superior to them in the very same thing in which I
was to the politicians.

Finally, then, I went to the manual artisans. For I was conscious
that I had knowledge of nothing, so to speak, but I knew that I   d
would discover that they, at least, had knowledge of many noble
things. And I was not played false about this: they did have knowledge of things which I did not have knowledge of, and in this way
they were wiser than I. But, men of Athens, the good craftsmen
also seemed to me to go wrong in the same way as the poets:
because he performed his art nobly, each one deemed himself
wisest also in the other things, the greatest things—and this discordant note of theirs seemed to hide that wisdom. So I asked myself   e
on behalf of the oracle whether I would prefer to be as I am, being
in no way wise in their wisdom or ignorant in their ignorance, or to
have both things that they have. I answered myself and the oracle
that it profits me to be just as I am.

This is the examination, men of Athens, from which I have incurred many hatreds, the sort that are harshest and gravest, so that   23a
many slanders have arisen from them, and I got this name of being
"wise." For those present on each occasion suppose that I myself
am wise in the things concerning which I refute someone else,
whereas it is probable, men, that really the god is wise, and that in
this oracle he is saying that human wisdom is worth little or nothing. And he appears to say this of Socrates and to have made use of

[35]The word for "make" here is *poiein*, which in this context also means "compose [poetry]."
The English and Greek words for poetry and poem derive from *poiein*. A poet who composes
"by a sort of nature" (in contrast to a man who possesses an art) writes without the guidance
of a plan or thought of which he is fully aware. "While inspired" (*enthousiazontes*) is from
entheos, "having a god within." Socrates elsewhere speaks of such poetic composition as
being directed by "divine allotment" (*Ion* 534c). He seems to mean that it is like the orderly
motions and works of nature, which are produced by no manifestly embodied intelligence.

my name in order to make me a pattern, as if he would say, "That   23b
one of you, O human beings, is wisest, who, like Socrates, has
become cognizant that in truth he is worth nothing with respect to
wisdom."

That is why even now I still go around seeking and investigating
in accordance with the god any townsman or foreigner I suppose
to be wise. And whenever someone does not seem so to me, I
come to the god's aid and show that he is not wise. And because of
this occupation, I have had no leisure, either to do any of the
things of the city worth speaking of or any of the things of my
family. Instead, I am in ten-thousandfold poverty because of my   c
devotion to the god.

In addition to these things, the young who follow me of their
own accord—those who have the most leisure, the sons of the
wealthiest—enjoy hearing human beings examined. And they
themselves often imitate me, and in turn they attempt to examine
others. And then, I suppose, they discover a great abundance of
human beings who suppose they know something, but know little
or nothing. Thereupon, those examined by them are angry at me,
not at themselves, and they say that Socrates is someone most   d
disgusting and that he corrupts the young. And whenever someone asks them, "By doing what and teaching what?" they have
nothing to say, but are ignorant. So in order not to seem to be at a
loss, they say the things that are ready at hand against all who
philosophize: "the things aloft and under the earth" and "not
believing in gods" and "making the weaker speech the stronger."
For I do not suppose they would be willing to speak the truth, that
it becomes quite clear that they pretend to know, but know nothing. So since they are, I suppose, ambitious and vehement and
many, and since they speak about me in an organized and persua-   e
sive way, they have filled up your ears, slandering me vehemently
for a long time.

From among these men, Meletus attacked me, and Anytus and
Lycon,[36] Meletus being vexed on behalf of the poets, Anytus on
behalf of the craftsmen and the politicians, and Lycon on behalf of   24a
the orators. Therefore, as I said when I began, it would be a wonder to me if I should be able in this short time to take away from
you this slander which has become so great. This is the truth for
you, men of Athens; I am hiding nothing from you either great or

---

[36]Little is known of Lycon; he may be the Lycon of Xenophon's *Symposium,* a slow-witted
but decent gentleman, whose son was beloved by Callias (n. 18).

small in my speech, nor am I holding anything back. And yet I   24a
know rather well that I incur hatred by these very things; which is
also a proof that I speak the truth, and that this is the slander
against me, and that these are its causes. Whether you investigate   b
these things now or later, you will discover that this is so.

So about the things which the first accusers accused me of, let
this be a sufficient defense speech before you. But against Meletus,
the "good and patriotic," as he says, and the later accusers, I will
try to speak next in my defense. Now again, just as though these
were other accusers, let us take up their sworn statement. It is
something like this: it asserts that Socrates does injustice by corrupting the young, and by not believing in the gods in whom the
city believes, but in other *daimonia*[37] that are novel. The charge is of   c
this sort.[38] But let us examine each one of the parts of this charge.

Now he asserts that I do injustice by corrupting the young. But I,
men of Athens, assert that Meletus does injustice, in that he jests
in a serious matter, easily bringing human beings to trial, pretending to be serious and concerned about things for which he never
cared[39] at all. That this is so, I will try to display to you as well.

Now come here, Meletus, tell me: do you not regard it as most   d
important how the youth will be the best possible?

[MELETUS][40] I do.

[SOCRATES] Come now, tell these men, who makes them better?
For it is clear that you know, since you care, at least. For since you
have discovered the one who corrupts them, as you say, namely
me, you are bringing me before these men and accusing me. But
the one who makes them better—come, tell them and reveal to
them who it is.

---

[37]*Daimonia*, the neuter plural of the adjective *daimonion* ("daimonic"), may be translated "daimonic things" or "daimonic beings," perhaps even "divinities." The word has been left untranslated wherever it is used as a substantive in order to leave open what the "daimonics" in question may be. As an adjective it will be translated "daimonic." For Socrates, "the daimonic" seems to be the realm between the divine (the gods) and the merely human. A daimon, as explained at 27d–e, is a being half-divine and half-human. See also *Symposium* 201d–204c.

[38]The original of the indictment seems best preserved in Diogenes Laertius II.40: "Socrates does injustice by not believing in the gods in whom the city believes, and by bringing in other *daimonia* that are novel; he also does injustice by corrupting the young." Xenophon's version differs in only one word: instead of "bringing in" he has "carrying in" (*Memorabilia* I.1.1). In Socrates' present version of the indictment (admittedly not accurate, since he says it is "some-thing like this"), (1) he reverses the original order of the impiety and corruption charges, and (2) he boldly drops the word "bringing in," changing the meaning of the charge from "intro-ducing" to "believing in" novel *daimonia*.

[39]"Care" is *meletē*; Socrates puns on Meletus' name by arguing that "Mr. Care doesn't really care." *Meletē* may also mean long practice, study, or attention.

[40]We have added the names of the speakers in brackets. They are not in the original text.

Do you see, Meletus, that you are silent and have nothing to   24d
say? And yet does it not seem to be shameful to you, and a sufficient proof of just what I say, that you have never cared? But tell,
my good man, who makes them better?

[MELETUS] The laws.

[SOCRATES] But I am not asking this, best of men, but rather what   e
human being is it who knows first of all this very thing, the laws?

[MELETUS] These men, Socrates, the judges.

[SOCRATES] What are you saying, Meletus? Are these men here
able to educate the young, and do they make them better?

[MELETUS] Very much so.

[SOCRATES] All of them, or some of them, and some not?

[MELETUS] All of them.

[SOCRATES] Well said, by Hera,[41] and you speak of a great abundance of benefiters. What then? Do the listeners here make them
better or not?

[MELETUS] These too.   25a

[SOCRATES] And what about the Councilmen?[42]

[MELETUS] The Councilmen too.

[SOCRATES] Well, Meletus, then surely those in the Assembly,[43]
the Assemblymen, do not corrupt the youth? Or do all those too
make them better?

[MELETUS] Those too.

[SOCRATES] Then all the Athenians, as it appears, make them
noble and good except me, and I alone corrupt them. Is this what
you are saying?

[MELETUS] I do say this, most vehemently.

[SOCRATES] You have charged me with great misfortune. Now
answer me. Does it seem to you to be so also concerning horses?
That all human beings make them better, while one certain one is   b
the corrupter? Or is it wholly opposite to this, that one certain one
is able to make them better—or very few, those skilled with
horses—while the many, if they ever associate with horses and use
them, corrupt them? Is this not so, Meletus, both concerning
horses, and all the other animals?

---

[41]"By Hera" is an oath usually used by women. Hera, a god of marriage and of the life of
women, is frequently connected with the birth and nurture of children.

[42]The Council (*boulē*) was an administrative body of five hundred members, which super-
vised the day-to-day domestic affairs of the city. Its members were selected by lot for a one-
year term of office.

[43]The Assembly (*ekklēsia*), the highest authority in democratic Athens, was composed of
whatever adult male citizens happened to attend any given meeting. All important questions
of public policy were determined by the Assembly.

Of course it is, altogether so, whether you and Anytus deny or   25b
affirm it. For it would be a great happiness for the young if one
alone corrupts them, while the others benefit them. But in fact,   c
Meletus, you have sufficiently displayed that you never yet gave
any thought to the young. And you are making your own lack of
care plainly apparent, since you have cared nothing about the
things for which you bring me in here.

But tell us further, Meletus, before Zeus, whether it is better to
dwell among upright citizens or villainous ones?

Sir, answer. For surely I am asking nothing hard. Do not the
villainous do something bad to whoever are nearest to them, while
the good do something good?

[MELETUS] Quite so.

[SOCRATES] Is there anyone, then, who wishes to be harmed by   d
those he associates with, rather than to be benefited?

Keep answering, my good man. For the law orders you to answer. Is there anyone who wishes to be harmed?

[MELETUS] Of course not.

[SOCRATES] Come then, do you bring me in here saying that I
voluntarily corrupt the young and make them more villainous, or
involuntarily?

[MELETUS] Voluntarily, I say.

[SOCRATES] What then, Meletus? Are you so much wiser at your
age than I at mine, that you have become cognizant that the bad
always do something bad to those who are closest to them, and the
good do something good; whereas I have come into so much igno-   e
rance that I am not even cognizant that if I ever do something
wretched to any of my associates, I will risk getting back something
bad from him? So that I do so much bad voluntarily, as you assert?
Of this I am not convinced by you, Meletus, nor, do I suppose, is
any other human being. But either I do not corrupt, or if I do
corrupt, I do it involuntarily, so in both cases what you say is false.   26a

And if I corrupt involuntarily, the law is not that you bring me in
here for such involuntary wrongs, but that you take me aside in
private to teach and admonish me. For it is clear that if I learn, I will
at least stop doing what I do involuntarily. But you avoided associating with me and teaching me, and you were not willing to, but
instead you brought me in here, where the law is to bring in those
in need of punishment, not learning.

But in fact, men of Athens, what I was saying is already clear,
that Meletus never cared about these things either much or little.   b
Nevertheless, speak to us, how do you say that I corrupt the

youth, Meletus? Or is it clear, according to the indictment that you   26b
brought, that it is by teaching them not to believe[44] in the gods in
whom the city believes, but in other *daimonia* that are novel? Do
you not say that it is by teaching these things that I corrupt them?

[MELETUS] I certainly do say this, most vehemently!

[SOCRATES] Then before these very gods, Meletus, about whom
our speech now is, speak to me and to these men still more plainly.   c
For I am not able to understand whether you are saying that I teach
them to believe that there are gods of some sort—and so I myself
do believe that there are gods and am not completely atheistic and
do not do injustice in this way—but that I do not believe in those in
whom the city believes, but in others, and this is what you charge
me with, that I believe in others. Or do you assert that I myself do
not believe in gods at all and that I teach this to others?

[MELETUS] This is what I say, that you do not believe in gods at
all.

[SOCRATES] Wondrous Meletus, why do you say this? Do I not   d
even believe, then, that sun and moon are gods, as other human
beings do?

[MELETUS] No, by Zeus, judges, since he declares that the sun is
stone and the moon is earth.

[SOCRATES] Do you suppose you are accusing Anaxagoras,[45] my
dear Meletus? And do you so much despise these men here and
suppose that they are so inexperienced in letters that they do not
know that the books of Anaxagoras of Clazomenae are full of these
speeches? Moreover, do the young learn these things from me,
when it is sometimes possible for them to buy them in the orchestra for a drachma,[46] if the price is very high, and then to laugh at   e
Socrates if he pretends that they are his own, especially since they

---

[44]The word translated "believe (in)" (*nomizein*) may also mean "acknowledge" or "respect." It is related to *nomos*, "custom" or "law." To believe in (*nomizein*) gods, then, may be
understood either as orthodoxy, the inward conviction that they exist, or as orthopraxy, the
outward demonstration of respect (by performance of the proper sacrifices, for example).
Socrates plays on this ambiguity of believe/acknowledge in the following cross-examination of
Meletus. (The word *hēgeisthai*, not related to *nomizein*, is usually translated "hold" but sometimes "believe.")

[45]The philosopher Anaxagoras, from the Greek city of Clazomenae, lived in Athens when
Socrates was a young man. He was a friend of Pericles and apparently taught that the nature
of things can be understood without reference to the city's gods. According to Plutarch,
Anaxagoras was indicted on a charge of impiety, but he avoided prosecution by fleeing the
city (*Pericles* 32). Socrates criticizes Anaxagoras' philosophical teachings, to which he was
attracted as a young man, in *Phaedo* 97b–99c.

[46]One drachma was the daily allowance for young men in training to be military officers, a
very modest sum. The "orchestra" was apparently an area of the marketplace where books
were sold.

are so strange? But before Zeus, is this how I seem to you? Do I   26e
believe there is no god?

[MELETUS] You certainly do not, by Zeus, not in any way at all!

[SOCRATES] You are unbelievable, Meletus, even, as you seem to
me, to yourself. This man seems to me, men of Athens, to be very
hubristic and unrestrained, and simply to have brought this indictment with a certain hubris and unrestraint and youthful rashness.
He is like someone testing me by putting together a riddle: "Will   27a
Socrates the 'wise' recognize that I am jesting and contradicting
myself, or will I deceive him and the rest of the listeners?" For he
himself appears to me to be contradicting himself in the indictment, as if he were to say, "Socrates does injustice by not believing
in gods, but believing in gods." And yet this is the conduct of one
who jokes.

Now consider with me, men, how he appears to me to be saying
this. And you answer us, Meletus. But you others, as I begged of
you from the beginning, please remember not to make distur-   b
bances if I make the speeches in my accustomed way.

Is there any human being, Meletus, who believes that there are
human matters, but does not believe in human beings?

Let him keep answering, men, and let him not make disturbances again and again. Is there anyone who does not believe in
horses, but believes in horse-matters? Or anyone who does not
believe in flute-players, but believes in flute-matters?

There is not, best of men. If you do not wish to answer, I say it
for you and for these others. But at least answer what comes next.
Is there anyone who believes that there are daimonic matters, but   c
does not believe in daimons?

[MELETUS] There is not.

[SOCRATES] How helpful you were by answering reluctantly
when compelled by these men! Now then, you say that I believe in
and teach *daimonia;* so whether they are novel or ancient, at any
rate I do believe in *daimonia* according to your speech, and you also
swore to this in the indictment. But if I believe in *daimonia*, then
surely there is also a great necessity that I believe in daimons. Is
this not so?

Of course it is. I set you down as agreeing, since you do not
answer. And do we not believe that daimons are either gods or   d
children of gods? Do you affirm this or not?

[MELETUS] Quite so.

[SOCRATES] Therefore if I do believe in daimons, as you say, and
if, on the one hand, daimons are gods of some sort, then this

would be what I say you are riddling and jesting about, when you   27d
say that I do not believe in gods, and again that I believe in gods,
since in fact I do believe in daimons.

On the other hand, if daimons are certain bastard children of
gods, whether from nymphs or from certain others of whom it is
also said they are born, then what human being would believe that
there are children of gods, but not gods? It would be as strange as if   e
someone believed in children of horses or asses—mules—but did
not believe that there are horses and asses.[47] But, Meletus, there is
no way that you did not bring this indictment either to test us in
these things, or else because you were at a loss about what true
injustice you might charge me with. There is no device by which
you could persuade any human being who is even slightly intelligent, that it is not the part of the same man to believe in both
daimonia and divine things, and further that this same man believes
in neither daimons nor gods nor heroes.[48]   28a

But in fact, men of Athens, that I do not do injustice according to
Meletus' indictment, does not seem to me to require much of a
defense speech, but even this is sufficient. But what I was saying
earlier—that I have incurred much hatred, and among many
men—know well that this is true. And this is what will convict me,
if it does convict me: not Meletus or Anytus, but the slander and
envy of the many. This has convicted many other good men too,
and I suppose it will also convict me. And there is no danger that it   b
will stop with me.

Perhaps, then, someone might say, "Then are you not ashamed,
Socrates, of having followed the sort of pursuit from which you
now run the risk of dying?"

I would respond to him with a just speech: "What you say is
ignoble, fellow,[49] if you suppose that a man who is of even a little

[47]An "ass" is *onos*, and a "mule" is *hemionos*, "half-ass." The word *hemionos* is analogous to, and in the present context reminds one of, *hemitheos*, "demigod" (literally, "half-god").

[48]Socrates concludes with a complex flourish. The last sentence means: if someone believes in *daimonia*, daimonic things, he also believes in *theia*, divine things; further, the same man must also believe in daimons, gods, and heroes. "Heroes" are demigods or "half-gods," children of one mortal and one divine parent. Socrates adds "heroes" here to prepare his introduction of the demigod Achilles, son of the goddess Thetis and the mortal Peleus. On heroes and daimons, see *Cratylus* 397d–398e, where Socrates presents the account of the *Apology* in a more playful manner.

[49]"Fellow" is literally "human being," an address that carries a somewhat contemptuous tone in Greek. "Human being" is *anthrōpos*, any member of the human race, as opposed to *anēr*, a "real man" or male human being. The life of an *anēr* (like Achilles) is distinguished by its dedication to manly excellence, which shows itself above all in politics and war. "Manli-ness"—*andreia*—is the Greek word for courage. Socrates is implicitly accused here of not bei. an *anēr*. Although Socrates proceeds to compare himself to Achilles, he implicitly proposes . standard of *human* excellence higher than that of mere manliness.

benefit should take into account the danger of living or dying, but   28b
not rather consider this alone whenever he acts: whether his actions are just or unjust, and the deeds of a good man or a bad. For
according to your speech, those of the demigods who met their   c
end at Troy would be paltry, especially the son of Thetis. Rather
than endure anything shameful, he despised danger so much that
when his mother (a goddess) spoke to him as he was eager to kill
Hector—something like this, as I suppose: 'Son, if you avenge the
murder of your comrade Patroclus and kill Hector, you yourself
will die; for straightway,' she says, 'after Hector, your fate is ready
at hand'—he, upon hearing this, belittled death and danger, fearing much more to live as a bad man and not to avenge his friends.   d
'Straightway,' he says, 'may I die, after I inflict a penalty on the
doer of injustice, so that I do not stay here ridiculous beside the
curved ships, a burden on the land.' Surely you do not suppose
that he gave any thought to death and danger?''[50]

This is the way it is, men of Athens, in truth. Wherever someone
stations himself, holding that it is best, or wherever he is stationed
by a ruler, there he must stay and run the risk, as it seems to me,

---

[50]Socrates refers in this passage to a crucial turning-point in the plot of Homer's *Iliad*, the
epic poem about the Greek war against Troy, whose story would have been familiar to every
Athenian. Achilles, whose youthful beauty and excellence as a warrior distinguish him from
the other heroes, withdraws from the war when he is publicly insulted by Agamemnon, the
commander of the Greek army. Achilles enlists the aid of Zeus, who supports his cause by
sustaining the Trojan army's success as long as Achilles remains absent from the war. But
when Patroclus, Achilles' closest friend, is killed by the Trojan hero Hector, Achilles' angry
desire for revenge leads him back into the fight, although he knows from a prophecy that
when he kills Hector, he must die soon thereafter. There follows a crescendo of violence
which culminates in Achilles' slaying of Hector, and the poem ends with the return of
Hector's body to the Trojans and his burial. Socrates' "quotation" from the *Iliad* departs
somewhat from the original text, which reads:

> "Swiftly doomed, child, you will be for me, since you say such things;
> for straightway after Hector, your fate is ready at hand."
> Greatly burdened, Achilles swift of feet addressed her:
> "Straightway may I die, since I was not
> to aid my comrade when he was killed. Very far from his fatherland
> he has perished; he needed me to become his protector from destruction.
> But now, since I am not returning to my dear fatherland's earth,
> and did not in any way become a light to Patroclus
> and to my other comrades, many of whom went down before glorious Hector,
> I sit beside the ships, a vain burden on the land."
> (XVIII.95–104)

Homer's Achilles chooses to avenge Patroclus out of grief and anger, while Socrates' Achilles,
more concerned with how he looks to others, fears doing anything shameful and appearing
"ridiculous." Further, in Homer the death of Patroclus is for Achilles the private loss of his
dearest friend, while Socrates transforms it into a crime that deserves punishment (and so
Hector rather than Patroclus is dwelt upon): Patroclus' death is a "murder" and Achilles will
"inflict a penalty [*dikē*, also the word for justice] on the doer of injustice."

and not take into account death or anything else compared to what   28d
is shameful. So I would have done terrible deeds, men of Athens,
if, when the rulers whom you elected to rule me stationed me in   e
Potidaea and Amphipolis and at Delium,[51] I stayed then where
they stationed me and ran the risk of dying like anyone else, but
when the god stationed me, as I supposed and assumed, ordering
me to live philosophizing and examining myself and others, I had
then left my station because I feared death or any other matter   29a
whatever.

Terrible that *would* be, and truly then someone might justly bring
me into a law court, saying that I do not believe that there are gods,
since I would be disobeying the divination, and fearing death, and
supposing that I am wise when I am not. For to fear death, men, is in
fact nothing other than to seem to be wise, but not to be so. For it is
to seem to know what one does not know: no one knows whether
death does not even happen to be the greatest of all goods for the
human being; but people fear it as though they knew well that it is
the greatest of evils. And how is this not that reproachable igno-   b
rance of supposing that one knows what one does not know? But I,
men, am perhaps distinguished from the many human beings also
here in this, and if I were to say that I am wiser than anyone in
anything, it would be in this: that since I do not know sufficiently
about the things in Hades,[52] so also I suppose that I do not know.
But I do know that it is bad and shameful to do injustice and to
disobey one's better, whether god or human being. So compared to
the bad things which I know are bad, I will never fear or flee the
things about which I do not know whether they even happen to be
good.

So that not even if you let me go now and if you disobey Any-   c
tus—who said that either I should not have been brought in here at
the beginning, or, since I was brought in, that it is not possible not
to kill[53] me (he said before you that if I am acquitted, soon your

[51]These three battles of the war between Athens and Sparta are described in Thucydides'
history (Potidaea: I.56–65, II.58, 70; Amphipolis: V.6–10; Delium: IV.90–101). Socrates is
reported to have aided Alcibiades when he was wounded at Potidaea and to have retreated
bravely at Delium (*Symposium* 220d–221b, *Laches* 189b). Potidaea was a costly and inconclusive
victory; Amphipolis and Delium were decisive defeats. George Anastaplo points out that on
each occasion the Athenian commander who stationed Socrates at his post died during the
battle. ("Human Being and Citizen: A Beginning to the Study of the *Apology of Socrates*," in
Human Being and Citizen, p. 24.)

[52]In Greek poetry Hades is the insubstantial abode for the shades or shadows of the dead
(*Odyssey* XI). Strictly speaking, Hades is Pluto, the god of the underworld, and the expression
translated "in Hades" is literally "in Hades' [house]." The name for Hades (*Haidēs*) is a
variant on the word "unseen" (*aidēs*).

[53]In Greek the word "kill," used in a legal context, may mean "condemn to death."

sons, pursuing what Socrates teaches, will all be completely cor-   29c
rupted)—if you would say to me with regard to this, "Socrates, for
now we will not obey Anytus; we will let you go, but on this
condition: that you no longer spend time in this investigation or
philosophize; and if you are caught still doing this, you will die"—   d
if you would let me go, then, as I said, on these conditions, I would
say to you, "I, men of Athens, salute you and love you, but I will
obey[54] the god rather than you; and as long as I breathe and am
able to, I will certainly not stop philosophizing, and I will exhort
you and explain this to whomever of you I happen to meet, and I
will speak just the sorts of things I am accustomed to: 'Best of men,
you are an Athenian, from the city that is greatest and best reputed
for wisdom and strength: are you not ashamed that you care for
having as much money as possible, and reputation, and honor, but   e
that you neither care for nor give thought to prudence, and truth,
and how your soul will be the best possible?' And if one of you
disputes it and asserts that he does care, I will not immediately let
him go, nor will I go away, but I will speak to him and examine and
test him. And if he does not seem to me to possess virtue, but only
says he does, I will reproach him, saying that he regards the things   30a
worth the most as the least important, and the paltrier things as
more important. I will do this to whomever, younger or older, I
happen to meet, both foreigner and townsman, but more so to the
townsmen, inasmuch as you are closer to me in kin.

"Know well, then, that the god orders this. And *I* suppose that
until now no greater good has arisen for you in the city than my
service to the god. For I go around and do nothing but persuade
you, both younger and older, not to care for bodies and money   b
before, nor as vehemently as, how your soul will be the best possible. I say: 'Not from money does virtue come, but from virtue
comes money and all of the other good things for human beings
both privately and publicly.' If, then, I corrupt the young by saying
these things, they may be harmful. But if someone asserts that
what I say is other than this, he speaks nonsense. With a view to
these things, men of Athens," I would say, "either obey Anytus or
not, and either let me go or not, since I would not do otherwise,
not even if I were going to die many times."   c

Do not make disturbances, men of Athens, but abide by what I
begged of you, not to make disturbances at the things I say, but to
listen. For, as I suppose, you will even be helped by listening. For

---

[54]Here and elsewhere the word "obey" is *peithesthai,* passive of *peithein,* "persuade." (Ex-
ception: "disobey" in 29c is *apistein,* literally, "not trust.")

in fact I am going to tell you certain other things at which you will   30c
perhaps cry out; but do not do this in any way. For know well that
if you kill me, since I am the sort of man that I say I am, you will
not harm me more than yourselves. For Meletus or Anytus would
not harm me—he would not even be able to—for I do not suppose
it is sanctioned that a better man be harmed by a worse. Perhaps,   d
however, he might kill or banish or dishonor[55] me. But this man no
doubt supposes, and others too, that these are great evils, while I
do not suppose that these are, but much rather doing what this
man here is now doing: attempting to kill a man unjustly.

So I, men of Athens, am now far from making a defense speech
on my own behalf, as someone might suppose. I do it rather on
your behalf, so that you do not do something wrong concerning
the gift of the god to you by voting to condemn me. For if you kill   e
me, you will not easily discover another of my sort, who—even if it
is rather ridiculous to say—has simply been set upon the city by
the god, as though upon a great and well-born horse who is rather
sluggish because of his great size and needs to be awakened by
some gadfly. Just so, in fact, the god seems to me to have set me
upon the city as someone of this sort: I awaken and persuade and
reproach each one of you, and I do not stop settling down every-   31a
where upon you the whole day. Someone else of this sort will
certainly not easily arise for you, men. Well, if you obey me, you
will spare me. But perhaps you may be vexed, like the drowsy
when they are awakened, and if you obey Anytus and slap me,
you would easily kill me. Then you would spend the rest of your
lives asleep, unless the god sends you someone else in his concern
for you.

That *I* happen to be someone of this sort, given to the city by the
god, you might apprehend from this: it does not seem human, on   b
the one hand, that I have been careless of all my own things and
that for so many years now I have endured that the things of my
family be uncared for; and on the other hand, that I always do your
business, going to each of you privately, as a father or an older
brother might do, persuading you to care for virtue. If I was getting
something out of this, and if I was receiving pay while I exhorted
you to these things, it would be somewhat reasonable. But as it is,
even you yourselves see that the accusers, who accused me so
shamelessly in everything else, in this have not been able to be-

---

[55]As a legal term, to "dishonor" someone is to deprive him of the rights and privileges
pertaining to citizenship.

come so utterly shameless as to offer a witness to assert that I ever   31c
took any pay or asked for it. For, I suppose, I offer a sufficient
witness that I speak the truth: my poverty.

Perhaps, then, it might seem to be strange that I do go around
counseling these things and being a busybody in private, but that
in public I do not dare to go up before your multitude to counsel
the city. The cause of this is what you have heard me speak of
many times and in many places, that something divine and daimonic[56] comes to me, a voice—which, of course, is also what   d
Meletus wrote about in the indictment, making a comedy over it.
This is something which began for me in childhood: a sort of voice
comes, and whenever it comes, it always turns me away from
whatever I am about to do, but never turns me forward.

This is what opposes my political activity, and its opposition
seems to me altogether noble. For know well, men of Athens, if I
had long ago attempted to be politically active, I would long ago
have perished, and I would have benefited neither you nor myself.
Now do not be vexed with me when I speak the truth. For there is   e
no human being who will preserve his life if he genuinely opposes
either you or any other multitude and prevents many unjust and
unlawful things from happening in the city. Rather, if someone
who really fights for the just is going to preserve himself even for a   32a
short time, it is necessary for him to lead a private rather than a
public life.

I for my part will offer great proofs of these things for you—not
speeches, but what *you* honor, deeds. Do listen to what happened
to me, so that you may see that I would not yield even to one man
against the just because of a fear of death, even if I were to perish
by refusing to yield. I will tell you vulgar things, typical of the law
courts, but true. I, men of Athens, never held any office in the city   b
except for being once on the Council. And it happened that our
tribe, Antiochis, held the prytany[57] when you wished to judge the
ten generals (the ones who did not pick up the men from the naval

---

[56]For other references to Socrates' *daimonion,* the "daimonic something" that comes to him,
see 40a–c below and *Euthyphro* 3b, *Republic* 496c, *Theaetetus* 151a, *Phaedrus* 242b–c, *Euthydemus*
272e, and *Theages* 128d–131a (the latter is an extended account). See also Xenophon, *Memorabilia* I.1.2–9 and his *Apology* 4, 12–13.

[57]The citizen-body of Athens was divided into ten administrative units called "tribes." Each
year fifty men were selected by lot from each of the tribes to serve on the Council (n. 42) for a
one-year term. The year was divided into ten parts called "prytanies," and each group of fifty
served as "prytanes" during one of these periods. Among their other responsibilities, the
prytanes arranged for meetings of the Council and Assembly. When the Assembly met,
certain of the prytanes were chosen by lot to be its chairmen.

battle) as a group—unlawfully, as it seemed to all of you in the time   32b
afterwards. I alone of the prytanes opposed your doing anything
against the laws then, and I voted against it. And although the
orators were ready to indict me and arrest me, and you were ordering and shouting, I supposed that I should run the risk with the   c
law and the just rather than side with you because of fear of prison
or death when you were counseling unjust things.[58]

Now this was when the city was still under the democracy. But
again, when the oligarchy came to be, the Thirty summoned five of
us into the Tholos, and they ordered us to arrest Leon the Salamin-
ian and bring him from Salamis to die.[59] They ordered many
others to do many things of this sort, wishing that as many as
possible would be implicated in the responsibility. Then, however,
I showed again, not in speech but in deed, that I do not even care   d
about death in any way at all—if it is not too crude to say so—but

[58]Athens and Sparta, the two leading cities of the Greek world, fought an exhausting
twenty-seven-year war which ended with a decisive Athenian defeat in 404 B.C., five years
before Socrates' trial in 399. The story of that war is told in Thucydides' history and in
Xenophon's *Hellenica* Books I and II. Two years before the end of the war, in 406, the Athenians won a major victory in a naval battle fought near the Aegean island of Arginusae.
However, on account of the confusion following the battle and a storm that arose soon
afterwards, the disabled ships and the Athenians still at the scene of the battle, both alive and
dead, could not be rescued as the ten generals had intended. When the generals returned to
Athens, eight of them were accused by Theramenes, an unscrupulous and ambitious politician, of neglecting their duty. One of the ten was not accused, and one had died after the
battle. (Socrates uses here the word *anairesthai* for "pick up"; in this context, the word can
mean particularly "to take up dead bodies for burial." This may imply that the most important
omission by the generals was the failure to pick up the dead for burial, a crucial rite in the
Greek tradition of piety.) Theramenes cleverly manipulated the Assembly of the people, and
it was led to condemn the eight to death as a group, although it was evident that many or
perhaps all of them were innocent of wrongdoing. Socrates happened to be one of the
prytanes who were chairmen of the Assembly, and he maintained that such a procedure was
against the law on the ground that the generals should have been tried separately. His protest
was ineffectual, for his fellow prytanes easily yielded to the loud threats of the politicians and
the Assembly. The six generals who were in Athens were executed. (Xenophon, *Hellenica*
I.6–7.)

[59]The arrest and execution without trial of Leon, who was reputed to be a perfectly just
man, was one of the harshest of the many injustices committed by the oligarchy. This regime,
later called the "Thirty Tyrants," was installed in Athens by the victorious Spartans at the end
of the Peloponnesian War. At first the Thirty confined their executions to unpopular informers and demagogues, but soon their scope extended to many former supporters of the
democracy as well as wealthy citizens and foreign residents, whose riches offered a tempting
target. Many of those who were sympathetic to the democracy left Athens and went into
exile. These exiles, among whom Anytus (later Socrates' accuser) was prominent, overthrew
the oligarchy by force of arms in 403 after it had ruled less than one year. Only in 401—two
years before Socrates' trial—did the partisans of the democracy finally overcome the oligarchs
themselves, who had withdrawn to a small town outside Athens. (Xenophon, *Hellenica* II.3–4
[Leon of Salamis is mentioned at II.3.39]; Aristotle, *Athenian Constitution* 34–40; Lysias, *Against
Agoratus* 78.)

The Tholos was a round building where, under the democracy, the prytanes met, sacrificed, and dined. The Thirty apparently made it one of their chief government buildings.

that my whole care is to commit no unjust or impious deed. That   32d
government, as strong as it was, did not shock me into doing
anything unjust. When we came out of the Tholos, the other four
went to Salamis and arrested Leon, but I departed and went home.
And perhaps I would have died because of this, if that government
had not been quickly overthrown. And you will have many witnesses of these things.   e

Do you suppose, then, that I would have survived so many
years if I had been publicly active and had acted in a manner
worthy of a good man, coming to the aid of the just things and, as
one ought, regarding this as most important? Far from it, men of
Athens; nor would any other human being.

But through all my life, if I was ever active in public at all, it is   33a
apparent that I was the sort of man (and in private I was the same)
who never conceded anything to anyone contrary to the just—
neither to anyone else, nor to any of those who my slanderers say
are my students.[60] I have never been anyone's teacher; but if anyone, whether younger or older, desired to hear me speaking and

---

[60]Socrates refers obliquely to the claim that several of his students later became prominent
in anti-democratic politics. According to Xenophon, Socrates' alleged corruption of Alcibiades
and Critias was a leading concern of his prosecutors (*Memorabilia* I.2.12–48). This claim probably could not be raised explicitly because the amnesty of 403, proclaimed when the democracy
was reestablished, prohibited prosecutions for crimes committed before that date.

Alcibiades, a brilliant and ambitious man who had associated with Socrates as a youth, was
involved in several scandalous actions that contributed to popular suspicion of Socrates. On
the night before an Athenian naval expedition departed on its disastrous attempt to conquer
Sicily (415), many of the statues of Hermes in Athens were mutilated. As the investigation of
this incident proceeded, it was alleged or discovered that certain wealthy and educated men
had privately made mockery of the Eleusinian Mysteries, a venerable Athenian rite whose
details were supposed to be kept secret from all except those formally initiated. The people of
Athens feared that these incidents portended a conspiracy against the democracy and evil for
the Sicilian venture. Among those implicated in the profanation of the Mysteries was Alcibiades, who had meanwhile departed for Sicily as one of the commanders chosen by the
Athenians for the expedition. His political enemies arranged for him to be tried in absentia for
impiety, and he was convicted and sentenced to death. Alcibiades then fled to Sparta, where
he successfully aided the Spartans in their war efforts against Athens. He was permitted to
return to Athens for a short period later in the war, after he had changed sides again and won
several naval victories for the Athenians. However, soon afterwards, suspected of anti-democratic intrigue, he was exiled for the last time. In sum, Alcibiades was said to be "the most
unrestrained and hubristic and violent of all those in the democracy" (*Memorabilia* I.2.12).

Critias and Charmides, two other former associates of Socrates, were involved in the
infamous oligarchy of the Thirty. (In the *Charmides* Plato portrays Socrates in a friendly
philosophical conversation with them that occurred in 431, many years before the trial.)
Critias, who had also been implicated in the mutilation of the Hermae, was the leading figure
in the Thirty; he was said to be "the most greedy and violent and murderous of all those in the
oligarchy" (*Memorabilia* I.2.12). Charmides, a younger relative of Critias, was one of the "Ten
in the Piraeus" who ruled Athens' seaport as deputies of the Thirty. Both men died violently
in a pitched battle with the exiled democrats. Both, incidentally, were relatives of Plato.
(Thucydides VI–VIII, esp. VI.17–29, 53, 60–61; Xenophon, *Hellenica* I.1–II.4; Andocides, *On
the Mysteries*.)

doing my own things, I never begrudged it to him. And I do not   33a
converse only when I receive money, and not when I do not re-   b
ceive it: rather, I offer myself to both rich and poor alike for questioning, and if anyone wishes to hear what I say, he may answer
me. And whether any of them becomes an upright man or not, I
would not justly be held responsible, since I have never promised
or taught any instruction to any of them. If someone says that he
has ever learned from me or heard privately anything that everyone else did not, know well that he does not speak the truth. But
why, then, do some enjoy spending so much time with me? You
have heard, men of Athens; I told you the whole truth. It is be-   c
cause they enjoy hearing men examined who suppose they are
wise, but are not. For it is not unpleasant.

I have been ordered to practice this by the god, as I affirm, from
divinations, and from dreams, and in every way that any divine
allotment ever ordered a human being to practice anything at all.
These things, men of Athens, are both true and easy to test.

Now if I for my part *am* corrupting some of the young, and have   d
already corrupted others, and if any of them, when they became
older, had recognized that I ever counseled them badly in anything
while they were young, then now, no doubt, they should have
come forward to accuse me and take their vengeance. If they themselves were not willing to, then some of their families—fathers and
brothers and their other relatives—should now have remembered
it and taken their vengeance if their families had suffered anything
bad from me.

In any event, there are present here many of them whom I see:
first of all Crito here, of my age and deme, the father of Critobulus   e
here; next, Lysanias the Sphettian, the father of Aeschines here;
further, here is Antiphon the Cephisean, the father of Epigenes.
Moreover, here are others whose brothers have spent time in this
way: Theozotides' son Nicostratus, the brother of Theodotus (and
Theodotus has met his end, so that he, at least, would not beg him
not to), and Demodocus' son Paralus, whose brother was Theages.
And here is Ariston's son Adeimantus, whose brother is Plato   34a
here, and Aeantodorus, whose brother is Apollodorus here.[61]

---

[61]These friends and acquaintances of Socrates were probably present as listeners (24e), not
jurors.

Crito: He was a sober, well-to-do gentleman of ordinary intelligence, a friend to Socrates
not because of philosophy, but because of their common life in proximity. They came from the
same "deme" (a neighborhood-sized political subdivision of Athens). Crito offers to pay for
Socrates' escape from prison in the *Crito*. He helps Socrates care for his body in the *Phaedo*,

And *I* can tell you of many others, from among whom Meletus   34a
should particularly have offered someone as a witness during his
own speech. If he forgot then, let him offer one now—I will yield—
and let him say if he has anyone of this sort at all. But you will
discover that it is wholly opposite to this, men; that everyone is
ready to come to aid *me,* the corrupter, the one who does evil to
their families, as Meletus and Anytus say. Now the corrupted ones
themselves would perhaps have a reason to come to my aid. But   b
the uncorrupted ones, their relatives, are now older men, so what
other reason would they have to come to my aid except the correct
and just one, that they are conscious that Meletus speaks falsely,
while I am being truthful?

Well then, men. These, and perhaps other such things, are about
all *I* would have to say in my defense. Perhaps someone among
you may be indignant when he recalls himself, if, in contesting a   c
trial even smaller than this trial, he begged and supplicated the
judges with many tears, bringing forward his own children and

---

concerning himself with Socrates' wife and children, his final bath, and his burial. He also
appears in the *Euthydemus* and in Xenophon, *Memorabilia* I.2.48, II.9.

Critobulus: Crito calls his son "puny" and despairs of educating him in *Euthydemus* 271b
and 306d–307a. Critobulus seems to be a rather silly boy who spends his time going to
comedies and has no serious friends (Xenophon, *Oeconomicus* 3.7, *Memorabilia* II.6; cf.
I.3.8–10, 3.13). He was present at Socrates' death (*Phaedo* 59b).

Lysanias is otherwise unknown. Sphettos was the name of an Athenian deme.

Aeschines wrote Socratic dialogues, of which a few fragments survive. He was once prosecuted for nonpayment of a debt. He was present at Socrates' death.

Antiphon is otherwise unknown. Cephisus was an Athenian deme.

Epigenes: Socrates exhorts him to remedy his poor bodily condition by exercise in Xenophon, *Memorabilia* III.12. He was present at Socrates' death (*Phaedo* 59b).

Nicostratus, Theozotides, Theodotus, and Paralus are otherwise unknown.

Demodocus: An older man than Socrates, he held in his lifetime many of the highest offices
in Athens (*Theages* 127e). In the *Theages* he requests that Socrates undertake to educate his son
Theages. There is a dialogue attributed to Plato, probably spurious, entitled *Demodocus*.

Theages: In the *Theages* Socrates is reluctant to accept him as a student. Socrates remarks in
the *Republic:* "In everything else Theages has been prepared to fall away from philosophy, but
the sickliness of his body, keeping him away from politics, holds him back" (496b–c).

Adeimantus: This elder brother of Plato converses with Socrates in the *Republic*. He is
presented there as a sober, pedestrian man without outstanding gifts.

Plato: The author mentions himself only three times in his dialogues; the other two places
are below, 38b, and *Phaedo* 59b, where he is said to have been prevented by sickness from
attending Socrates on the day he died.

Aeantodorus is otherwise unknown.

Apollodorus: Xenophon says he was a great admirer of Socrates, but "otherwise simple"
(*Apology* 28). A companion once told him, "You are always alike, Apollodorus. For you
always speak badly of yourself and others, and you seem to me to believe that simply
everyone, beginning with yourself, is wretched except Socrates" (*Symposium* 173d). When
Apollodorus cannot control his lament at the sight of Socrates dying, Socrates chastises him,
as well as the others attending him, for their womanlike conduct (*Phaedo* 117d).

many others of his family and friends, so as to be pitied as much as   34c
possible, while I will do none of these things, although in this too I
am risking, as I might seem, the extreme danger. Perhaps, then,
someone thinking about this may be rather stubborn toward me,
and, angered by this very thing, he may set down his vote in
anger. If there is someone among you like this—for I, at least, do   d
not deem that there is, but if there is—to me it seems decent for me
to say to this man, "I, best of men, surely do have some family; for
this is also just what Homer says: not even I have grown up 'from
an oak or a rock,' but from human beings."[62] So that I do have a
family, and sons too, men of Athens, three of them, one already a
youth, and two still children. Nevertheless I will bring none of
them forward here in order to beg you to vote to acquit me.

Why, then, will I do none of these things? Not because I am
stubborn, men of Athens, nor because I dishonor you. Whether I   e
am daring with regard to death or not is another story; but at any
rate as to reputation, mine and yours and the whole city's, to me it
does not seem to be noble for me to do any of these things. For I am
old and have this name; and whether it is true or false, it is reputed
at least that Socrates is distinguished from the many human beings   35a
in some way. If, then, those of you who are reputed to be distinguished, whether in wisdom or courage or any other virtue at
all, will act in this way, it would be shameful. I have often seen
some who are just like this when they are judged: although they
are reputed to be something, they do wondrous deeds, since they
suppose that they will suffer something terrible if they die—as
though they would be immortal if you did not kill them. They seem
to me to attach shame to the city, so that a foreigner might take it
that those Athenians who are distinguished in virtue—the ones   b
whom they pick out from among themselves for their offices and
other honors—are not at all distinguished from women. For those
of you, men of Athens, who are reputed to be something in any
way at all, should not do these things; nor, whenever we do them,
should you allow it. Instead, you should show that you would
much rather vote to convict the one who brings in these piteous
dramas and makes the city ridiculous than the one who keeps
quiet.

[62]The phrase "from an oak or a rock" occurs twice in Homer. (1) In the *Odyssey*, when
Penelope asks her husband Odysseus, who has returned home in disguise, to tell her of his
ancestry, she says, "for you are not of an oak of ancient story, or a rock." Odysseus responds
with a tale full of "many falsehoods" (XIX.163, 203). (2) In the *Iliad* Hector utters this phrase
pathetically in his last speech to himself before he is killed by Achilles (XXII.126).
The word for "I have grown up" (*pephyka*) contains the same root as *physis*, "nature."

Apart from reputation, men, to me it also does not seem to be   35b
just to beg the judge, nor to be acquitted by begging, but rather to   c
teach and to persuade. For the judge is not seated to give away the
just things as a gratification, but to judge them. For he has not
sworn to gratify whoever seems favorable to him, but to give judgment according to the laws. Therefore we should not accustom you
to swear falsely, nor should you become accustomed to it. For
neither of us would be pious.[63]

So do not deem that I, men of Athens, should practice such
things before you which I hold to be neither noble nor just nor
pious, and certainly, by Zeus, above all not when I am being pros-   d
ecuted for impiety by Meletus here! For plainly, if I should persuade and force you by begging, after you have sworn an oath, I
would be teaching you not to hold that there are gods, and in
making my defense speech I would simply be accusing myself of
not believing in gods. But that is far from being so. For I believe,
men of Athens, as none of my accusers does. And I turn it over to
you and to the god to judge me in whatever way it is going to be
best both for me and for you.

[*The jury votes on Socrates' innocence or guilt, and a majority finds him
guilty as charged. Meletus then makes a speech proposing the death penalty, and Socrates must offer a counterproposal.*][64]

Many things contribute to my not being indignant, men of Ath-   e
ens, at what has happened—that you voted to convict me—and   36a
one of them is that what has happened was not unexpected by me.
But I wonder much more at the number of the votes on each side.
For I at least did not suppose it would be by so little, but by much.
But as it is, as is likely, if only thirty of the votes had fallen differ-
ently, I would have been acquitted. So as it seems to me, I have
even now been acquitted as far as Meletus is concerned; and not
only have I been acquitted, but it is clear to everyone that if Anytus
and Lycon had not come forward to accuse me, he would have had
to pay a fine of a thousand drachmae, since he would not have   b
gotten a fifth of the votes.[65]

---

[63]"Pious" here translates *eusebes*, and "impiety" in the next paragraph is *asebeia*. However,
"pious" at 35d is *hosion*, and "impious" at 32d is *anosion*. For the difference between the Greek
words, see *Euthyphro* nn. 17 and 18.

[64]The italicized explanatory remarks inserted into the translation are by the translators.

[65]In order to discourage frivolous or malicious prosecutions, Athenian law prescribed a fine
against the accuser if less than one-fifth of the jury voted for conviction. If there were 500 men
in Socrates' jury, 280 voted for conviction and 220 for acquittal. (Two hundred eighty is one-

At any rate, the man proposes death as my desert.[66] Well, then.   36b
What counterproposal shall I make to you, men of Athens? Or is it
not clear that it should be whatever I am worthy of? What then?
What am I worthy to suffer or to pay because I did not keep quiet
during my life and did not care for the things that the many do—
moneymaking and household management, and generalships,
and popular oratory, and the other offices, and conspiracies and
factions that come to be in the city—since I held that I myself was
really too decent to survive if I went into these things? I did not go   c
into matters where, if I did go, I was going to be of no benefit either
to you or to myself; instead, I went to each of you privately to
perform the greatest benefaction, as I affirm, and I attempted to
persuade each of you not to care for any of his own things until he
cares for himself, how he will be the best and most prudent possible, nor to care for the things of the city until he cares for the city
itself, and so to care for the other things in the same way. What,
then, am I worthy to suffer, being such as this? Something good,   d
men of Athens, at least if you give me what I deserve according to
my worth in truth—and besides, a good of a sort that would be
fitting for me. What, then, is fitting for a poor man, a benefactor,
who needs to have leisure to exhort you? There is nothing more
fitting, men of Athens, than for such a man to be given his meals in
the Prytaneum, much more so than if any of you has won a victory
at Olympia with a horse or a two- or four-horse chariot.[67] For he
makes you seem to be happy, while I make you be so; and he is not   e
in need of sustenance, while I am in need of it. So if I must propose

---

half of 500 plus 30: Socrates says that a change of 30 votes would have acquitted him.) When
he says that Meletus would not have gotten one-fifth of the votes without the other two
accusers, Socrates seems to be assuming playfully that each accuser contributed precisely one-
third of the total votes for conviction. (One-fifth of the votes is 100; one-third of 280 is ninety-
three, seven less than 100.) Or Socrates may simply be attributing most of the vote to convict
to the persuasive authority of the politician Anytus.

[66]The Greek word for "propose as (one's) desert" is *timasthai*, whose root meaning is simply
"estimate or value at a certain publicly recognized price," or "honor or reward [someone with
something]" (cf. *timē*, "honor" or "price"). By extension the word came to be used in court to
mean "assess the punishment due." But Socrates insists upon using the word in its original,
nonjudicial sense, whereby it may refer to the worth or value of a man, good or bad. When
Socrates says, "What shall I propose [as my punishment]?" he is also saying, "What [good or
bad thing] do I deserve?" or "How shall I honor myself?" This ambiguity cannot be translated, but the reader should keep it in mind throughout this section. (The word "counterproposal," *antitimēsis*, has the same ambiguity.) *Timasthai* will be variously translated as
"propose as [my] desert," "propose [i.e., as a penalty or reward]," "give [me] what I
deserve."

[67]On the Prytaneum, see Introduction, p. 21 bottom.

what I am worthy of in accordance with the just, I propose this: to   36e
be given my meals in the Prytaneum.   37a

Perhaps, then, when I say this, I seem to you to speak in nearly
the same way as when I spoke about lament and supplication—
quite stubbornly. It is not like that, men of Athens, but rather like
this: I am convinced that I do not do injustice to any human being
voluntarily, but I am not persuading you of this. For we have
conversed with each other a short time. Since, as *I* suppose, if you
had a law like other human beings, not to judge anyone in a matter
of death in one day alone, but over many, you would be per-   b
suaded.[68] But as it is, it is not easy in a short time to do away with
great slanders.

I, being convinced indeed that I do not do injustice to anyone,
am far from doing injustice to myself, and from saying against
myself that I myself am worthy of something bad, and from proposing this sort of thing as my desert. What would I fear? That I
might suffer what Meletus proposes for me, about which I say that
I do not know whether it is good or bad? Or instead of this, should
I choose something from among the things that I know well are
bad and propose that? Should it be prison? And why should I live
in jail, enslaved to the authority that is regularly established there,   c
the Eleven?[69] Or money, and imprisonment until I pay? But for me
this is the same as what I was saying just now, for I have no money
to pay.

Well, should I propose exile, then? For perhaps you would grant
me this as my desert. I would certainly be possessed by much love
of soul,[70] men of Athens, if I were so unreasonable that I were not
able to reason that you who are my fellow citizens were not able to
bear my ways of spending time and my speeches, but that instead   d
they have become quite grave and hateful to you, so that you are
now seeking to be released from them: will others, then, bear them
easily? Far from it, men of Athens. Noble indeed would life be for
me, a human being of my age, to go into exile and to live exchang-
ing one city for another, always being driven out! For I know well
that wherever I go, the young will listen to me when I speak, just
as they do here. And if I drive them away, they themselves will
drive me out by persuading their elders. But if I do not drive them   e

[68]Sparta, the arch-enemy of Athens, had such a policy.

[69]"The Eleven" were the administrators, chosen by lot, in charge of the prison and
executions.

[70]The term "love of soul" (*philopsychia*) has a collateral sense of "cowardice."

away, their fathers and families will drive me out because of these   37e
same ones.

Perhaps, then, someone might say, "By being silent and keeping
quiet, Socrates, won't you be able to live in exile for us?" It is
hardest of all to persuade some of you about this. For if I say that
this is to disobey the god and that because of this it is impossible to
keep quiet, you will not be persuaded by me, on the ground that I   38a
am being ironic.[71] And on the other hand, if I say that this even
happens to be a very great good for a human being—to make
speeches every day about virtue and the other things about which
you hear me conversing and examining both myself and others—
and that the unexamined life is not worth living for a human being,
you will be persuaded by me still less when I say these things. This
is the way it is, as *I* affirm, men; but to persuade you is not easy.

And at the same time, I am not accustomed to deem myself
worthy of anything bad. For if I had money, I would have pro-   b
posed as much money as I could pay, for that would not harm me.
But as it is, I do not have any—unless, of course, you wish me to
propose as much money as I am able to pay. Perhaps I would be
able to pay you, say, a mina of silver. So I propose that much.

But Plato here, men of Athens, and Crito and Critobulus and
Apollodorus bid me to propose thirty minae,[72] and they will stand
as guarantors. So I propose that much, and they will be trustwor-
thy guarantors of the money for you.

[*Voting between the penalties proposed by the accuser and the accused,
the jury condemns Socrates to death. He has time to make some further
remarks before he is taken away to prison to await execution.*]

For the sake of a little time, men of Athens, you will get a name   c
and be charged with the responsibility, by those wishing to revile
the city, for having killed Socrates, a wise man. For those wishing
to reproach you *will* assert that I am wise, even if I am not. At any
rate, if you had waited a short time, this would have come about
for you of its own accord. For you see that my age is already far
advanced in life and close to death. I say this not to all of you, but
to those who voted to condemn me to death.   d

I also say the following to these same ones. Perhaps you sup-

---

[71]"To be ironic" (*eirōneuesthai*) is to dissemble, to say less than one thinks, to present oneself
as less than one is. The opposite of irony is boastfulness, claiming to be more than one is.

[72]A mina consists of 100 drachmae (n. 46), a fairly small amount for a fine. Thirty minae is a
quite substantial sum of money.

pose, men of Athens, that I have been convicted because I was at a   38d
loss for the sort of speeches that would have persuaded you, if I
had supposed that I should do and say anything at all to escape the
penalty.[73] Far from it. Rather, I have been convicted because I was
at a loss, not however for speeches, but for daring and shameless-
ness and willingness to say the sorts of things to you that you
would have been most pleased to hear: me wailing and lamenting,
and doing and saying many other things unworthy of me, as *I*   e
affirm—such things as you *have* been accustomed to hear from
others. But neither did I then suppose that I should do anything
unsuitable to a free man because of the danger, nor do I now regret
that I made my defense speech like this: I much prefer to die
having made my defense speech in this way than to live in that
way.

For neither in a court case nor in war should I or anyone else
devise a way to escape death by doing anything at all. In battles it   39a
often becomes clear that one might escape death, at least, by letting
go of his arms and turning around to supplicate his pursuers. And
there are many other devices to escape death in each of the dangers, if one dares to do and say anything at all. But I suspect it is
not hard, men, to escape death, but it is much harder to escape
villainy. For it runs faster than death.[74] And now I, since I am slow   b
and old, am caught by the slower, while my accusers, since they
are clever and sharp, are caught by the faster, by evil. And now I
go away, condemned by you to pay the penalty of death, while
they have been convicted by the truth of wretchedness and injustice. And I abide by my penalty, and so do they. Perhaps these
things even had to be so, and I suppose there is due measure in
them.

After this, I desire to deliver oracles to you, O you who voted to   c
condemn me. For in fact I am now where human beings particularly deliver oracles: when they are about to die.[75] I affirm, you
men who condemned me to death, that vengeance will come upon
you right after my death, and much harsher, by Zeus, than the sort

---

[73]"Escape" in this passage translates *pheugein* and cognates, more literally "flee." This
word also means "be prosecuted," just as "pursue" below may also mean "prosecute" (cf.
Euthyphro 3e–4a). The word for "penalty" is *dikē*, "justice" (also in 39b). This term is also
translated "lawsuit" (19c) and "court case" (38e).

[74]"It runs faster than death" is an alliterative jingle in Greek: *thatton thanatou thei.*

[75]Socrates may allude here to two famous death scenes in Homer's *Iliad*: Patroclus' last
words when he is slain by Hector, and Hector's last words when he is slain by Achilles. In
each case the man about to die oracularly forecasts the death of his slayer. (*Iliad* XVI.843–857,
XXII.355–363.)

you give me by killing me. For you have now done this deed   39c
supposing that you will be released from giving an account[76] of
your life, but it will turn out much the opposite for you, as *I* affirm.
There will be more who will refute you, whom I have now been   d
holding back; you did not perceive them. And they will be harsher,
inasmuch as they are younger, and you will be more indignant. For
if you suppose that by killing human beings you will prevent
someone from reproaching you for not living correctly, you do not
think nobly. For that kind of release is not at all possible or noble;
rather, the kind that is both noblest and easiest is not to restrain
others, but to equip oneself to be the best possible. So, having
divined these things for you who voted against me, I am released.

But with those who voted for me I would be pleased to converse   e
on behalf of this affair which has happened, while the officials are
occupied and I do not yet go to the place where, when I do go, I
must die. Please stay with me, men, for this much time; nothing
prevents our telling tales[77] to one another as long as it is possible.
For I am willing to display to you, as to friends, what ever this   40a
thing means which has occurred to me just now. For to me, judges—for by calling you judges I would address you correctly[78]—
something wondrous has happened. For my customary divination
from the *daimonion* was always very frequent in all former time,
opposing me even in quite small matters if I were about to do
something incorrectly. Now, you yourselves see what has occurred
to me, these very things which someone might suppose to be, and
are believed to be, extreme evils. But the sign of the god did not   b
oppose me when I left my house this morning, nor when I came up
here to the law court, nor anywhere in the speech when I was
about to say anything, although in other speeches it has often
stopped me in the middle while I was speaking. But as it is, it has
nowhere opposed me either in any deed or speech, concerning this
action. What, then, do I take to be the cause of this? I will tell you.
Probably what has occurred to me has turned out to be good, and
there is no way that those of us take it correctly who suppose that
being dead is bad. In my view, a great proof of this has happened.   c
For there is no way that the accustomed sign would not have
opposed me unless I were about to do something good.

[76]Literally, "giving a refutation" (*elenchon didonai*), grammatically analogous to the common
Greek expression, "paying the penalty" (*dikēn didonai*).

[77]"To tell tales" is *diamythologein*, which contains the word *mythos*, "tale" or "story," often
associated with the tales told by the poets.

[78]Throughout the trial Socrates has carefully avoided the usual practice of addressing the
jurors by the name of "judges" (as Meletus does at 26d).

Let us also think in the following way how great a hope there is   40c
that it is good. Now being dead is either of two things. For either it
is like being nothing and the dead man has no perception of anything, or else, in accordance with the things that are said, it happens to be a sort of change and migration of the soul from the place
here to another place.

And if in fact there is no perception, but it is like a sleep in which   d
the sleeper has no dream at all, death would be a wondrous gain.
For *I* suppose that if someone had to select that night in which he
slept so soundly that he did not even dream and had to compare
the other nights and days of his own life with that night, and then
had to say on consideration how many days and nights in his own
life he has lived better and more pleasantly than that night, then I
suppose that the Great King[79] himself, not to mention some private man, would discover that they are easy to count in compari-   e
son with the other days and nights. So if death is something like
this, I at least say it is a gain. For all time appears in this way
indeed to be nothing more than one night.

On the other hand, if death is like a journey from here to another
place, and if the things that are said are true, that in fact all the
dead are there, then what greater good could there be than this,
judges? For if one who arrives in Hades, released from those here   41a
who claim to be judges, will find those who are judges in truth—
the very ones who are said to give judgment there, Minos and
Rhadamanthys, and Aeacus, and Triptolemus,[80] and those of the

---

[79]The King of Persia, called the "Great King" by the Greeks, was popularly believed to be
the happiest of men because of his enormous wealth and empire.

[80]Minos: In Homer's *Odyssey* Odysseus pays a visit to Hades; among those he says he saw
there was Minos, "brilliant son of Zeus, holding a golden sceptre, and seated, giving laws to
the dead, while they, seated and standing around the lord through the wide-gated dwelling
of Hades, asked for judgments" (XI.568–571). Minos was said to be an ancient king of Crete,
the first to clear the seas of pirates (Thucydides I.4, I.8). There was a tradition that he exacted
an annual Athenian tribute of seven youths and seven maidens, whom he would feed to a
great beast. Theseus freed Athens from the tribute by going to Crete and killing this Minotaur
(see *Crito* n. 3). Minos was said to have been the original lawgiver for the Cretans and to have
been a just man while he lived (*Minos* 318d–321b; *Laws* beginning).

Rhadamanthys: The brother of Minos, he too had a reputation for great justice. (See above
references to *Minos* and *Laws*.) The poet Pindar speaks of the "straight counsel" of Rhadamanthys, who was placed in authority in the Isles of the Blessed, where men who have lived justly
go to live after their deaths (*Olympian* II.68–77).

Aeacus: Pindar (in *Isthmian* VIII.22–24) says that he was "most careful" of mortals and
"gave judgments even to gods."

Triptolemus: Legendary king of Eleusis, near Athens, he learned from the goddess Demeter
the mysteries of the seasonal growth and harvest of grain; he passed on to men these "Eleusinian Mysteries" (which centered upon the worship of Demeter and her daughter Persephone)
and the art of farming. Athenian vase-painting depicts Triptolemus, Rhadamanthys, and

other demigods who turned out to be just in their own lives—   41a
would this journey be a paltry one? Or again, to associate with
Orpheus and Musaeus and Hesiod and Homer,[81] how much
would any of you give? For *I* am willing to die many times if these
things are true, since especially for myself spending time there   b
would be wondrous: whenever I happened to meet Palamedes and
Telemonian Ajax,[82] or anyone else of the ancients who died because of an unjust judgment, I would compare my own experi-
ences with theirs. As *I* suppose, it would not be unpleasant. And
certainly the greatest thing is that I would pass my time examining
and searching out among those there—just as I do to those here—
who among them is wise, and who supposes he is, but is not. How
much would one give, judges, to examine him who led the great
army against Troy, or Odysseus, or Sisyphus,[83] or the thousand   c
others whom one might mention, both men and women? To converse and to associate with them and to examine them there would
be inconceivable[84] happiness. Certainly those there surely do not

---

Aeacus as judges of the dead (Minos was apparently left out because he was thought harsh
and unjust by the Athenians on account of the tribute). Socrates seems to have been the first
to include both Minos and Triptolemus among the judges of the dead. In the *Gorgias* he
speaks at length about the judgments of the dead (523e–527a). There he names Minos,
Rhadamanthys, and Aeacus as the judges. See also *Crito* 54b–c.

[81]These are the four seminal poets of the Greeks, although little is known of Orpheus and
Musaeus, and they may be merely legendary. Hesiod's chief poems are *Works and Days* and
Theogony. In Aristophanes' *Frogs* the four poets are mentioned in the same order as here:

> For Orpheus showed us our rites, and how to hold back from murders,
> Musaeus cures for diseases, and oracles; Hesiod
> how to work the earth, and seasons of harvest and tilling; and the divine Homer,
> did he not get his fame from teaching uprightness,
> orders [of battle], virtues, and armings of men?
> (1032–1036)

[82]The legendary Palamedes was the subject of several lost tragedies. Gorgias (n. 17) wrote
an *Apology* ["Defense"] *of Palamedes* which has been compared to the *Apology of Socrates.*
Palamedes' famous cleverness brought him into conflict with Odysseus, either because Odysseus was jealous of him or because Palamedes shrewdly foiled Odysseus' scheme to avoid
serving in the Trojan War. (The story has several variants.) Odysseus implicated Palamedes in
a plot to betray the Greeks to the Trojans, and Palamedes was stoned to death by the army.
Ajax, one of the foremost Greek warriors at Troy, was outwitted and tricked by Odysseus in a
contest over the arms of Achilles, which had been set for a prize after Achilles' death.
Odysseus apparently won the contest by some underhanded device. Ajax sought to avenge
the defeat by killing Odysseus and Agamemnon, but instead, in a fit of madness visited on
him by the goddess Athena, he slaughtered a flock of sheep. When he came to his senses,
Ajax committed suicide from shame and humiliation. (*Odyssey* XI.541–562; Sophocles, *Ajax.*)

[83]"The one who led the great campaign" was Agamemnon, whose quarrel with Achilles
touches off the action of the *Iliad*. Sisyphus in Hades labors to move a huge stone over a hill,
but it always rolls down again just as he reaches the hilltop (*Odyssey* XI.593–600). In the *Iliad*
Sisyphus is called "craftiest of men" (VI.153).

[84]*Amēchanon*, translated "inconceivable," is literally "unable to be devised."

kill on this account. For those there are happier than those here not   41c
only in other things but also in that they are immortal henceforth
for the rest of time, at least if the things that are said are in fact true.

But you too, judges, should be of good hope toward death, and
you should think this one thing to be true: that there is nothing bad
for a good man, whether living or dead, and that the gods are not   d
without care for his troubles. Nor have my present troubles arisen
of their own accord, but it is clear to me that it is now better, after
all, for me to be dead and to have been released from troubles. This
is also why the sign did not turn me away anywhere, and I at least
am not at all angry at those who voted to condemn me and at my
accusers. And yet it was not with this thought in mind that they
voted to condemn me and accused me: rather, they supposed they
would harm me. For this they are worthy of blame.   e

This much, however, I beg of them: when my sons grow up,
punish them, men, and pain them in the very same way I pained
you, if they seem to you to care for money or anything else before
virtue. And if they are reputed to be something when they are
nothing, reproach them just as I did you: tell them that they do not
care for the things they should, and that they suppose they are
something when they are worth nothing. And if you do these
things, we will have been treated justly by you, both I myself and   42a
my sons.

But now it is time to go away, I to die and you to live. Which of
us goes to a better thing is unclear to everyone except to the god.[85]

---

[85] A variant manuscript reading would change "except" (*plēn ē*) to "unless" (*plēn ei*). If the
latter reading is correct, Socrates would be professing doubt even about the god's knowledge
of what is best. The word "thing" in this sentence is *pragma,* translated "matter," "trouble,"
or "affair" elsewhere (n. 25).

Plato's *Crito*

[*Or, On What Is to Be Done*]¹

SOCRATES. Why have you arrived at this hour, Crito?² Or isn't it 43a still early?

CRITO. It certainly is.

SOCRATES. What is the hour?

CRITO. Just before daybreak.

SOCRATES. I wonder how it is that the guard of the prison was willing to let you in.

CRITO. He is accustomed to me by now, Socrates, because of my frequent visits here; and besides, he has been done a certain benefaction by me.

SOCRATES. Have you just come, or have you been here long?

CRITO. Fairly long.

SOCRATES. Then why didn't you wake me up right away, instead b of sitting beside me in silence?

CRITO. No, by Zeus, Socrates, nor would I myself willingly be in such great sleeplessness and pain! But I have long been wondering at you, perceiving how pleasantly you sleep. And I kept from waking you on purpose, so that you would pass the time as pleasantly as possible. And though I have of course often previously regarded you through your whole life as happy in your temperament, I do so especially in the present calamity now, so easily and mildly do you bear it.

---

¹"Or, On What Is to Be Done" may be Plato's subtitle or, more likely, may have been added by a later Greek editor.

²On the man Crito, see *Apology* n. 61. The name Crito comes from a Greek word that means "discern" or "judge."

SOCRATES. That's because it would be discordant, Crito, for   43b
someone of my age to be vexed if he now must meet his end.

CRITO. Others of your age, Socrates, are also caught in such   c
calamities, but their age does not release them from being vexed at
their present fortune.

SOCRATES. This is so. But why *have* you arrived so early?

CRITO. To bear a message, Socrates, that is hard—not hard for
you, as it appears to me, but for me and for all your companions it
is a hard and grave one. And I, as it seems to me, would bear it the
most gravely of all.

SOCRATES. What is it? Or has the ship arrived from Delos, after
whose arrival I must die?[3]   d

CRITO. It hasn't arrived yet, but it does seem to me that it will
come today, from the report of some men who have come from
Sunium and left it there.[4] So it is clear from these messengers that
it will come today, and tomorrow it will be necessary, Socrates, for
you to end your life.

SOCRATES. Well, may it be with good fortune, Crito; if such is
dear to the gods, such let it be. However, I don't suppose it will
come today.

CRITO. From what do you infer this?   44a

SOCRATES. I will tell you. Surely I must die on the day after the
ship comes.

CRITO. That's at least what those having authority over these
things say.

SOCRATES. Then I do not suppose it will come on the day that is
upon us, but on the next. I infer it from a certain dream I had a little
earlier tonight. And there's probably something opportune in your
not having awakened me.

CRITO. But what *was* the dream?

[3]See Plato, *Phaedo* 58a–c: "This is the ship, as the Athenians say, in which Theseus once
went to Crete leading the 'twice seven' and saved them and was saved himself. [According to
tradition the Athenians had been obliged to send Crete a periodic tribute of seven youths and
seven maidens. Theseus, the founder of Athens, went to Crete and, by some accounts, saved
himself and the others by defeating the Minotaur.] They made a vow to Apollo then, as is
said, that if they were saved, they would send a mission each year to Delos [the Aegean island
sacred to Apollo], and because of that they always send it annually to the god and still do
now. Now whenever they begin the mission, it is their law to purify the city during this time
and to conduct no public executions until the ship arrives at Delos and comes back here again.
This occasionally takes a long time, whenever the winds happen to hold them back. The
beginning of the mission is whenever the priest of Apollo crowns the stern of the ship. This
happened, as I say, on the day before the trial. Because of this Socrates was in jail a long time
between his trial and his death."

[4]Sunium is the cape of the Athenian territory of Attica, and a ship returning from Delos
would pass by it and might be detained there if the winds were unfavorable.

SOCRATES. It seemed that a certain woman approached me, beau-   44a
tiful and well formed, dressed in white, and that she called me by   b
name and said: "Socrates, on the third day thou would'st arrive in
fertile Phthia."[5]

CRITO. The dream is strange, Socrates.

SOCRATES. No, quite manifest, at least as it seems to me, Crito.

CRITO. Too much so, as is likely. But, daimonic[6] Socrates, even
now obey[7] me and save yourself, since if you die, for me it is not
just one calamity: apart from being deprived of such a companion[8]
as I will never discover again, I will also seem to many, those who
don't know you and me plainly, to have been able to save you if I   c
had been willing to spend money, but not to have cared. And yet
what reputation would be more shameful than to seem[9] to regard
money as more important than friends? For the many will not be
persuaded that you yourself were not willing to go away from here
although we were eager for it.

SOCRATES. But why do we care in this way, blessed Crito, about
the opinion of the many? For the most decent men, whom it is
more worthy to give thought to, will hold that these things have
been done in just the way they were done.

CRITO. But surely you see that it is necessary, Socrates, to care   d
also about the opinion of the many. The present situation now

---

[5]In the *Iliad* (IX.363) Achilles says to Odysseus, "And if the famous Earth-shaker grants me
a good sailing, on the third day I would arrive in fertile Phthia." Achilles is refusing Odysseus' request that he be reconciled with Agamemnon, his ruler. He is threatening to leave the
army at Troy and go home to Phthia, an area of Thessaly. But Socrates also dreamed that he
was addressed by a beautiful woman, which may be an allusion to a later event in the *Iliad*
(XVIII.94ff.): "In a central passage of the *Apology of Socrates* (28c2–d5) where Socrates presents
Achilleus as a model of noble conduct, he speaks of a beautiful woman, the goddess Thetis,
saying to her son Achilleus that he will die straightway after Hektor; Achilleus chose to die
nobly rather than to live in disgrace—which he would surely do by returning to Phthia. In
Socrates' dream the two Homeric passages are combined with the result that a beautiful
woman prophesies to him that he would come to Phthia, or advises him to go to Phthia, i.e.,
to Thessaly. . . . But Phthia being Achilleus' fatherland, the dream could as well mean that
Socrates will come on the third day to his true fatherland, i.e., to Hades." Quoted from Leo
Strauss, "On Plato's *Apology of Socrates* and *Crito*," in Strauss, *Studies in Platonic Political
Philosophy* (Chicago: University of Chicago Press, 1984), p. 55. A pun may also be intended:
"Phthia" suggests the verb *phthiein*, "waste away, decay, die."

[6]As an address, "daimonic" usually conveys a sense of ironic reproach, meaning something like "you marvellous fellow," "strange sir." On the literal meaning of daimon and the
daimonic, see *Apology* n. 37.

[7]Here and throughout, the word "obey" (*peithesthai*) may also mean "be persuaded."

[8]"Companion" is *epitēdeios*; this word which Crito uses for "friend" connotes someone
"useful" or "serviceable."

[9]Here and elsewhere, "seem" (*dokein*) may also be translated "be reputed." The word
"opinion" (*doxa*) in Socrates' reply is formed from the same root as *dokein*. On *doxa*, see
Apology n. 29.

makes it clear that the many can produce not the smallest of evils   44d
but almost the greatest, if someone is slandered among them.

SOCRATES. Would that the many *could* produce the greatest evils,
Crito, so that they could also produce the greatest goods! That
would indeed be noble. But as it is, they can do neither. For they
aren't capable of making someone either prudent or imprudent,[10]
but do whatever they happen to do by chance.

CRITO. Let these things be so. But, Socrates, tell me this. Surely   e
you aren't worrying, are you, on behalf of me and the rest of your
companions, over the prospect that if you leave here, the
informers[11] will make trouble for us on the ground that we stole
you away from here, and we will be compelled to lose either our
whole substance[12] or a lot of money, or even to suffer something
else besides this? If you fear some such thing, leave it aside. For   45a
surely it is just for us to save you and run this risk, and one still
greater than this, if need be. But obey me and do not do otherwise.

SOCRATES. I am worrying over the prospect of these things,
Crito, and of many others.

CRITO. Then do not fear these things. For in fact it is not even
much money that certain people are willing to take to save you and
lead you out of here. Furthermore, don't you see how easily these
informers are bought, and that they wouldn't need much money?
My money is available to you, and is, as I suppose, sufficient.   b
Furthermore, even if out of some concern for me you suppose I
shouldn't spend mine, these foreigners who are here are ready to
spend theirs. And one of them has brought sufficient money for
this very thing, Simmias of Thebes; and Cebes[13] is ready too, and
very many others.

So as I say, don't hesitate to save yourself because you fear these
things, and don't let it be hard for you to accept, as you were
saying in the court, because you wouldn't know what to do with
yourself[14] if you left. For there are many places where they will   c
greet you with affection when you arrive. And if you wish to go to
Thessaly, I have guest-friends there who will regard you as impor-

---

[10]"Prudent or imprudent": see *Apology* n. 33.

[11]"Informers" (*sykophantes*) were private citizens who personally profited from their honest or dishonest prosecutions, especially of the wealthy.

[12]"Substance" is *ousia*, literally "beinghood" or "beingness," but used to refer to a man's monetary estate or "real estate."

[13]Simmias and Cebes from Thebes were companions and admirers of Socrates in Athens at this time; they are Socrates' two leading interlocutors in the *Phaedo*.

[14]Literally, "you wouldn't have [any notion of] whatever you would use yourself [for]."

tant and offer you safety, so that no one throughout Thessaly will cause you pain.[15]

45c

Besides, Socrates, you seem to me to be attempting a thing that isn't even just: you are betraying yourself, although it is possible to be saved. And you are hastening the coming to pass of the very things concerning yourself which your very enemies would hasten on, and did hasten on in their wish to ruin[16] you. In addition to these things, you seem to me at least to be betraying your own sons, too, whom you will leave and abandon, although it is possible for you to nurture and educate them. As far as it lies in you, they will do whatever they happen to do by chance, and chance will bring them, as is likely, just the sorts of things that usually happen to orphans when they are orphaned. Now one either should not have children or should endure the hardship of nurturing and educating them. But you seem to me to be choosing the most easygoing course.

d

Instead, one should choose just what a good and manly[17] man would choose, particularly if one has claimed to care for virtue through his whole life. For my part I am ashamed for you and for us, your companions, that the whole affair concerning you will seem to have been conducted with a certain lack of manliness on our part: the way the lawsuit was introduced into the law court, even though it was possible for it not to be introduced; the way the judicial contest itself took place; and now this, the ridiculous conclusion of the affair, will seem to have escaped us completely because of a certain badness and lack of manliness on our part, since we didn't save you, nor did you save yourself, although it was possible and feasible if we had been of even a slight benefit. So see to it, Socrates, that these things be not shameful as well as bad both for you and for us.

e

46a

But take counsel—rather, there is no longer time to take counsel, but to have taken counsel. And there is only one counsel. For all these things must be done during the coming night. If we wait any longer, it will be impossible and can no longer be done. But in every way, Socrates, obey me and in no way do otherwise.

---

[15]Thessaly is an area of Greece north of Thermopylae, about 100 miles northwest of Athens. Being relatively isolated from the rest of Greece, it was somewhat rude and uncivilized.

[16]*Diaphtheirein* ("ruin") is elsewhere translated as "corrupt," as in the expression, "corrupt the youth."

[17]The word translated "manly" (*andreios*) may also mean "courageous." The word derives from *anēr*, "man" (*Apology* n. 49).

SOCRATES. Dear Crito, your eagerness is worth much if some   46b
correctness be with it. If not, the greater it is, the harder it is to deal
with. So we should consider whether these things are to be done or
not, since I, not only now but always, am such as to obey nothing
else of what is mine than that argument which appears best to me
upon reasoning. The arguments that I spoke in the past I am not
able to throw out now that this fortune has come to pass for me.
Instead, they appear rather alike to me, and I venerate and honor
the same ones I did before. If we have no better argument to say at   c
present, know well that I will certainly not yield to you, not even if
the power of the many scares us like children with more hobgob-
lins than those now present, sending against us imprisonments
and executions and confiscations of money.

How then would we consider this with all due measure? By taking
up first this argument you are making about opinions. Was it said
nobly on each occasion or not, that one should pay mind to some   d
opinions, but not others? Or was it said nobly before I had to die,
while now it has become very clear that it was said pointlessly just
for the sake of argument, and that in truth it was child's play and
drivel? I desire to consider in common with you, Crito, whether the
argument appears at all different to me, now that I am in this
position, or the same; and whether we shall leave it aside or obey it.

On each occasion, as I suppose, those who supposed that they
had something to say somehow used to speak as I was speaking
just now: of the opinions which human beings opine, some must
be regarded as important, others not. Before the gods, Crito, does   e
this not seem to you to be nobly spoken? For you, humanly speaking, are not about to die tomorrow, and the present calamity   47a
wouldn't lead you astray. Consider, then. Doesn't it seem to you
adequately spoken, that one should not honor all the opinions of
human beings, but some and not others? What do you say? Isn't
this nobly spoken?

CRITO. Nobly.[18]

SOCRATES. To honor the upright opinions, but not the villainous?

CRITO. Yes.

SOCRATES. Aren't the upright ones those of the prudent, and the
villainous ones those of the imprudent?

CRITO. Of course.

---

[18]*Kalon* is translated "noble" or "beautiful" throughout the *Crito*. When *kalon* is applied to
speech, as here, it may mean merely "well" spoken, or it may have the stronger sense of
"honorably." See *Apology* n. 16 on *kalon*.

SOCRATES. Come then, again, how were such things spoken of?   47a
Does a man who is exercising and practicing gymnastics pay mind   b
to the praise and blame and opinion of every man, or of one only,
who happens to be a doctor or trainer?

CRITO. Of one only.

SOCRATES. Therefore he should fear the blame and welcome the
praises of the one, but not those of the many.

CRITO. Clearly.

SOCRATES. He is to practice and exercise, then, and to eat and
drink as seems fitting to the one—the overseer and expert—rather
than to all the others.

CRITO. This is so.

SOCRATES. Well, then. If he disobeys the one and dishonors his   c
opinion and praises, while honoring those of the many who have
no expertise, won't he suffer evil?

CRITO. Of course.

SOCRATES. What is this evil? And where and at what does it aim
among the things belonging to him who disobeys?

CRITO. Clearly at his body, for this is what it destroys.

SOCRATES. Nobly spoken. Aren't the other things also like this
(so that we don't have to go through all of them)? And in particular, concerning the just and unjust and shameful and noble and
good and bad things, about which we are now taking counsel,
must we follow the opinion of the many and fear it rather than that   d
of the one—if there is such an expert—whom we must be ashamed
before and fear more than all the others? And if we don't follow
him, we will corrupt and maim that thing which, as we used to
say, becomes better by the just and is destroyed by the unjust.[19] Or
isn't there anything to this?

CRITO. I, at least, suppose that there is, Socrates.

SOCRATES. Come then, if we destroy that which becomes better
by the healthful and is corrupted by the diseaseful, because we
don't obey the opinion of the experts, is life worth living for us
when it has been corrupted? Surely this is the body, isn't it?   e

CRITO. Yes.

SOCRATES. So is life worth living for us with a wretched and
corrupted body?

CRITO. In no way.

---

[19]Words exactly corresponding to "as we used to say" are not in the Greek, but they are
implied by Socrates' use of the imperfect tense (literally, "used to become better by the just
and used to be destroyed by the unjust").

SOCRATES. But is life worth living for us with that thing corrupted   47e
which the unjust maims and the just profits? Or do we hold that
thing to be more paltry than the body—whatever it is of the things
that belong to us which both injustice and justice concern?   48a

CRITO. In no way.

SOCRATES. But more honorable?

CRITO. Much more so.

SOCRATES. Then we ought not at all, O best of men, to give so
much thought to what the many will say of us, but rather to what
the expert concerning the just and unjust things—to what the one,
and truth itself—will say. So first, it's not correct for you to introduce the claim that we must give thought to the opinion of the
many concerning things just and noble and good and their
opposites.

"But the fact is," someone might say, "the many are able to kill
us."

CRITO. Yes, clearly this is so. For it might be said, Socrates. What   b
you say is true.

SOCRATES. But, you wondrous man, the argument that we have
gone through still seems to me, at least, like it did before. Consider, again, whether the following also still stays so for us or not: not
living, but living well, is to be regarded as most important.

CRITO. It does stay so.

SOCRATES. And that living well and nobly and justly are the
same. Does it stay so or does it not stay?

CRITO. It stays so.

SOCRATES. Therefore from the things agreed upon, it must be
considered whether it is just for me to try to go out of here although the Athenians are not permitting me to go, or not just. And   c
if it appears just, let us try, but if not, let's leave it aside. As for the
considerations that you speak of concerning spending of money
and reputation and nurture of children, I suspect that in truth,
Crito, these are considerations of those who easily kill and, if they
could, would bring back to life again, acting mindlessly: namely,
the many. Since this is how the argument holds, nothing else is to
be considered by us except what we were saying just now: whether
we will do just things by paying money and gratitude to those who
will lead me out of here, or whether in truth we will do injustice by   d
doing all these things—those of us who are leading out as well as
those of us who are being led out. And if it is apparent that these
deeds of ours are unjust, we must take nothing into account com-

pared to the doing of injustice, even if we must die by staying here 48d and keeping quiet or must suffer anything else whatever.

CRITO. You seem to me to speak nobly, Socrates; but see what we are to do.

SOCRATES. Let us consider in common, my good man, and if there is some way you can contradict my argument, contradict it e and I will obey you. But if not, blessed man, then stop telling me the same argument again and again, that I ought to go away from here although the Athenians are unwilling. For I regard it as important to act after persuading you, not while you are unwilling. Now see if this beginning of the consideration is stated adequately for you, and try to answer what is asked in whatever way you most 49a suppose it to be.

CRITO. I will try.

SOCRATES. Do we assert that in no way ought injustice to be done voluntarily, or that in one way injustice ought to be done, but in another way not? Or is doing injustice in no way good or noble, as we have often agreed in the past, and which was also said just now? Or have all those former agreements of ours been poured away in these few days? And although at our age, Crito, we old men have long been seriously conversing with each other, were we unaware, then, that we ourselves are no different from children? b Or is it so for us now more than ever just as it was spoken then? Whether the many say so or not, and whether we must suffer things still harder than these or maybe milder, does doing injustice nevertheless happen to be bad and shameful in every way for the one who does injustice? Do we affirm it or not?

CRITO. We affirm it.

SOCRATES. Then one must in no way do injustice.

CRITO. Of course not.

SOCRATES. And even he who has been done injustice, then, must not do injustice in return, as the many suppose, since one must in no way do injustice.

CRITO. Apparently not. c

SOCRATES. What then? Should one do evil or not, Crito?

CRITO. Doubtless one must not, Socrates.

SOCRATES. What then? Is it just or not just for the one to whom evil is done to do evil in return, as the many say?

CRITO. In no way.

SOCRATES. For surely there is no difference between human beings doing evil and doing injustice.

CRITO. What you say is true.   49c

SOCRATES. Then no human being should do injustice in return or do evil, whatever he suffers from others. And see to it, Crito, that by agreeing to this, you aren't agreeing contrary to your opinion.   d
For I know that this seems and will seem so only to a certain few. So there is no common counsel for those who hold this opinion and those who do not: it is necessary that they will have contempt for each other when they see each others' counsels. So you too consider very well whether you share this opinion in common with me and whether we should begin taking counsel from here: that it is never correct to do injustice, or to do injustice in return, or for someone to whom evil is done to defend himself by doing evil in return. Or do you stand aloof and not share this beginning? For to me it has long seemed so and still does now, but if it has seemed   e
some other way to you, speak and teach me. But if you abide by the things from before, hear what comes after this.

CRITO. I do abide by them and it does seem so to me as well. But speak.

SOCRATES. Again, I'll say what comes after this, or rather ask. Ought someone to do the things he agrees upon with someone—if they are just—or ought he to evade them by deception?

CRITO. He ought to do them.

SOCRATES. Observe what follows from these things. If we go away from here without persuading the city, do we do evil to   50a
some—indeed to those whom it should least be done to—or not? And do we abide by the things we agreed to—if they are just—or not?

CRITO. I have no answer to what you ask, Socrates. For I don't understand.

SOCRATES. Consider it as follows. What if the laws and the community of the city should come and stand before[20] us who are about to run away (or whatever name we should give it) from here and ask: "Tell me, Socrates, what do you have in mind to do? By this deed that you are attempting, what do you think you're doing,   b
if not destroying us laws and the whole city, as far as it lies in you? Or does it seem possible to you for a city to continue to exist, and not to be overturned, in which the judgments[21] that are reached have no strength, but are rendered ineffective and are corrupted by private men?"

[20]Dreams were frequently said to "stand before" (epistēnai) the person dreaming.
[21]The words "judgments" and "trials" in this speech render the Greek dikai, the plural of dikē, "justice." See also Apology n. 73 on dikē.

What shall we say, Crito, to these and other such things? For   50b
someone, especially an orator, would have many things to say on
behalf of this law if it were destroyed—the law that orders that the
judgments reached in trials be authoritative. Or shall we tell them,
"The city was doing us injustice and did not pass judgment cor-   c
rectly"? Shall we say this, or what?

CRITO. Yes, this, by Zeus, Socrates!

SOCRATES. Then what if the laws should say, "Socrates, has it
been agreed to by us and by you to do this, or to abide by whatever
judgments the city reaches in trials?"

If, then, we should wonder at their saying this, perhaps they
would say, "Socrates, do not wonder at what is said, but answer,
since you have been accustomed to make use of questioning and
answering. Come now, what charge are you bringing against us
and the city that you are attempting to destroy us? First, didn't we   d
beget you, and didn't your father take your mother and bring you
forth through us? Tell us, then, do you in some way blame those of
us laws that concern marriages, for not being noble?"

"I do not blame them," I would say.

"What about those that concern the nurture and education (in
which you too were educated) of the one born? Or didn't those
laws among us which have been ordered for this end order your
father nobly when they passed along the command to him to educate you in music and gymnastic?"[22]   e

"Nobly," I would say.

"Well, then. Since you were born and nurtured, and educated,
too, could you say, first, that you are not ours, both our offspring
and slave, you yourself as well as your forebears? And if this is so,
do you suppose that justice is equal for you and for us? And do you
suppose that it is just for you to do in return whatever we attempt
to do to you? Now with regard to your father (or a master, if you
happened to have one), justice was not equal for you, so that you
didn't also do in return whatever you suffered: you didn't contradict him when he spoke badly of you, nor did you beat him in   51a
return when you were beaten, or do any other such thing. So is it
then permitted to you to do so with regard to the fatherland and
the laws, so that if we, believing it to be just, attempt to destroy
you, then you too, to the extent that you can, will attempt to

---

[22]"Music and gymnastic" are the elements of the education of a free man. For the Greeks
"music" (*mousikē*, that which concerns the Muses) meant especially poetry. Compare *Republic*
Books II–III and VI–VII.

destroy us laws and the fatherland in return? And will you say that   51a
in doing this you are acting justly, you who in truth care for virtue?
Or are you so wise that you have been unaware that fatherland is
something more honorable than mother and father and all the
other forebears, and more venerable, and more holy, and more
highly esteemed among gods and among human beings who are   b
intelligent? And that you must revere and give way to and fawn
upon a fatherland more than a father when it is angry with you,
and either persuade it or do whatever it bids, and keep quiet and
suffer if it orders you to suffer anything, whether to be beaten or to
be bound? Or that if it leads you into war to be wounded or killed,
this must be done? And that this is just and that you are not to give
way or retreat or leave your station, but that in war and in court
and everywhere, you must do whatever the city and fatherland
bid, or else persuade it what the just is by nature?[23] And that it is
not pious to do violence to mother or father, and still less by far to
the fatherland than to them?"

What shall we say in reply to these things, Crito? That what the
laws say is true or not?

CRITO. It seems so to me, at least.

SOCRATES. "Then consider, Socrates," the laws would perhaps
say, "that if what we say is true, the things you are attempting to
do to us are not just. For although we begat, nourished, and educated you, and gave you and all the other citizens a share in all the   d
noble things we could, nevertheless we proclaim, by making it
possible for any Athenian who wishes, once he has been admitted
to adulthood and has seen the affairs in the city and us laws, that if
we do not satisfy him, he is allowed to take his own things and go
away wherever he wishes. And none of us laws is an obstacle or
forbids anyone from going wherever he wishes, keeping his own
things, whether one of you wishes to go to a colony (if we and the
city are not satisfactory) or to go and settle in another home some-   e
where. But to whoever of you stays here and sees the way that we
reach judgments and otherwise manage the city, we say that he
has already agreed with us in deed to do whatever we bid. And
when he does not obey, we say that he does injustice in three
ways: in that he does not obey us who begat him; nor us who
nurtured him; and in that although he agreed to obey us, he neither obeys nor persuades us if we do something ignobly, although
we put forward an alternative to him and do not order him crudely   52a

---

[23]"Is by nature" translates *pephyka*, the perfect tense of *phyein*, "to grow."

to do whatever we bid, but permit either of two things—either to 52a
persuade us or to do it—but he does neither of these.

"To these charges, Socrates, we say that you too will be liable if
you do what you have in mind, and you not least of the Athenians,
but more than anyone among them."

If then I should say, "Because of what?" perhaps they would
accost me justly and say that more than anyone among the Athenians I happen to have agreed to this agreement. They would say,
"Socrates, we have great proofs that both we and the city were b
satisfactory to you. For you would never have exceeded all the
other Athenians in staying at home in it unless it had satisfied you
exceedingly. You never went out of the city to see the sights except
once to the Isthmus, nor did you ever go anywhere else except
when you were with the army on campaign somewhere.[24] Nor did
you ever make any other journey, as other human beings do, nor
did a desire ever take hold of you to know another city or other
laws: we and our city were sufficient for you. So vehemently were c
you choosing us and agreeing to be governed in accordance with
us that among other things you also had children in it, as though
the city was satisfactory to you. Furthermore, in the trial itself you
could have proposed exile as your penalty if you had wished, and
what you are attempting now when the city is unwilling, you could
have done then when it was willing. But you were then pluming
yourself on not being vexed if you should have to die, and you
chose death, as you said, before exile; while now you are not
ashamed of those speeches, nor do you heed us laws, since you are
attempting to corrupt us. And you are doing just what the paltriest d
slave would do: attempting to run away contrary to the contracts
and agreements according to which you contracted with us to be
governed.

"So first, answer us this very thing: whether what we say is true
or not true when we claim that you have agreed in deed, but not in
speech, to be governed in accordance with us?"

What are we to say in reply to this Crito? Shall we not agree?

CRITO. Necessarily, Socrates.

SOCRATES. "So are you not transgressing," they would say,
"your contracts and agreements with us, although you did not e

---

[24]"To see the sights" translates *epi theorian,* literally, "for contemplation." A *theoria* may
also be a religious or other festival, and the reference to "the Isthmus" is probably to the
Isthmian games, athletic contests held periodically at Corinth. (The phrase "except once to
the Isthmus" is missing from some manuscripts, and it may be an interpolation.) Socrates'
military campaigns are mentioned in *Apology* 28e.

agree to them under necessity and were not deceived? Nor were   52e
you compelled to take counsel in a short time, but during seventy
years in which you could have gone away if we were not satisfactory or if the agreements did not appear to be just to you. But you
chose instead neither Lacedaemon nor Crete—and you yourself on
occasion say that *they* have good laws[25]—nor any other of the
Greek cities or the barbarian ones. Rather, you took fewer journeys   53a
away from the city than the lame and blind and the other cripples,
so exceedingly did it and we laws satisfy you more than the other
Athenians, clearly. For whom would a city satisfy without laws?
But will you in fact not abide now by what you have agreed to? You
will, if you obey us, Socrates; and you will not become ridiculous
by going out from the city.

"For consider, if you transgress these things and commit any of
these wrongs, what good will you produce for yourself or your
own companions? For it is rather clear that your companions will   b
themselves risk being exiled and being deprived of their city or
losing their substance. And as for yourself, first, if you go to one of
the nearest cities, to Thebes or Megara[26] (for both have good laws),
you will come as an enemy, Socrates, to their political regime, and
those very ones among them who are concerned for their own
cities will look askance at you, believing that you are a corrupter of
the laws. And you will confirm the judges in their opinion, so that
they will seem to have judged the lawsuit correctly. For whoever is   c
a corrupter of laws would surely seem very much to be a corrupter
of young and mindless human beings. So will you flee the cities
with good laws and the most decorous men? And if you do this,
will life be worth living for you? Or will you consort with these
men and shamelessly converse with them? With what speeches,
Socrates? The ones that you speak here, that virtue and justice are
of the most worth to human beings, and customs and laws? And
do you not suppose the affair of Socrates[27] will appear unseemly?   d
One must suppose so.

[25]In *Republic* Book VIII Socrates calls the Spartan and Cretan political order "timocracy,"
and he appears to rank this order as the best of the political regimes not ruled by philosophers
(544c, 547b–548d). Aristotle describes Sparta and Crete in detail in his *Politics* Book II. *Eu-
nomeisthai*, here translated "have good laws," could also mean "are law abiding."

[26]Thebes and Megara, which had been enemies of Athens during the Peloponnesian War,
apparently were governed at the time of Socrates' incarceration by narrowly oligarchical
constitutions; the regime at Thebes was overthrown with great popular rejoicing several years
later.

[27]"The affair (*pragma*) of Socrates"; compare *Apology* 20c and n. 25.

"But will you depart from these places and come to the guest-   53d
friends of Crito in Thessaly? There, of course, is very much disor-
der and lack of restraint, and perhaps they would be pleased to
hear from you how laughably you ran away from the prison by
covering yourself with some disguise—putting on either a leather
skin or other disguises such as those who run away usually use—
and by altering your own figure. Is there no one who will say that
you, an old man with only a little time left in his life, as is likely,
dared so greedily to desire to live by transgressing the greatest   e
laws? Perhaps not, if you don't cause pain to anyone. Otherwise,
Socrates, you will hear many things unworthy of yourself. You will
live by fawning upon all human beings and being their slave. And
what else will you be doing but feasting well in Thessaly, as
though you had journeyed to Thessaly for dinner? Where will
those speeches concerning justice and the rest of virtue be for us   54a
then?

"Is it rather that you wish to live for your children's sake, so that
you may nurture and educate them? What then? Will you take
them to Thessaly to nurture and educate them, making them foreigners, so that they will have this advantage too? Or if not this, if
they are nurtured here, will they be better nurtured and educated
because you are alive when you won't be with them? No, for your
companions will take care of them for you. Will they take care of
them if you journey to Thessaly but not take care of them if you
journey to Hades? If in fact those who claim to you to be your
companions are of any benefit at all, one must suppose, at least,   b
that they will.

"But, Socrates, obey us, your nurturers, and do not regard children or living or anything else as more important than justice, so
that when you go to Hades you will have all these things to say in
your defense before those who rule there. For if you do these
things, it does not appear to be better or more just or more pious
here, either for you or for anyone else of those who are yours, nor
will it be better for you when you arrive there. If you depart[28]
now,
you will depart having been done injustice not by us laws, but by   c
human beings. But if you go away so shamefully doing injustice in
return and doing evil in return, transgressing your own agreements and contracts with us and doing evil deeds to those to

---

[28]"If you depart": that is, to Hades. In the next sentence, "But if you go away" means into
exile.

whom they should least be done—yourself and friends and father-   54c
land and us—then we will be angry with you while you live, and
our brothers, the laws in Hades, will not receive you favorably
there, knowing that you even attempted to destroy us as far as it
lay in you. But let not Crito persuade you to do what he says rather   d
than what we say."

Know well, my dear comrade Crito, that these things are what *I*
seem to hear, just as the Corybantes seem to hear the flutes,[29] and
this echo of these speeches is booming within me and makes me
unable to hear the others. Know that insofar as these things seem
so to me now, if you speak against them, you will speak in vain.
Nevertheless, if you suppose that you will accomplish anything,
speak.

CRITO. But, Socrates, I have nothing to say.

SOCRATES. Then let it go, Crito, and let us act in this way, since in   e
this way the god is leading.

---

[29]In connection with worship of the goddess Cybele a rite was developed to cure nervous-
ness and hysteria by means of dancing to frenzied music played on the flute and kettledrum.
Participants in this psychiatric exercise were called Corybantes. The present passage suggests
that the music echoes, probably with a calming effect, in the memory of those who have
undergone the cure.

Aristophanes' *Clouds*

Characters of the Drama

Strepsiades	Creditor
Pheidippides	Second Creditor
Slave of Strepsiades	Second Student of Socrates
Student of Socrates	Hermes
Socrates	Witness (non-speaking part)
Chorus of Clouds	Xanthias, Slave of Strepsiades
Just Speech	(non-speaking part)
Unjust Speech	

[*For the opening scene of the play, one side of the stage represents a bedroom of Strepsiades' house. Two or three statues of gods are visible. Strepsiades and his son Pheidippides are in their beds. At stage center, toward the back, a small, unkempt dwelling can be seen: Socrates' "thinkery." The time is night, just before dawn.*][1]

STREPSIADES [*sitting up in bed*]. Oh! Oh!
O Zeus the King, how long the nights are!
Boundless! Will day never come?
I heard the cock long ago,
but the servants are still snoring. They wouldn't have before. 5
Perish, then, O war, because among many other things,
now I can't even punish my servants![2]

---

[1]All stage directions and other remarks in brackets are by the translators. The Greek text contains nothing but designations of the respective speakers and the words spoken by them. This prose translation makes no attempt to imitate Aristophanes' poetic meter. However, the translation has been divided into distinct lines that correspond as closely as feasible to the lines of the Greek text.

[2]During the Peloponnesian war between Athens and Sparta (431–404 B.C.), when the Athenian territory of Attica outside the city walls was frequently occupied by the enemy, slaves were easily able to desert to the other side.

[*Points to Pheidippides.*]
Nor does this upright youth here
wake up at night; he farts away,
enwrapped in five blankets.   10
But if it is so resolved,[3] let's cover ourselves up and snore.
[*He pulls the blankets up over his head and tries to sleep, but starts
tossing, and finally sits up again.*]
But I can't sleep, wretched me, I'm being bitten—
by expenses and stables and my debts
because of this son of mine. He with his long hair
rides horses and drives a chariot,   15
and dreams of horses, while I am ruined
as I see the moon bringing on the twenties:
the interest mounts up.[4] [*Calls to a slave offstage.*]
                              Boy! Light the lamp
and bring out the ledger so I can take it and read
how many I'm in debt to and reckon the interest.   20
[*A slave enters with an oil lamp and slate, holding the lamp for Strepsiades
to read by.*]
Come, let me see, what do I owe? "Twelve minae to Pasias."
Twelve minae to Pasias for what? What did I use it for?
It was when I bought the koppa-horse.[5] Oh me, alas,
I'd sooner have my eye knocked out by a stone!
    PHEIDIPPIDES [*in his sleep*].
Philon, that's unjust! Drive in your own course!   25
    STREP. This is it, the evil that has ruined me.
Even in his sleep he dreams of horsemanship.
    PHEID. [*asleep*]. How many courses will the war-chariots drive?
    STREP. You're driving me, your father, many courses!
But "what debit hath come"[6] on me after Pasias?   30
"Three minae to Amynias for a chariot-frame and a pair of
        wheels."
    PHEID. [*still sleeping*].
Give the horse a roll and lead it home.

---

[3]*Ei dokei*, literally "if it seems (fitting)." The word *dokei* ("it seems to [the people of Athens]," i.e., "it is resolved . . .") was used at the beginning of enactments passed by the Assembly.

[4]The "twenties" were the last ten days of the month. Interest on loans was typically collected monthly and fell due on the last day.

[5]A koppa-horse is probably some sort of thoroughbred, branded with the letter koppa (our Q) to designate his pedigree. In the next line the word for "knocked out" is *exekopēn*, with a pun on *koppa*.

[6]These words are probably quoted from a lost play of the tragic poet Euripides.

STREP. My dear, you've rolled *me* out of my belongings,
now that I've been losing lawsuits and now that others are saying
they'll have my property seized for the interest.

PHEID. [*now awake*].   Really, father!   35
Why are you upset? And why do you twist and turn[7] the whole
    night?

STREP. Some sort of public official is biting me from the
    bedclothes.

PHEID. Let me have a little sleep, you daimonic[8] man.
[*Goes back to sleep.*]

STREP. All right, sleep! But know that these debts
will fall, all of them, on your head.   40
    Oh, would that the matchmaker might perish evilly,
she who stirred me up to marry your mother!
Mine was a rustic life, most pleasant:
squalid, unswept, lying down at random,
teeming with bees and sheep and olive-cakes.   45
Then I married a niece of Megacles the son of Megacles.[9]
I was a rustic, she from the town:
classy, luxurious, aristocratic.[10]
When I married her, I lay down together with her,
I smelling of new wine, fig crates, wool, abundance,   50
she in turn of perfume, saffron, kisses with the tongue,
expenses, gluttony, Colias, Genetyllis.[11]
But I certainly won't say she was idle; she *did* weave.
And I would show her this cloak
as an occasion and say, "Woman, you weave too closely."[12]   55
[*The lamp goes out.*]

[7]"Twist and turn" translates the verb *strephein*, from which Strepsiades' name is formed. Other occurrences of "twisting" or "turning" (the word can also mean "cheating") are found at lines 88, 335, 434, 450, 554, 776, 792, 1455.

[8]As an address, "daimonic" usually conveys a sense of ironic reproach. A daimon may be an offspring of divine and human parents, or, as sometimes in this play and elsewhere in Greek poetry, a god may be called a "daimon." On the daimonic, see *Apology* n. 37.

[9]Megacles ("famed for greatness") is a grand, aristocratic-sounding name that belonged to several members of the venerable Alcmeonid family. There was a wealthy Megacles of this family living in Athens when the *Clouds* was produced.

[10]"Aristocratic" translates a word meaning, literally, "Coisyrified." Coisyra is the name of a real or legendary aristocratic woman of the sort described here, probably the mother of Megacles, which would make her the grandmother of Strepsiades' wife.

[11]Colias is the name of an Athenian temple for Aphrodite, goddess of love; Genetyllis is a minor love-goddess who is associated with Aphrodite Colias.

[12]"Weave" (*spathan*) is literally "pack down the woof with the blade." When the thread is packed too tightly, it is wasted. Thus the expression "weave too closely" means "be extravagant," "waste money." We may guess that the cloak that Strepsiades holds up is old, thin, and perhaps full of holes.

SERVANT. There's no oil in our lamp.

STREP. Oh me! Why did you light the drunkard lamp?
Come here, that you may weep!

SERVANT.   But why should I weep?

STREP. Because you put in one of the thick wicks.[13]

[*The servant keeps out of reach and runs inside.*]

After that when this son here was born to us—   60
to me, yes, and to the good woman—
we railed at each other over his name.
She was for adding *hippos* to the name—
Xanthippus or Charippus or Callippides[14]—
while I put in for Pheidonides,[15] after his grandfather.   65
So for a while we disputed it. Then, after a time,
we got together and settled on Pheidippides.[16]
She would take this son of hers and fondle him, saying,
"When you are big and drive a chariot to the city,
like Megacles, wearing a festal robe. . . ."[17] But I would say,   70
"Rather, when you bring the goats away from the rocky ground,
like your father, clad in leather. . . ."
But he wasn't persuaded by my speeches at all:
he's been pouring horse-itis upon my money.

So after thinking all night about a way out,   75
now I've discovered one straight path, daimonically preternatural,
and if I can persuade *him* to it, I'll be saved.
But first I wish to wake him up.
How could I wake him most pleasantly? How?

[*He goes over to his son's bed and coos sweetly.*]

Pheidippides! Pheidippiddy![18]

PHEID. [*waking up*].   What, father?   80

STREP. Kiss me and give me your right hand.

PHEID. [*does so*].

[13]Strepsiades threatens to beat his servant because the thick wick makes the lamp "drunk-ard," i.e., guzzle too much oil. The point is that Strepsiades can barely afford oil for his lamp.

[14]These names formed from *hippos* ("horse") have a proud tone. Athenian aristocrats were called *hippeis*, "knights": horsemanship was a traditional badge of wealth and authority.

[15]Pheidon means "thrifty" (the name of Strepsiades' father: line 134); Pheidonides is "off-spring of Pheidon."

[16]Pheidippides: "thrifty horseman," an oxymoron, like "stingy big-spender." According to some manuscripts of Herodotus, Pheidippides was the name of the Athenian runner sent to Sparta to ask for military aid when the Persians landed at Marathon (n. 162). He ran 150 miles in two days, but the Spartans sent no help until after the battle was over (VI.105).

[17]She refers to the Panathenaic festival honoring Athena, when the rich would ride in their saffron robes up to the "city," i.e., the acropolis. See n. 72.

[18]The Greeks sometimes added a diminutive ending to a name, indicating endearment or fawning.

There. What is it?

STREP.   Tell me, do you love me?

PHEID. [*stands up, gesturing toward a statue of the god*].

Yes, by this Poseidon of horses!

STREP. Please, not by this god of horses, in no way!

For he is responsible for my evils.   85

But if you really love me from the heart,

my boy, obey.[19]

PHEID.   What should I obey you in?

STREP. Turn your own ways inside out as quickly as possible:

go and learn what I will advise.

PHEID.

Speak, what do you bid me?

STREP.   And will you obey at all?   90

PHEID. I will obey, by Dionysus.[20]

STREP. [*pointing to the house at the back of the stage, which is now fully
visible in the growing light of dawn*].

                                        Look over here, now.

Do you see that little door and little house?

PHEID. I see them. So really, what is it, father?

STREP. That is a thinkery of wise souls.[21]

In there dwell men who by speaking   95

persuade one that the heaven is a stove

and that it is around us, and we are charcoals.[22]

If someone gives them money, they teach him

how to win both just and unjust causes by speaking.

PHEID. Who are they?

[19]The Greek word for "obey" (*peithesthai*) is the passive of the word "persuade," and may
also mean "be persuaded." See also line 119.

[20]As the god of banquets and of the vine, Dionysus is a compromise between the horseman's Poseidon (83) and the farmer's Demeter (121) (Leo Strauss, *Socrates and Aristophanes*
[New York: Basic Books, 1966], p. 13).

[21]"Thinkery" is *phrontisterion*, coined by Aristophanes on the model of such words as
dikasterion ("law court," from *dikē*, "justice"). "Think-tank" is an alternate translation. Words
with this *phron-* root occur frequently in the *Clouds*, and they are translated consistently with
"think" or "thought" although they also convey the sense of "worry." See *Apology* n. 8.
"Soul" (*psychē*), in popular usage, may also mean "ghost."

[22]*If* the Socrates of this play holds the doctrine that Strepsiades attributes to him, he may
have learned that heaven is *like* a stove (*pnigeus*, a dome-shaped oven for baking bread) from
the minor philosopher Hippon (so says a medieval *scholium* or explanatory note in one of the
manuscripts) or from the astronomer Meton (Aristophanes, *Birds* 1001). The philosopher
Heraclitus compared men to charcoals in the following way: just as charcoals glow when filled
with fire and turn black when fire is withdrawn, so we partake of "the common and divine
logos" when the things surrounding us come into our mind through the passages of the
senses—less when asleep, more when awake. (Hermann Diels and Walther Kranz, *Fragmente
der Vorsokratiker* [16th ed.; Dublin: Weidmann, 1972], A16.)

STREP.   I don't know their names precisely.   100
Pondering thinkers—noble and good men.[23]

   PHEID. Ugh! Villains, I know. They're boasters,
pale, shoeless men that you're speaking of,
and among them that miserably unhappy Socrates and Chaere-
      phon.[24]

   STREP. Now, now, be silent. Don't say anything foolish.   105
But if you have any concern for your father's barley,[25]
give up your horsemanship and for my sake become one of them.

   PHEID. I wouldn't, by Dionysus, not even if you gave me
the pheasants that Leogoras is raising.[26]

   STREP. Go, I beseech you, dearest of human beings to me,   110
go and be taught.

   PHEID.   And what shall I learn for you?

   STREP. It's said that they have two speeches,
the stronger, whatever it may be, and the weaker.
One of these speeches, the weaker,
wins, they say, although it speaks the more unjust things.   115
So if you learn this unjust speech for me,
I wouldn't give anyone back even an obol[27]
of those debts that I owe because of you.

   PHEID. I won't obey, for I wouldn't dare to see
the horsemen after I've lost my complexion.[28]   120

   STREP. Then by Demeter, you won't eat of *my* belongings,
not you yourself, not your chariot horse, and not your
      thoroughbred!
I'll drive you out of my house to the crows![29]

   PHEID. But my uncle Megacles won't let me go horseless!
I'm going inside, and I won't give any thought to you!   125
[*Exit Pheidippides into the interior of the house.*]

   STREP. But neither will *I* stay down, even if I have taken a fall.
After I pray to these gods here, I will be taught.
I'll go into the thinkery myself.
[*He sets off toward the thinkery, but along the way he hesitates.*]

---

[23]"Noble and good men": see *Apology* n. 19. In the *Clouds, kalon* is always "noble" or "beautiful."

[24]Chaerephon: see *Apology* 21a and n. 27 there.

[25]Barley: i.e., your father's daily bread, his livelihood.

[26]Pheasants were rare in Athens, and only a very rich man like Leogoras (father of the orator Andocides) could afford to keep them.

[27]Obol: a small Athenian coin, one-sixth of a drachma (*Apology* nn. 46 and 72).

[28]Pheidippides anticipates that he would lose his manly horseman's tan by spending time studying indoors.

[29]"To the crows!" is a Greek imprecation meaning something like "To the dogs!" or "Go hang yourself!"

Now how, since I am an old man, forgetful and slow,
am I going to learn the splinters of precise speeches? [*Pauses.*]   130
One must go. [*Starts again, then stops before the door.*]
       Why do I keep hanging back like this
and not knock on the door? [*Knocks.*] Boy! Little boy![30]
  STUDENT [*within*].
Throw yourself to the crows! Who is it that knocked on the door?
  STREP. Strepsiades the son of Pheidon, from Cicynna.[31]
  STUDENT [*opening the door*].
Unlearned too, by Zeus, for you've   135
kicked the door so very unponderingly
that you've made a thought I had discovered miscarry.
  STREP. Forgive me, for I dwell far off in the country.
But tell me the matter that's miscarried.
  STUDENT. It's not sanctioned to say, except to the students.   140
  STREP. Be bold and tell me now. For I've come
here to the thinkery as a student.
  STUDENT. I'll tell you, but you must believe these things are
    Mysteries.[32]
Just now Socrates was asking Chaerephon
how many of its own feet a flea could leap.   145
For after biting Chaerephon on the eyebrow,
it jumped onto Socrates' head.
  STREP. How did he measure it?
  STUDENT.   Most shrewdly.
He melted some wax, then took the flea
and dipped two of its feet into the wax;   150
as it cooled, Persian slippers[33] grew around them.
He took these off and was measuring the space.[34]
  STREP. O Zeus the King, what subtlety of the wits!
  STUDENT. What, then, if you should find out another thought of
    Socrates?
  STREP. What? I beseech you, tell me.   155

---

[30]Expecting a slave to answer, Strepsiades calls out "boy" in the usual Greek manner. But the Socratics, who have to steal their dinner if they are to eat at all (175–179), are too poor to keep slaves.

[31]Cicynna is the name of the *deme* or neighborhood division of Attica where Strepsiades was born. (Sphettos, line 156, is the name of another deme.) Strepsiades introduces himself as though reporting to the authorities.

[32]"Mysteries" are religious rites, knowledge of which was permitted only to initiates. In the Platonic dialogues Socrates frequently applies the language of Mystery-initiation to philosophy: e.g., *Symposium* 209e–212a, *Phaedrus* 250c–d.

[33]"Persian slippers" (literally, "Persians") are a kind of female footwear.

[34]The student seems to mean that Socrates was carefully measuring the space occupied by the flea's foot in the wax "slipper" when Strepsiades knocked and spoiled the attempt.

STUDENT. Chaerephon from Sphettos was asking him
which notion[35] he held: do gnats
hum through their mouth or through their behind?
    STREP. What, then, did he say about the gnat?
    STUDENT. He declared that the gnat's intestine is   160
narrow, and because it is slender, the breath
goes violently straight to its behind.
There the anus, hollow where it lies near the narrow part,
resounds from the violence of the wind.
    STREP. Then the gnats' anus is a trumpet.   165
O thrice-blessed for intestinal insight!
How easily would a defendant escape the penalty
if he thoroughly knew the intestine of the gnat!
    STUDENT. But lately he was robbed of a great notion
by a lizard.
    STREP.   In what way? Tell me.   170
    STUDENT. As he was investigating the courses
and revolutions of the moon and was gaping upwards,
a lizard (it was night) crapped on him from the roof.
    STREP. [laughing].
I'm pleased by a lizard crapping on Socrates.
    STUDENT. Yesterday evening we had no dinner.   175
    STREP. Well, well. Then how did he contrive for barley?[36]
    STUDENT. He sprinkled fine ash on the table,
bent a meat-spit, then taking it as a compass
he made away with the cloak from the wrestling school.[37]
    STREP. Why then do we wonder at Thales?[38]   180
Open up, open up the thinkery, hurry,
and show me Socrates as quickly as possible,
for I'm going to be a student! Open up the door!
[The student opens the doors, revealing the courtyard of the house, where
the students are discovered in various odd poses.]
Heracles! Where do these beasts come from?
    STUDENT. Why do you wonder? What do they seem like to you?   185

---

[35]"Notion" is gnomē, a prominent term in the Clouds. It is sometimes translated "judgment."

[36]Barley: see n. 25.

[37]Scholars disagree about what it is that Socrates did. The point seems to be that he succeeded in his "attempt to supply his starving group with a frugal dinner by cleverly executing an act of petty theft while pretending to do geometry" (Strauss, Socrates and Aristophanes, p. 14).

[38]Thales is believed to have been the first Greek philosopher and was popularly admired for his great wisdom, both theoretical and practical.

STREP. Like the Laconian captives from Pylos.[39]
[*Observing one group in an attitude of deep thought.*]
But why ever are these over here looking down at the earth?
    STUDENT. They're investigating the things beneath the earth.
    STREP.   Then it's vegetable bulbs.
[*Addressing them.*] Don't give it any more thought now,
for I know where there are big and beautiful ones.   190
[*Turning to another group with their heads fixed on the ground and their behinds in the air.*]
But what are they doing over there who are so stooped over?
    STUDENT. They are delving into Erebus under Tartarus.[40]
    STREP. Why then is the anus looking at the heaven?
    STUDENT. It itself by itself[41] is being taught astronomy.
[*To the other students.*]
Go inside, so that *he* won't happen upon us.   195
    STREP. Not yet, not yet! Let them stay, so
I can share a little matter of mine with them.
    STUDENT. But it's not possible for them to spend
very much time outside in the air.
                              [*Other students exit into the thinkery.*]
    STREP. [*catching sight of the instructional equipment*].
Before the gods, what are these things? Tell me.   200
    STUDENT. This is astronomy.
    STREP.   And what is this?
    STUDENT. Geometry.
    STREP.   So what's the use of it?
    STUDENT. To measure the earth.
    STREP.   For the land-allotment?
    STUDENT. No, all of it.
    STREP.   That's a pretty trick
you speak of: for it's populist and useful.[42]   205
    STUDENT. Here's a map of the whole earth. See?
Here's Athens.

---

[39]The Spartans captured by the Athenians in their victory at Pylos in 425 were kept at Athens for four years; they must have been pale and emaciated from the long siege and from their captivity (Thucydides IV.29–41, V.24). Apparently Socrates' students practice an almost inhuman asceticism.

[40]In Greek poetry, Erebus and Tartarus are names for the underworld, or for different aspects of it.

[41]"It itself by itself" is an expression that Socrates uses frequently in Plato's dialogues (e.g. *Phaedo* 64c).

[42]Athens sometimes distributed titles to the land of its conquered enemies to a number of citizens selected by lot. Strepsiades thinks they are using geometry to divide up the earth in a huge *clerurchy* or land-allotment. "Trick" is *sophisma*, from *sophon*, "wise."

STREP.   What are you saying? I'm not persuaded,
since I don't see any judges sitting.[43]

    STUDENT. Truly, this *is* the area of Attica.

    STREP. And where are my fellow demesmen of Cicynna?   210

    STUDENT. They're in here. And Euboea here, as you see,
is long and laid out quite far.

    STREP. I know, for it was laid out by us and Pericles.[44]
But Lacedaemon—where is it?

    STUDENT.   Where is it? Here.

    STREP. So near us! Give thought to how   215
to take it quite far away from us.

    STUDENT.
But that's impossible.

    STREP.   By Zeus, you'll lament, then!
[*Socrates comes into view aloft, suspended in a basket.*]
Come, who is this man in the basket?

    STUDENT. Himself.

    STREP.   Who is "himself"?

    STUDENT.   Socrates.

    STREP. [*Calling to him*].   Socrates!
[*To the student.*] Come, you shout to him loudly for me.   220

    STUDENT. You call him yourself. I haven't the leisure. [*Exit.*]

    STREP. Socrates! Socratesie!

    SOCRATES. Why are you calling me, ephemeral one?

    STREP. First, I beseech you, tell me what you're doing.

    SOC. I tread on air and contemplate the sun.   225

    STREP. Then you look down[45] on the gods from a perch
and not from the earth?—if that's what you're doing.

    SOC.   I would never
discover the matters aloft correctly
except by suspending mind and subtle thought
and mixing them with their like, the air.   230
If I considered the things above from below on the ground,
I would never discover them. For the earth forcefully

---

[43]Strepsiades alludes to the litigiousness for which Athenians were notorious.

[44]Euboea, a long narrow island off the coast of Attica, was ruthlessly subjugated by an Athenian force of which Pericles was a commander (Thucydides I.114). This expedition occurred over twenty years before the first performance of the *Clouds*, so Strepsiades' "us" refers to "the older generation."

[45]In the previous line "contemplate" is literally "think around," i.e., "look at from all sides" (*periphronein*), and may also mean "despise." Strepsiades explains Socrates' meaning by using a related word (*hyperphronein*, repeated at 1400) that definitely means "despise" or "look down on" (literally, "over-think"). Strepsiades' comment indicates that he, like almost all men, regards the sun as a god (cf. *Apology* 26d).

pulls to itself the moisture from the thought.
The same thing happens also to water cress.[46]
STREP. What are you saying?   235
Does thinking pull the moisture into the water cress?
Come now, Socratesie, come down to me.
And teach me what I've come for.
SOC. [*descends and gets out of the basket*].
Why did you come?
STREP.   I wish to learn to be a speaker.
I am plundered, I am pillaged[47] by interest and   240
most peevish creditors; my property is being seized for debts.
SOC. How is it that you were unaware of yourself becoming
    indebted?
STREP. Horse-disease ground me down, devouring me terribly.
But teach me one of the two speeches,
the one that pays nothing back. Whatever fee   245
you set, I swear by the gods to pay you.[48]
SOC. What gods indeed will you swear by! For first of all,
we don't credit gods.[49]
STREP.   What do you swear with?
Iron coins, as in Byzantium?[50]
SOC. Do you wish to know divine matters plainly,   250
to know correctly what they are?
STREP.   Yes, by Zeus, if in fact it's possible.
SOC. And to associate in speech with the Clouds,
our daimons?

---

[46]Water cress seeds were known to absorb moisture, just as (according to Socrates) the earth does. The opinion that moisture impedes thought was held by the philosopher Diogenes of Apollonia, who lived and wrote at the same time as Socrates (Diels-Kranz, *Fragmente der Vorsokratiker*, A19, §44).

[47]"Plunder and pillage," literally "lead and carry" (*agein kai pherein*), is an expression used of troops looting in wartime, *leading* off slaves and cattle and *carrying* property away.

[48]It is noteworthy that Socrates shows no interest at all in Strepsiades' offer to pay but only seeks to disabuse him of his old-fashioned religious convictions. This, along with the fact that Socrates and his students live in dire poverty (175), shows that Strepsiades' uninformed opinion that Socrates teaches for pay (98)—an opinion with which many modern scholars agree—is incorrect. The gift that Strepsiades gives Socrates at line 1147 is spontaneous. See also n. 149.

[49]Literally, "gods are not *nomisma* for us." Socrates appears to be using the word *nomisma* in its root meaning, "something believed in," but Strepsiades indicates in his confused response that he understands *nomisma* in its usual sense of "money." Socrates was accused of not "believing in" the gods of the city (*Apology* 24b–c); the word "believe in" is *nomizein*, related to *nomisma*. (Alan H. Sommerstein, ed., Aristophanes, *Clouds* [Warminster: Aris & Phillips 1982], p. 173.)

[50]Unlike other Greek cities at this time, which used precious metals, Byzantium minted its coins from iron.

STREP.   Very much so.

SOC. [*leading him to a low bench*].

Then sit down on the sacred couch.

STREP. There, I'm seated.

SOC. [*placing a wreath on his head*].

Now, take this crown.   255

STREP. Why a crown? Oh me, Socrates,

don't sacrifice me like Athamas![51]

SOC. No, we do all these things to the initiates.

STREP. What will I gain, then?

SOC. You will become a smooth, rattling, fine-as-flour speaker.   260

But hold still.

[*Sprinkles flour on him from a can by the bench.*]

STREP.   By Zeus, you're not going to be false with me,

for I will become fine as flour when I'm sprinkled!

SOC. The old man must hush and listen to the prayer.

[*Solemnly.*] O master and lord, measureless Air, who holds the
    earth aloft,

and bright Aether, and august goddesses Clouds sending thunder
    and lightning,   265

arise, appear, O Ladies, aloft for the thinker.

STREP. [*covering his head with his cloak*].

Not yet, not yet, until I fold this around me, so I won't be
    drenched.

O miserably unhappy me, to come from home without even a cap!

SOC. Come then, much-honored Clouds, to display yourselves
    to this man,

whether you are seated on the sacred snow-beaten peaks of
    Olympus,   270

or setting up a sacred chorus with the nymphs in the gardens of
    father Oceanus,[52]

or drawing waters in golden vessels at the mouths of the Nile,

or keeping to Lake Maeotis or the snowy look-out of Mimas[53]—

hear, receive the sacrifice, and rejoice in the sacred rites.

---

[51]In the *Athamas*, a lost tragedy of Sophocles, Athamas, crowned with a wreath, was about to be sacrificed on an altar when he was rescued by Heracles. Strepsiades may also have been reminded of Athamas because of the name of Athamas' wife: Nephele ("Cloud"). This section (254–262) is a parody of the initiation rites into the Mysteries at Athens (n. 32).

[52]In Hesiod (*Theogony* 133) Oceanus is the child of Earth and Heaven (but not father of the Clouds). His gardens were supposed to be in the sea far to the west of Greece.

[53]Lake Maeotis is the present-day Sea of Azov in the northeast corner of the Black Sea. Mimas juts out from the coast of Asia Minor just north of the island of Chios. The four lines that state the possible locations of the Clouds describe the four points of the compass: north (Olympus), west (Oceanus' gardens), south (the Nile), and east (Maeotis and Mimas).

CHORUS [*song, offstage*].
Ever-flowing Clouds,   [*Strophe.*[54]]   275
let us arise, clearly apparent in our
dewy, shining nature,
from deep-resounding father Oceanus
up to lofty mountain peaks
shaggy with trees, so that   280
we may gaze upon look-out points apparent from afar,
and sacred land with well-watered fruits,
and roarings of rivers most divine,
and deep-thundering, roaring sea.
For the untiring eye   285
of Aether blazes
with glistering rays.
But let us shake off the rainy cloud
from our immortal form, and let us give
the earth to our far-seeing eye.   290
  SOC. O greatly august Clouds, it is apparent that you heard me
       calling you.
[*To Strepsiades.*] Did you perceive a voice and bellowing thunder,
       divinely august?
  STREP. Yes, and I revere you, much honored ones, and wish to
       fart in response
to the thunder, so much do I tremble and fear before them.
And if it is sanctioned—right now, in fact, even if it isn't sanc-
       tioned—I want to take a crap.   295
  SOC. Do not mock, and don't do what those trygic daimons[55] do,
but hush. For a great swarm of goddesses is in motion with songs.
  CHORUS [*song, still at a distance*].
Rain-bearing virgins,   [*Antistrophe.*]
let us go to the sleek land
of Pallas, to see the well-manned earth   300
of Cecrops,[56] much beloved,
where there is reverence for sacred things unspeakable;

---

[54]"Strophe" is the name given to a song sung by the Chorus, to which an "antistrophe" answers (line 298). The names strophe ("turning") and antistrophe ("turning back") are thought to refer to the practice of having the Chorus dance in one direction during the strophe and in the reverse during the antistrophe (not here, however, for the Chorus is still offstage).
[55]"Trygedy" (mocking "tragedy") is a comic term for comedy, from *trygē*, "grape vintage," alluding to Dionysus, god of wine and of drama (line 519). The word translated "trygic daimon" is *trygodaimon*, coined by Aristophanes in imitation of *kakodaimon*, "miserably unhappy," but perhaps also suggesting the comic poets' claim to be daimons (gods).
[56]"Well-manned" (*euandron*) means either "having good men" or "abounding in men." Cecrops is the legendary first king of Athens.

where the halls that receive the Mysteries
are displayed in holy initiation-rites.[57]
Gifts to heavenly gods are there,   305
lofty-roofed temples and statues,
most sacred processions for the blessed ones,
and well-crowned sacrifices
and festivals for gods
in all manner of seasons.   310
And as spring comes on, there is Bromian[58] rejoicing,
and contentions of well-sounding choruses,
and deep-thundering music of flutes.

    STREP. Before Zeus, I beseech you, tell me, Socrates, who are
       these
who have uttered this august thing? They aren't anything like
      heroines,[59] are they?   315
    SOC. Not in the least: they're heavenly Clouds, great goddesses
      for idle men,
who provide us with notions and dialectic and mind,
and marvel-telling and circumlocution and striking and seizing.[60]
    STREP. That's why, on hearing their utterance, my soul is taking
      flight,
and it already seeks to speak subtly and to quibble about smoke,   320
to oppose a speech with another speech by pricking a notion with a
      sharper notion.
So if it's somehow possible, I desire to see them now clearly
      apparent.
    SOC. Look over here toward Parnes.[61] For I already see them
quietly descending.

[*The Chorus of Clouds begins to enter from the side entrance.*]

    STREP.   Where? Show me.
    SOC.   Quite many are coming
through the hollows and the thickets—there, at the side.
    STREP. [*peering*].   What's the matter?   325
I don't see them.

---

    [57]The Chorus refers to the Eleusinian Mysteries celebrated at Athens and famous through-
out Greece. See *Apology* n. 80 on Triptolemus.

    [58]"Bromius" is Dionysus. These last three lines of the song refer to the comic and tragic
poetry contests held in the spring at Athens in honor of Dionysus.

    [59]The terms "hero" and "heroine" were popularly applied to the outstanding protagonists
in the Trojan and Theban wars described in poetry. As descendants of gods, they were held in
great respect. Cf. *Apology* n. 48.

    [60]These four terms are technical jargon from current rhetorical theory. The precise meaning
of "striking" and "seizing" is unknown.

    [61]Parnes: a mountain in Attica.

SOC.   By the entrance!

STREP.   Now I do, but just barely.

[*The Chorus of twenty-four Clouds is now fully on stage.*]

SOC. By now you must see them, unless your eyes are oozing pumpkins.

STREP. By Zeus, I do. O much-honored ones! They're already covering the whole place.

SOC. But did you neither know nor believe that they are goddesses?

STREP. No, by Zeus. I held them to be mist and dew and smoke.   330

SOC. Then you don't know, by Zeus, that they nourish most of the sophists,

Thurian diviners,[62] practicers of the art of medicine, idle-long-haired-onyx-ring-wearers.[63]

Song-modulators of circling choruses—men who are impostors about the things aloft—

idle do-nothings they nourish too, because they make poetry and music about these Clouds.[64]

STREP. This is why poets have composed "twisting-radiant burning impetus of wet clouds,"   335

and "tresses of hundred-headed Typhus"[65] and "hard-blowing tempests";

and then, "air-swimming, crooked-clawed birds of the liquid aire,"

and "rains of waters from dewy clouds." And then, in return for making these phrases, they gulp down

slices of great good fish and birds' flesh of thrushes.

SOC. That's why, of course. And isn't it just?

STREP.   Tell me, what's happened to them   340

(if in fact they truly are clouds), that they are like mortal women?

For those in the sky are not such as these.

SOC.   Well, what sorts of things are those?

STREP. I don't plainly know. Anyway, they're like spread-out wool,

not women, by Zeus, not at all. These have noses.

---

[62]The founding of the Greek colony of Thurii in southern Italy in 443 would have provided an occasion for divinations and prophecy, much of it no doubt fraudulent.

[63]This word (*sphragidonychargokomētai*), coined by the poet, means "foppish, sophisticated intellectuals and aesthetes."

[64]This and the preceding line refer to poets of dithyrambs, a form of lyric poetry sung by choruses at public contests.

[65]Typhus, son of Earth, was buried beneath the earth and generated storm winds (Hesiod, *Theogony* 820–880). His "tresses" must be clouds. Strepsiades is recalling snatches of dithyrambic poetry that speak metaphorically of clouds.

SOC.
Now answer whatever I ask.

    STREP.   Say quickly what you wish.   345

    SOC. While looking upward have you ever seen a cloud like a
        centaur
or leopard or wolf or bull?

    STREP.   By Zeus, I have. What about it?

    SOC. They become all things that they wish. And so if they see a
        long-hair,
one of those shaggy "rustics," like the son of Xenophantus,
they mock his madness and make themselves look like centaurs.[66]   350

    STREP. What if they catch sight of Simon,[67] a plunderer of public
        property: what do they do?

    SOC. They make his nature apparent by suddenly becoming
        wolves.

    STREP. That's it, then—that's why yesterday, when they saw
        Cleonymus, who abandoned his shield in battle,
they became deer because of seeing this great coward.[68]

    SOC. [*gesturing to the Chorus*]. Yes, and now, you see, they've
        become women because they saw Cleisthenes.[69]   355

    STREP. Then hail, Ladies! And now, if you ever do so for anyone
        else,
for me too let your voice burst forth the length of heaven, O queens
        of all!

    CHORUS [*the leading Cloud speaks for the Chorus*].
Hail, elderly man born long ago, hunter of Muse-loving speeches.
And you, priest of subtlest babble, tell us what you want.
For we wouldn't listen to anyone else of those who are now soph-
        ists-of-the-things-aloft   360
except for Prodicus: to him because of his wisdom and judgment,
        to you
because you swagger in the streets and cast your eyes from side to
        side,

---

[66]"Rustics" is slang for homosexuals. The son of Xenophantus may be Hieronymus, a foppish dithyrambic poet of no particular merit. Centaurs were mythical creatures—half-man, half-beast, shaggy and rustic in appearance—that indulged their heterosexual and homosexual appetites shamelessly.

[67]Simon is otherwise unknown, except that he was also a perjurer (line 399).

[68]Cleonymus, apparently cowardly and poor (line 675), was frequently ridiculed by Aristophanes. The deer is proverbially timid.

[69]Cleisthenes, a notorious homosexual, was effeminate in appearance, apparently being unable to grow a beard. He appears as a character in Aristophanes' *Thesmophoriazusae* 574–654 and is ridiculed in several other plays.

and barefooted you endure many evils and put on a solemn face
    for us.

    STREP. O Earth, what a voice! How sacred and august and
        portentous!

    SOC. Yes, for they alone are goddesses; everything else is drivel.   365

    STREP. Come now, by the Earth, isn't Olympian Zeus a god for
        us?

    SOC. What Zeus! Don't babble. Zeus doesn't even exist.

    STREP.   What are you saying?

Who makes it rain? First of all make this apparent to me.

    SOC. [*indicating the Clouds*].

They do, of course. I'll teach it to you by great signs.

Come, where have you ever beheld it raining without clouds?   370

Yet Zeus should be able to make it rain in the clear air by himself,
    while they are away.

    STREP. By Apollo, you've certainly clinched *that* by your present
        argument.

Yet before, I supposed that in truth Zeus was pissing through a
    sieve.

But tell me who it is that thunders—which makes me tremble.

    SOC. *They* thunder, as they roll.

    STREP.   In what way, you all-daring man?   375

    SOC. When they are filled up with much water and are
        compelled[70]

to be borne along by necessity, hanging down full of rain, then
they heavily fall into each other, bursting and clapping.

    STREP. And who is it that compels them to be borne along? Isn't it
        Zeus?

    SOC. Not in the least. It's ethereal vortex.

    STREP.   Vortex? I hadn't noticed that   380

Zeus doesn't exist, and that instead of him Vortex is now king.[71]

But you haven't yet taught me anything about the clapping and the
    thunder.

    SOC. Didn't you hear me say that the clouds full of water

fall into each other and clap because of their density?

    STREP. Come, how am I to trust this?

---

[70]The word "compel" (here and 379) is literally "necessitate." Socrates' explanation of rain
(and thunder: 405) in terms of necessity indicates his deterministic view of the nature of the
Clouds.

[71]Strepsiades is thinking of the dethroning of Ouranos by Kronos, and of Kronos by Zeus
(see *Euthyphro* 6a). He thinks that Zeus (*Dios* in the genitive) has been overthrown by Vortex
or Whirl (*Dinos*).

SOC.   I will teach you from yourself.   385
Have you ever been filled up with stew at the Panathenaea,[72] and
 then your belly was stirred up,
and suddenly an agitation rumbled through it?
 STREP. Yes, by Apollo, right away it acts terribly and it's been
  stirred up in me;
the stew claps just like thunder and clamors terribly:
softly at first, "pappax, pappax," and then it leads to
 "papapappax,"   390
and when I crap, it absolutely thunders, "papapappax," just like
 them.
 SOC. Then consider, since you have farted so much from such a
  little belly,
[*gesturing toward the sky*] isn't it likely that this air, being boundless,
  should thunder greatly?
 STREP. So that's also why the names "thunder" and "fart" are
  similar to each other.[73]
But teach me where the thunderbolt, bright with fire, comes from,   395
which burns us to ashes when it strikes, and scorches the living.
For it is apparent indeed that Zeus hurls it at perjurers.
 SOC. You fool, smelling of the age of Kronos,[74] you're out of
  date.
If in fact he strikes perjurers, then how is it that he didn't burn up
  Simon
or Cleonymus or Theorus?[75] Yet they are vehement perjurers.   400
But he strikes his own temple and Sunium, the cape of Athens,
and tall oak trees. Why? An oak, at least, doesn't perjure itself.
 STREP. I don't know. But you appear to speak well. Then what *is*
  the thunderbolt?
 SOC. Whenever a dry wind is raised aloft and gets shut up into
  these clouds,

---

[72]The Panathenaic festival was held annually in honor of Athena, the patron goddess of Athens. A procession to the acropolis (see line 69), sacrifices (that is, a feast), and games were held. See *Euthyphro* n. 24.

[73]"Thunder" is *brontē*, "fart" is *pordē*. *Brontē* may have been pronounced *borntē*; otherwise the wordplay is forced, which may be the point. Dover and most manuscripts assign line 394 to Socrates (K. J. Dover, ed., Aristophanes, *Clouds* [Oxford: Clarendon Press, 1968]); we follow the other manuscripts and Leonard Woodbury, "Strepsiades' Understanding: Five Notes on the *Clouds*," *Phoenix* 34 (1980), 112.

[74]Kronos, who ruled the gods before Zeus (n. 71), was a byword for "old fashioned." The belief that Zeus punishes perjurers (those who violate their solemn oaths in court) was an old tradition.

[75]Simon and Cleonymus were mentioned at lines 351 and 353. Theorus is represented in Aristophanes' *Wasps* (42–45, 418–419) as a flatterer.

it puffs them up inside like a bladder; then by necessity   405
it bursts them and goes rapidly outside because of its density,
and by its rushing and impetus it itself kindles itself.
   STREP. Yes, by Zeus! At any rate, this is just what happened to
      me once at the Diasia.[76]
I was roasting a thick sausage for my kinfolk, and I carelessly failed
      to slit it;
it got puffed up and, suddenly breaking open,   410
it spattered my eyes with crap and burned my face.
   CHORUS [*addressing Strepsiades*].
O human being, desiring great wisdom from us,
how happy you will become among Athenians and the Greeks!—
if you have a good memory, and are a thinker, and have hard labor
in your soul, and aren't wearied either by standing or walking,   415
and aren't too much annoyed when you shiver with cold, and have
      no desire to dine,
and keep away from wine and gymnastics and the other mindless
      things,
and believe that it is best (which is likely for a shrewd man)
to win by being active and taking counsel and warring with your
      tongue.
   STREP. As for a solid soul and sleep-disturbing pondering,   420
and a thrifty, life-consuming belly that dines on bitter herbs,
have no care: as for these things, I would boldly offer to be forged
      on an anvil.
   SOC. Now won't you believe in no god but ours:
this Chaos, and the Clouds, and the Tongue, these three?[77]
   STREP. I simply wouldn't converse with the others even if I
      should meet them,   425
nor would I sacrifice or pour libations or offer incense to them.
   CHORUS. Now tell me boldly what we may do for you. For you
      won't fail to get it
if you honor and admire us and seek to be shrewd.
   STREP. O Ladies, I beg of you then this one very little thing:
to be the best speaker of the Greeks by a hundred stadia.[78]   430
   CHORUS. This you will have from us, so that henceforth from
      now on

[76]The Diasia is a festival in honor of Zeus marked by family gatherings.

[77] Chaos: the word means "space" or "sky." In Hesiod Chaos is that which first comes into being, before all gods (*Theogony* 116). Tongue: Socrates refers to speech or the ability to speak well. When he names the three gods, he probably points to the sky, the Chorus, and his own mouth.

[78]Stadia: a "stadium" is about one-ninth of a mile.

no one will win more proposals in the Assembly of the people than
  you.
  STREP. Don't speak to me of great proposals. For I have no desire
    for them,
but only to twist justice enough to give my creditors the slip.
  CHORUS. Then you'll get what you yearn for, since you have no
    desire for great things.   435
Give yourself boldly to our ministers.
  STREP. I'll do this, trusting in you. For necessity weighs me down
because of the koppa-horses and the marriage that has crushed
    me.
So let them simply use me as they wish.
I offer them this body of mine   440
to be beaten, to hunger, to thirst,
to be squalid, to shiver with cold, to be flayed alive—
if only I am going to escape my debts
and be reputed by human beings to be
a bold, glib-tongued, daring go-getter,   445
a stinking concocter of falsehoods,
a phrase-finding lawsuit shyster,
a statute-book, a rattler, a fox, a sharpster,
supple, ironic, slippery, boastful,
a stinging, disgusting, twisting pest,   450
a cheater.
If those who meet me call me these things,
let them[79] simply do to me whatever they want.
And if they wish,
by Demeter, let them serve up a sausage   455
made out of me to the thinkers!
  CHORUS.[80] This man has a mettle
that is not without daring, but ready.
[To Strepsiades.] Know that
when you learn these things, from me   460
you will have glory among mortals
the length of heaven.
  STREP. What will happen to me?
  CHORUS. For all time you will lead with me
a life most enviable of human beings.   465
  STREP. But will I ever see this?

---

[79]"Them" refers to Socrates and his fellows in the thinkery (as also in lines 439–440).
  [80]Most manuscripts assign lines 457–462, 464–465, and 467–475 to Socrates. We follow all
modern editors in assigning them to the Chorus.

CHORUS. Yes, and consequently
many will always be sitting
at your gates
wishing to consult   470
and come to speak,
taking counsel with you
over affairs and indictments
concerning many talents,[81]
things worthy of your wit.   475
[*To Socrates.*]
But attempt first to teach the elderly man whatever you're going to,
and set his mind in motion, and try out his judgment.
    SOC. Come then, describe your own way[82] to me,
so that when I know what sort it is,
I may next bring novel devices to bear on you.   480
    STREP. What? Do you have it in mind, before the gods, to lay
        siege to me?
    SOC. No, but I wish to ask you in brief
whether you have a good memory.
    STREP.   Yes, in two ways, by Zeus!
If something is owed me, I have quite a memory;
but if, miserably, I owe, I'm quite forgetful.   485
    SOC. Do you have it in your nature to be a speaker?
    STREP. To be a speaker isn't in it, but to be a cheat is.
    SOC. Then how will you be able to learn?
    STREP.   Beautifully, have no care.
    SOC. Come now, so that whenever I throw out something wise
about the things aloft, you'll snatch it up right away.   490
    STREP. What, then? Am I going to feed on wisdom like a dog?
    SOC. This human being is unlearned and barbaric.
I fear, elderly one, that you'll need blows.
Come, let me see, what do you do if someone beats you?
    STREP.   I let myself be beaten,
and then, after holding on a little while,[83] I call the bystanders as
    witnesses;   495
then, again after waiting a moment, I bring a lawsuit.

---

[81]A "talent" is a large measure of silver, worth 6,000 drachmae.

[82]"Way" is *tropos,* meaning here "bent," "turn of mind," or "temperament" (same word in line 483). The point is that different pupils, having various natures, need different approaches.

[83]To make a stronger case in court, Strepsiades lets himself suffer for a while.

SOC. [*ready to take Strepsiades indoors for instruction*].
Come now, take off your cloak.

STREP.   Have I done some injustice?[84]

SOC. No, but it's the custom to enter stripped.

STREP. But I'm not going in to search for stolen property.[85]

SOC. Take it off. Why are you being silly?

STREP. [*taking off his cloak*].   Tell me this, now: 500
If I am diligent and learn eagerly,
which of the students will I resemble?

SOC. Your nature won't be any different from Chaerephon's.[86]

STREP. Oh me, miserably unhappy, I'll become half dead!

SOC. Stop chattering. Follow me and   505
hurry over here, quickly. [*Leads him up to the door.*]

STREP.   First put a honey-cake
into my hands, for I fear
going down inside, as if I were going into the cave of Trophonius.[87]

SOC. Go on! Why do you keep poking about the door?
[*They enter the thinkery.*]

CHORUS. Go and farewell,   510
since you have this courage.
[*The door closes behind the two men.*]
May there be good fortune for this
human being, because, proceeding
into the depth of his age,
he colors his own nature with matters   515
fit for those younger than he
and toils at wisdom.
[*Parabasis. The leading Cloud comes forward and addresses the audience.*][88]

---

[84]Strepsiades thinks he is being stripped to be given a beating. "Stripped" here means only "without one's cloak"; he is being asked to remove his jacket, so to speak.

[85]Athenian citizens had the right to search the houses of others for stolen goods, provided that they wore no clothing in which they could smuggle the articles in so as to pretend to discover them there.

[86]Chaerephon's "nature" was pale and gaunt.

[87]The cave of Trophonius, located between Thebes and Delphi, was visited by those who wished to obtain oracles from the dead hero Trophonius. It was believed that the snakes that infested the cave could be appeased with honey-cakes.

[88]The interlude that follows (to line 626) while Socrates is instructing Strepsiades indoors is called the *parabasis* ("digression"), in which the Chorus speaks directly to the audience. (Almost all of Aristophanes' comedies feature a parabasis.) Its first part (518–562) is delivered by the leading Cloud, through whom Aristophanes speaks in his own name and in the first person. This identification of Aristophanes with the Chorus in the *Clouds* is unique among his plays.

Spectators, to you I will freely speak out
the truth, by Dionysus who nurtured me.
As I would win[89] and be believed wise,   520
so also, since I hold you to be shrewd spectators
and this to be the wisest of my comedies,
I deemed it worthy that you first should taste afresh the one that
    provided me
the most work. At that time I retreated, worsted by vulgar men,
although I didn't deserve it.[90] For this, then, I blame you,   525
the wise, for whose sake I busied myself over it.
But I will never voluntarily betray the shrewd among you.
From the time when my Moderate Man and my Pederast
were spoken of as best here by men whom it is pleasant even to
    speak of,[91]
—that was when I was still a virgin and wasn't yet permitted to
    have children;   530
I exposed it, but some other girl got it and took it up,
while you nobly nurtured and educated it[92]—
from that time you have been keeping for me sworn pledges of
    your judgment.
So now, in the manner of Electra, this comedy
has come seeking, if she is fortunate enough to find spectators so
    wise: 535
she will recognize, if she sees it, the lock of her brother.[93]
So consider how moderate she is by nature: first,
she has not come with a hanging leather phallus stitched on,
thick and red at the top, to make little boys laugh;
nor does she mock the bald-headed, nor dance the cordax;   540

---

[89]"Win": i.e., win the contest against the other two competing comedies. The three comedies presented at a festival were ranked by a panel of judges in order of merit.

[90]Aristophanes is rebuking his audience for the bad reception it gave to the *Clouds* at its first performance (it placed third, i.e., last). Apparently he rewrote this first part of the parabasis (518–562) some time after the first presentation of the play (see nn. 96, 109).

[91]Aristophanes refers to the characters of the *Banqueters*, his first comedy, which is no longer extant.

[92]Aristophanes means that he was too young to produce plays ("children") in his own name, so, like a girl with an illegitimate baby, he willingly concealed his authorship (left it to die in an exposed place). Another "girl" (an older playwright) found it and the family "she" brought it to (the Athenian audience) has since fostered it.

[93]In Aeschylus' *Choephorae* Electra longs for a sign of her lost brother Orestes. His return is heralded by a lock of his hair, which Electra discovers on the tomb of their father Agamemnon. Just as Electra hopes that Orestes will return and kill their mother, who had killed Agamemnon, so Aristophanes hopes that the wise spectators who approved the *Banqueters* will return to him and redeem the earlier defeat of the *Clouds* by granting the first prize to this second production. (The word "comedy" in Greek is feminine in gender.)

nor does the elderly man while speaking his words
beat whoever is present with his staff to hide poor jokes;
nor does she dart in holding torches or shout "Oh! Oh!"—
no, she has come trusting only in herself and her words.[94]
And I, a man who is such a poet, am no long-hair,[95]   545
nor do I seek to deceive you by leading in the same things two and
     three times:
I always sophisticate by bringing in novel forms
not at all like one another—and all shrewd.
When Cleon[96] was greatest, I am the one who hit him in the belly
and did not dare to jump on him again when he was down.   550
But they,[97] now that Hyperbolus[98] has given them a grip,
are always trampling on him, the wretch, and his mother.
Eupolis,[99] the very first, dragged in his *Maricas*;
being bad, he badly turned our *Knights* inside out,
adding to it only a drunken hag for the sake of the cordax.   555
(Phrynichus[100] put her in a poem long before, for the sea-monster
     to eat.)
Then Hermippus in turn wrote a poem against Hyperbolus,
and now all the others are bashing away against Hyperbolus,
imitating my images of the eels.[101]
So whoever laughs at these, let him not delight in mine.   560
But if you enjoy me and these discoveries of mine,
in times to come you will be reputed to think well.

[94]In fact, of course, Aristophanes employs in the *Clouds* many of the low devices mentioned here, although less so than in his other comedies. The "cordax" is an undignified, perhaps licentious dance used in comedy.

[95]"Long-hair": see n. 63. The line has a second meaning if, as seems probable from ancient evidence, Aristophanes was bald.

[96]Cleon was a crude but powerful demagogue, the leading figure in Athenian politics for a time after Pericles' death (Thucydides III.36–40, IV.21–22). He was "greatest" after the capture of the Spartans at Pylos (n. 39), when Aristophanes attacked him strongly in his *Knights*. His preeminence in Athens ended when he was killed in battle in 422 (Thucydides V.1–10), about a year after the first performance of the *Clouds*.

[97]"They" are Aristophanes' rival comic poets.

[98]Hyperbolus was a demagogue, prominent in Athens after Cleon, and even more vulgar than his predecessor. The line means, "once Hyperbolus opened himself to criticism by his deplorable actions, my rivals started attacking him without restraint."

[99]Eupolis, Cratinus, and Aristophanes were the three leading comic poets of the age (Horace, *Satires* I.4.1).

[100]Phrynichus, another rival poet (somewhat older than Aristophanes, like Hermippus, next line) wrote a comedy which apparently parodied the legend of Andromeda, a beautiful girl threatened by a sea-monster.

[101]In his *Knights* (864) Aristophanes compared Cleon to eel-catchers, who stir up mud in order to increase their catch.

[*Ode, sung by the Chorus.*]
Lofty guardian, great   [*Strophe.*]
Zeus, tyrant[102] of gods,
I first call upon to join the Chorus;   565
and the great-strengthed director of the trident,
wild heaver of
earth and salty sea;[103]
and our great-named father,
Aether most revered, life-nurturer of all;   570
and the steerer of horses,[104] who
covers with rays exceedingly bright
the plain of earth, a daimon great
among gods and mortals.
[*Epirrhema.*[105] *The leading Cloud again speaks to the audience.*]
O most wise spectators, apply your minds,   575
for we have been done injustice and blame you to your faces.
For although we of all gods benefit the city most,
to us alone of daimons you do not sacrifice or pour libations—
we who watch over you. If there is ever some mindless
expedition, then we thunder or drizzle.[106]   580
Further, when you were about to choose as general the enemy of
        gods,
the Paphlagonian tanner,[107] we drew our eyebrows together
and sent forth terrible things; thunder burst through lightning;
the moon was abandoning her courses; and the sun
quickly drew his wick back into himself,[108]   585
declaring that he would not appear for you if Cleon were to be
        general.
Nevertheless, you chose him. They say that bad counsel
belongs to this city, but that the gods,
whenever you go wrong, turn it to the better.

[102]The term "tyrant" is not always as strongly disparaging as it sounds in English, although it certainly conveys the notion of illegitimacy or usurpation. (Consider what Zeus did to his father: *Euthyphro* 5e–6a and note).

[103]Poseidon.

[104]Helios, the sun, was represented as a charioteer guiding his horses across the sky.

[105]This section of the parabasis is called the epirrhema, "afterword" (575–594). The leading Cloud now speaks on behalf of the Clouds as goddesses.

[106]The Clouds claim that they warn the Athenians against foolish military campaigns in their war with Sparta. The Greeks took rain as an inauspicious sign.

[107]The "Paphlagonian tanner" is Cleon, who was the son of a tanner and was presented in the *Knights* as a slave from Paphlagonia, a barbaric region of Asia Minor.

[108]I.e., the stormy weather obscured the moon and sun.

And that this[109] too will be profitable, we will easily teach you.   590
If you convict the vulture Cleon of taking bribes and of stealing,
and then muzzle his neck in the stocks,
you will again find, as in the old days, that even if you did go
          wrong somewhat,
the affair will turn out to the better for the city.
[Antode, sung by the Chorus.][110]
Further, come to me, lord Phoebus,   [Antistrophe.]   595
Delian one, holding the lofty-horned
Cynthian rock;[111]
and you, blessed one, who hold the all-golden
house of Ephesus, wherein Lydian maids
greatly revere you;[112]   600
and our local goddess,
aegis-driving Athena, protector of the city;
and you who hold the rock Parnassus
and blaze with pine-torches,
conspicuous among the Delphic Bacchants,   605
reveler Dionysus.[113]
[Antepirrhema. Spoken by the leading Cloud.]
When we were preparing to start on our way here,
the Moon happened to meet us and enjoined us
first to greet the Athenians and their allies.
Next she declared she was angry and had suffered terrible things,   610
although she has benefited all of you, not in words, but
          manifestly.
First, thanks to her, you save no less than a drachma each month
          for torches,
so that everyone, as he is going out in the evening, says,
"Don't buy a torch, boy, the moon's light is beautiful."

---

[109]"This" is the election of Cleon as general. The fact that Cleon is spoken of here as alive indicates that the epirrhema remains as it stood in the play's original version (see n. 90). Scholars therefore doubt whether Aristophanes ever completed his revision and whether the play was ever performed a second time at a major festival.

[110]This *antode* ("song answering an ode") continues the ode of 563–574, as the *antepirrhema* that follows it continues the epirrhema.

[111]"Phoebus" is Apollo; Delos is the island sacred to him, on which was found a rocky height called Cynthus.

[112]The reference is to Artemis, whose worship centered at Ephesus, a Greek city on the coast of Asia Minor. Artemis of Ephesus was highly regarded in Lydia, a non-Greek inland country to the east of Ephesus.

[113]Parnassus is the mountain facing Delphi, site of the oracle of Apollo. For three months of the year this region was given over to Dionysus and to the revels of his female worshippers, the Bacchants.

She says she does other good things for you, and yet you do not
    keep the days   615
at all correctly;[114] you wreak confusion up and down,
so that the gods, she says, threaten her each time
they are cheated of their dinner and go home
without getting the feast appropriate to a reckoning of the days.
So whenever you should be sacrificing, you are inflicting
    tortures[115] and contesting lawsuits;   620
and often when we gods are keeping a fast,
lamenting Memnon or Sarpedon,[116]
you are pouring libations and laughing. In return for this, Hyper-
    bolus, chosen by lot
this year to be the Sacred Recorder, was
stripped of his crown by us gods.[117] Thus he will know better   625
that he ought to keep the days of his life according to the moon.
[*The Chorus now retires from center stage. In the choral interlude an
indefinite length of time has passed, during which Strepsiades has been
receiving instruction indoors. Socrates now enters from the thinkery.*]
    SOC. By Respiration, by the Chaos, by the Air![118]
Nowhere have I seen a man so rustic,
so resourceless, so dull, so forgetful
that he has forgotten the petty little quibbles he was learning   630
before he learned them! Nevertheless I'll
call him outdoors here to the light.
[*Calling into the thinkery.*]
Where's Strepsiades? Come out and bring your bed.
    STREP. [*emerging with a flea-infested mattress and blanket*].
But the bugs won't let me carry it out.
    SOC. Hurry up, put it down and apply your mind.
    STREP. [*sets down the bed and edges away from it*].   There!   635

---

[114]The Greek calendar year was shorter than the solar year by about eleven days. Hence the time of year when a given month might fall varied considerably, since every few years an extra month had to be inserted into the calendar to restore the months to their proper seasons. So the festivals, at which sacrifices were presented to the gods, never took place at exactly the same seasonal time from one year to the next.

[115]The Athenians permitted the torture of slaves in the gathering of evidence for trials.

[116]Memnon, the son of Dawn, and Sarpedon, the son of Zeus, were killed at Troy (Pindar, *Pythian Ode* VI.28–42; Homer, *Iliad* XVI.463–526).

[117]A "Sacred Recorder" was sent from various Greek cities to the Amphictionic council, which oversaw the management of the Delphic oracle and other sacred matters. How Hyperbolus lost his badge of office, the wreath, is unclear. He may have been removed from office; or perhaps the Clouds mean that the wind literally blew the wreath off.

[118]Socrates swears here by three "gods" all of whom seem to be equivalent to air.

soc. Come now, what do you first wish to learn now
of the things that you've never been taught at all? Tell me:
about meters, or about words, or rhythms?

strep. Meters[119] for me. For lately
I was swindled of two quarts by a barley-meal huckster.   640

soc. I'm not asking you that, but which you believe is
the most beautiful meter, the trimeter or the tetrameter?[120]

strep. To me, nothing is preferable to a half-sixth.[121]

soc. You're speaking nonsense, fellow.[122]

strep.   Now make me a bet
that a tetrameter is not a half-sixth.   645

soc.
To the crows! How rustic you are and poor at learning!
Perhaps you would be able to learn about rhythms.

strep. But how will rhythms benefit me in getting my barley?

soc. First, they will make you elegant in company,
an expert in what sort of rhythm is   650
"enoplion," and again, what sort is "dactylic."[123]

strep. "Dactylic?" By Zeus, I know that.

soc.   Then tell me.

strep. [holding up his index finger].
What else but this finger?
[He extends his middle finger in a vulgar gesture.]
Before, when I was still a boy, like so.

soc. You're crude and a dullard.

strep.   No, you dreary man, I'm not,   655
for I have no desire to learn any of these things.

soc.   What, then?

strep. This! This! The most unjust speech!

soc. But you must learn other things before that:
what quadrupeds are correctly called males.

strep. I do know the males, if I'm not mad: 660
ram, goat, bull, dog, chicken.

---

[119]"Meters" is also the word for "measures."

[120]These are poetic meters; Strepsiades thinks (or pretends to think) measures of quantity are meant.

[121]A "half-sixth" is equivalent to four quarts, the measure on which Strepsiades' next remark is based (the word tetrameter means "four-measure").

[122]"Fellow": see *Apology* n. 49.

[123]Enoplion ("warlike") is a stirring martial rhythm which some believe to be: $-/ \text{---}/ \text{---}/-$. Such a rhythm is sometimes employed, for example, in Sousa's marches. Dactylic ("finger"): each measure of this rhythm consists of a long and two shorts (---). For an account of these rhythms, see Dover, p. 180.

SOC. Do you see what's happened to you? You call the
female "chicken," in the same way as you do the male.

STREP. Come now, how so?

SOC.   How? "Chicken" and "chicken."

STREP. Yes, by Poseidon! Then what should I call them now?   665

SOC. "Chickeness," and the other, "rooster."[124]

STREP. "Chickeness?" Well done, by the Air!
In return for this teaching alone,
I'll fill up your kneading-pan with a circle of barley meal.

SOC. See, again, there's another one. You call "pan"   670
male when it's female.[125]

STREP.   In what way?
Am I calling "pan" male?

SOC.   Certainly.
just as if you were to say "Cleonymos."

STREP.   How so? Tell me.

SOC. For you, "pan" (kardop*os*) amounts to the same as
       "Cleonym*os*."

STREP. But, my good man, Cleonymos didn't even have a knead-
       ing pan.   675
He kneaded his dough in a little round bowl.[126]
But what should I call it from now on?

SOC.   What?
"Panette" (kardop*ē*), just as you say Sostratē.[127]

STREP. "Panette," as female?

SOC.   Yes, you're speaking correctly.

STREP. And that would be: "panette," "Cleonymē.[128]   680

SOC. But furthermore, you must learn about names:
which of them are male, and which are female.

STREP. But I, at least, know the ones that are female.

SOC.   Then tell me.

STREP. Lysilla, Philinna, Cleitagora, Demetria.

---

[124]The Greek word for chicken, *alektryon*, had a male variant in general use, *alektor*, here
translated "rooster." But Socrates has to coin a word for female chicken, *alektryaina*,
"chickeness."

[125]Some Greek nouns, such as "kneading pan" (*kardopos*), are feminine in gender but have
a masculine ending in -*os*. The usual feminine ending for such nouns would be -*ē*.

[126]Strepsiades may understand the Greek of Socrates' previous sentence to say: "The same
thing: for you, a kneading pan can belong to Cleonymos." Strepsiades is perhaps thereby
reminded of Cleonymos' poverty (he cannot afford a kneading pan); the joke is unclear.

[127]*Sostratē*: a common name for a woman.

[128]Strepsiades gives Cleonymos' name a feminine ending, probably alleging some
effeminacy in him.

SOC. And what sorts of names are male?

STREP.   Ten thousand: 685
Philoxenus, Milesias, Amynias.[129]

soc. But, villain, these aren't male.

STREP. Aren't they male in our view?

SOC.   In no way, for
how would you call Amynias if you met him?

STREP. How? Like this: "Come here, come here, Amynia,"[130]   690

SOC. You see? You're calling Amynias a woman.

STREP. Isn't it just, since she isn't serving in the army?
But why am I learning things that we all know?

SOC. For nothing, by Zeus!

[*Leading Strepsiades over to his bed, he pulls back the flea-bitten blanket and gestures to him to get in.*]

                    But lie down here—

STREP.   To do what?

SOC. —and think out one of your own troubles.   695

STREP. Oh no, I supplicate you, not there! But if I *must* lie down,
let me think out these very things on the ground.

SOC. There's no other way but this.

STREP. [*reluctantly gets into the bed and covers himself up*].
                              Miserably unhappy me!
Such a penalty I will pay to the bugs today!

SOC. [*song*].
Think and examine: 700
concentrate yourself in every way
and spin yourself around.
Swiftly, whenever you fall into
perplexity, jump to another
thought of wit and keep sweet-spirited sleep   705
away from your eyes.

STREP. [*he has been tossing and squirming under the bedclothes, and now lies silently for a moment, but suddenly cries out in pain*].
Attatai! Attatai!

SOC. What are you suffering? What ails you?

STREP. [*under the covers*].

---

[129]These three Athenians were probably known to be effeminate or homosexual. Philoxenus and Amynias are mentioned in the *Wasps*, Philoxenus as a passive homosexual, Amynias as a wealthy gambler who fell into poverty (74, 84, 1266). Amynias was one of Strepsiades' creditors (*Clouds* 31).

[130]Greek has a *vocative* case, used to address someone directly. The vocative of Amynias happens to end in -*a*, a typical feminine ending.

Wretched me, I'm perishing! From my couch
the Corinthians[131] are creeping out and biting me,   710
and devouring my sides,
and drinking out my soul,
and pulling out my balls,
and digging through my anus,
and destroying me!   715
   soc. Now don't grieve too heavily.
   strep. [*still under the covers*].
How can I not, when
gone is my money, gone my complexion,
gone my soul, gone my shoe,
and further, besides these evils,   720
as I sing while I'm on watch,[132]
I am almost gone!
[*Pause. Strepsiades settles down. Socrates waits for a moment, then
    speaks.*]
   soc. You there! What are you doing? Aren't you thinking?
   strep. [*sticking his head out*].   Me?
Yes, by Poseidon!
   soc.   And what did you think of, then?
   strep. Whether anything will be left of me by the bugs!   725
   soc. You will perish most evilly!
   strep.   But, my good man, I have already just perished!
   soc. You must not be soft, but cover yourself up;
for you must discover an intellection abstractional[133]
and fraudulent. [*Covers him up again with the sheepskin blanket.*]
   strep.   Oh me! If only someone would throw on me,
instead of sheepskins, an abstracting notion!   730
[*Pause.*]
   soc. Come now, first I'll observe what he's doing.
[*To Strepsiades.*]
You there! Are you sleeping?
   strep. [*under the covers*].   No, by Apollo, not I!
   soc. Have you got hold of anything?

---

[131]Corinth was fighting on the side of Sparta, and its army regularly ravaged Athenian
territory. There is a pun on *kores*, bugs. This passage parodies Heracles' death throes in
Sophocles, *Trachiniae* 1052–1057.
[132]"To sing while on watch" may be an idiomatic expression meaning "to pass the time in
difficult or tedious circumstances."
[133]"An intellection abstractional": with a second meaning, "a cheating insight." Dover
assigns this speech, which in the manuscripts is Socrates', to the Chorus.

STREP.   No, by Zeus, I certainly don't!
SOC.   Nothing at all?
STREP. [*poking out his head*].
Nothing but the dick in my right hand.

SOC. Won't you quickly cover yourself up and think of
    something?   735

STREP. What about? You tell me this, Socrates.

SOC. You yourself first discover and say what you wish.

STREP. You've heard ten thousand times what I wish:
about the interest, how I can pay nobody back.

SOC. Go now, cover up, let your subtle thought loose;   740
think about your troubles in small parts,
distinguishing and considering them correctly.

STREP. [*Under the blanket again, he is again beset by the bugs.*]
                                        Oh wretched me!

SOC. Keep still! And if you're perplexed over any of your
    intellections,
leave it, go away, then set your judgment back
in motion again and weigh it up.   745

[*Another long pause. Suddenly Strepsiades leaps out of bed.*]

STREP. O dearest Socratesie!

SOC.   What, old man?

STREP. I have a notion abstractional of the interest!

SOC. Display it.

STREP.   Now tell me—

SOC.   What?

STREP. What if I should buy a Thessalian witch
and draw down the moon by night,[134] then   750
close it up in a round feather-box
like a mirror,[135] and then keep watch over it?

SOC. How would this benefit you?

STREP.   Because
if the moon would no longer rise anywhere,
I wouldn't have to pay back the interest.

SOC.   Why?   755

STREP. Because money is lent out by the month.

SOC. Well done! But again, I'll throw out another shrewd thing
    for you.

---

[134]A Greek tradition had it that witches of Thessaly could perform this feat (*Gorgias* 513a).

[135]Perhaps Strepsiades thinks of the moon as a mirror because he has learned that the moon's light is a reflection of sunlight, as the pre-Socratic philosopher Empedocles taught (Diels-Kranz, *Fragmente der Vorsokratiker*, B42, 43).

If someone should indict you in a five-talent lawsuit,
tell me how you would make it disappear.[136]
    STREP. How? How? I don't know. But it must be sought.   760
    SOC. Don't always coop up your judgment around yourself,
but slack your thought away into the air,
like a beetle thread-tied by the foot.
    STREP. [*after a pause*].
I've discovered a most wise way of making the lawsuit disappear:
you'll agree with me yourself.
    SOC.   What sort of thing is it?   765
    STREP. Have you ever seen that stone at the drug-dealers',
the beautiful one, transparent,
from which they kindle fire?
    SOC.   Are you speaking of a glass lens?
    STREP. I am. Come, what if I were to take it,
while the scribe was writing down the indictment,   770
and were to stand farther off, like this, toward the sun,
and melt away the letters of my lawsuit?[137]
    SOC. Wisely done, by the Graces![138]
    STREP.   Oh me, how pleased I am
that my five-talent lawsuit has been written off!
    SOC. Come, quickly snatch up this one.
    STREP.   What?   775
    SOC. If you were a defendant and were about to lose
because you had no witnesses present, how would you twist away
        from the lawsuit?
    STREP. Most simply and easily.
    SOC.   Then tell me.
    STREP.   I am telling you.
What if, while one lawsuit was still pending
before mine was called, I would run away and hang myself?   780
    SOC. You're talking nonsense.
    STREP.   I'm not, by the gods, since
no one will bring a lawsuit against me if I'm dead.
    SOC. You're talking foolishness. Go away. I won't teach you any
        more.
    STREP. Why? Do teach me, before the gods, Socrates!

---

[136]To "make a lawsuit disappear" is a legal expression for *quashing* it. Strepsiades applies the expression literally.

[137]The suit would have been entered on a wax tablet.

[138]Dwelling with the Muses, the Graces were goddesses of song and dance (Hesiod, *Theogony* 64). Swearing by the Graces was not common.

soc. But you forget right away whatever you learn.   785
What were you taught first just now? Tell me.
    strep. Come, let me see, what *was* first? What was first?
What was it in which we knead our barley-meal?
Oh me, what was it?
    soc.   Won't you go to the crows and get lost,
you most forgetful and dull oldster?   790
    strep. Oh me! What ever will happen to me, a miserable wretch?
For I'll perish if I haven't learned tongue-twisting.
[*He turns to the Clouds.*]
O Clouds, give me some useful counsel.
    chorus [*the leading Cloud speaking*].
We counsel you, elderly man,
if you have a grown-up son,   795
to send him to learn instead of yourself.
    strep. I do have a son, noble and good.
But since he's not willing to learn, what should I do?
    chorus. Do you give in to him?
    strep.   Yes, for he's brawny-bodied and robust,
and he's born of women who are high-flying and aristocratic.[139]   800
But I'll go after him, and if he's not willing,
there's no way I won't drive him out of the house!
[*To Socrates.*]
Go in and wait for me a little while.
[*Exit Strepsiades into his house.*]
    chorus [*song, addressed to Socrates*].
Do you perceive that you'll soon
have very many good things because of us   805
alone of the gods? For he's ready
to do everything you bid him to.
And you—recognizing that the man is
astounded and manifestly excited—
quickly lap up   810
as much as you can.
For somehow such things are wont
to turn in another direction.
[*Exit Socrates into the thinkery. Commotion inside Strepsiades' house.
Enter Strepsiades, driving Pheidippides before him.*]

---

[139]"Aristocratic": literally "Coisyras," plural of Coisyra: see n. 10.

STREP. By the Mist, you won't stay here any longer!
Go and eat the pillars of Megacles![140]   815
    PHEID. Daimonic man, what's the matter with you, father?
Your mind isn't well,[141] by Olympian Zeus.
    STREP. See! See! "Olympian Zeus"! What foolishness!
Believing in Zeus at your age!
    PHEID. Really! Why do you laugh at that?
    STREP.   I was pondering   820
that you're a little child and think ancient things.
[*Motions to Pheidippides to come closer.*]
Nevertheless, come here so you'll know more,
and I'll tell you a certain matter, and when you learn it, you'll be a
       man.
But don't teach it to anyone!
    PHEID. [*comes up next to him*].
There. What is it?
    STREP.   You swore just now by Zeus.   825
    PHEID. I did.
    STREP.   Do you see, then, how good it is to learn?
There is no Zeus, Pheidippides.
    PHEID.   Who, then?
    STREP. Vortex is king, having driven out Zeus.
    PHEID. Ugh! What are you babbling?
    STREP.   Know that this is so!
    PHEID. Who says this?
    STREP.   Socrates the Melian,[142]   830
and Chaerephon, who knows the footsteps of fleas.
    PHEID. Have you come into such great madness
that you're persuaded by bilious men?[143]
    STREP.   Hold your tongue
and do not disparage men who are shrewd
and intelligent: because of their thrift,   835
none of them has ever had his hair cut or oiled himself
or gone to a bath-house to wash. But *you*
are washing up my life as if I were dead.[144]
Now go as quickly as possible and learn in my place.

---

[140]I.e., go and beg for sustenance in the marble halls of your wealthy uncle Megacles.
[141]"Your mind isn't well": literally, "you don't think well."
[142]Diagoras of Melos was a notoriously atheistic philosopher or poet. Hence Socrates is a "Melian."
[143]In Greek medicine madness was sometimes attributed to an excess of bile.
[144]I.e., you are squandering my livelihood as if I no longer needed it.

PHEID. What could someone learn from them that is of any use?   840
   STREP. Truly? Whatever is wise among human beings.
And you will know yourself—how unlearned and dense you are.
But wait here for me a little while.
[*Suddenly rushes back into the house.*]
   PHEID. Oh me! What'll I do, my father's out of his wits!
Shall I take him to court and get him convicted of being out of his
       mind,   845
or shall I announce his madness to the coffin-makers?[145]
[*Strepsiades hurries out of the house, leading a slave holding a rooster and
a hen.*]
   STREP. Come, let me see. What do you believe this is? Tell me.
       [*Points to the rooster.*]
   PHEID. A chicken.
   STREP.   Beautiful! And what is this? [*Pointing to the hen.*]
   PHEID. A chicken.
   STREP.   Both the same? You're ridiculous.
Not so, from now on. Call this one   850
"chickeness" and that one "rooster." [*Exit slave.*]
   PHEID. "Chickeness"? Are these the shrewd things you learned
when you went inside just now to the earth-born?[146]
   STREP. Yes, and many other things. But whatever I'd learn on
       each occasion
I forgot right away because of the multitude of my years.   855
   PHEID. Is *that* why you also lost your cloak?
   STREP. I didn't lose it, I thought it away.
   PHEID. And what did you do with your shoes, you mindless
       man?
   STREP. Like Pericles, I lost them for something needful.[147]
[*He leads his son over to the thinkery; Pheidippides follows reluctantly.*]
But come, walk, let's go. After you obey   860
your father, do wrong if you like. I know that I too
once obeyed you, a lisping six-year-old.
With the first obol I got for jury-duty,
I bought you a little wagon at the Diasia.[148]
   PHEID. Verily, in time you will be indignant about these things.   865

[145]I.e., perhaps he is about to die.
[146]The expression may mean only "stupid clods," but strictly speaking the "earth-born" are
the Giants who once stormed Olympus to overthrow the gods (Sommerstein, p. 202).
[147]Pericles secretly bribed the Spartan king in 445 to withdraw his army from Attica. He
later rendered account of the public money to Athens with the famous phrase, "spent for
something needful." (Plutarch, *Pericles* 22–23.)
[148]Diasia: see n. 76.

STREP. It's well that you've obeyed.
[*Knocks on the thinkery door.*]   Come here, come here, Socrates,
come out! I'm bringing you this son of mine,
I've persuaded him against his will.
[*Socrates comes out.*]
SOC.   Yes, he's still a childling
and isn't used to the baskets here.
  PHEID. [*with casually incorrect enunciation*].
You'd be properly used yourself if you were hung in a basket!   870
  STREP. To the crows! Are you rude to your teacher?
  SOC. See there, "basket." How foolishly he uttered it,
and with his lips loosely apart!
How would he ever learn acquittal of a lawsuit
or summons or persuasive puffery?   875
And yet Hyperbolus learned this for a talent.[149]
  STREP. Have no care, teach him. He's wise-spirited by nature.
Even when he was a little boy—only so big—
he'd fashion houses and carve ships indoors
and produce little leather wagons   880
and make frogs out of pomegranate peel—how does that seem to
      you?
He's to learn those two speeches:
the stronger, whatever it may be, and the weaker,
which argues the unjust things and overturns the stronger.
If not both, he's to learn at least the unjust one by every art.   885
  SOC. He'll learn them himself from the two speeches themselves;
I will leave.
  STREP.   Now remember this: he's to be able
to speak against all the just things.
[*Socrates goes into the thinkery. Enter from the same door Just Speech,
perhaps dressed in simple, old-fashioned clothing that is a little
threadbare.*]
  JUST SPEECH[150] [*calling into the open door*].
Come out here! Show yourself
to the spectators: you're so bold.   890
[*Unjust Speech follows, perhaps foppishly and fashionably attired.*]

---

[149]I.e., if even the stupid Hyperbolus (n. 98) could learn forensic rhetoric (to be sure, with
the help of an extremely large fee), there is hope for Pheidippides. Some editors take this line
as proof that Socrates taught rhetoric for pay, but Socrates does not say that he himself taught
Hyperbolus.
   [150]Just Speech and Unjust Speech, personifications of two ways of speaking and ways of
life, are called Stronger Speech and Weaker Speech in Dover's edition, contrary to the
manuscripts.

UNJUST SPEECH. Go wherever you want. For I'll
destroy you much more by speaking among the many.
 JUST. You'll destroy me? Who are you?
 UNJUST.   A speech.
 JUST.   Yes, a weaker one.
 UNJUST. But I'll defeat you who claim to be stronger than I.
 JUST. By doing what wise thing?   895
 UNJUST. By discovering novel notions.
 JUST. Yes, these things are flourishing
because of these mindless ones here. [*Points to the audience.*]
 UNJUST. No, they're wise.
 JUST.   I'll destroy you badly.
 UNJUST. Tell me, by doing what?
 JUST.   By speaking the just things. 900
 UNJUST. I'll overturn them by speaking against them,
for I quite deny that Justice[151] even exists.
 JUST. You deny that it exists?
 UNJUST.   Yes, for come, where is it?
 JUST. With the gods.
 UNJUST.   If Justice exists, then why didn't Zeus
perish when he bound his father?[152]   905
 JUST. Ugh! This is the evil
that's spreading around. Give me a basin.[153]
 UNJUST. You're an old fogy and out of tune.
 JUST. You're a pederast and shameless!
 UNJUST. You've spoken roses of me.
 JUST.   You're ribald!   910
 UNJUST. You crown me with lilies.
 JUST.   And a parricide!
 UNJUST. You don't recognize that you're sprinkling me with gold.
 JUST. Before, this wasn't gold, but lead.
 UNJUST. But as it is now, this is adornment for me.
 JUST. You're too bold.
 UNJUST.   And *you* are ancient.   915
 JUST. Because of you, none of the lads
is willing to go to school.
And someday the Athenians will recognize
what sorts of things you teach the mindless.

---

[151]Justice here is *Dikē*, the goddess or idea. In Hesiod, *Works and Days* 256–262, she sits
beside her father Zeus and tells him of men's injustices.
[152]See *Euthyphro* 6a and note for the story.
[153]A basin: to vomit in.

UNJUST. You're shamefully squalid.[154]

JUST.   And *you* are faring well,   920
although before, you were a beggar
claiming to be Telephus the Mysian,
gnawing on the notions of Pandeletus
from your little pouch.[155]

    UNJUST. Oh, the wisdom that you've remembered!   925

    JUST. Oh, the madness—yours and that of the city
which nourishes you
who harm the lads.

    UNJUST [*pointing to Pheidippides*].
You won't teach *him*, you Kronos!

    JUST. Yes I will, at least if he should be saved   930
and not just practice chattering.

    UNJUST [*to Pheidippides*].
Come here, and let him rave.

    JUST. You'll weep if you lay a hand on him!
[*With Just Speech and Unjust Speech about to come to blows, the leading
Cloud steps forward.*]

    CHORUS. Stop your battling and raillery! But display,
[*to Just Speech*]
you, what you used to teach them in the past,   935
[*to Unjust Speech*]
and you, the novel education, so that he,
[*indicating Pheidippides*]
when he's heard you both speaking against each other,
may decide and go to school.

    JUST. I'm willing to do this.

    UNJUST.   I too am willing.

    CHORUS. Come, then, which one will speak first?   940

    UNJUST. I'll let him.
And then, from whatever things he says,
I'll shoot him down with
novel phraselets and thoughts.[156]
And in the end, if he keeps on muttering,   945

---

[154]I.e., Just Speech is so far out of favor in Athens that he has been reduced to the condition
of a beggar.

[155]Telephus, the king of Mysia (north of Lydia in Asia Minor), appeared disguised as a
beggar in Euripides' *Telephus*. (The play has not survived.) Just Speech means that in the past
Unjust Speech lived beggar-like off meager scraps of food in a pouch, and that the "scraps"
were legalistic and sophistic quibbles. Pandeletus may have been a contemporary politician
and informer.

[156]The image is of a bow shooting arrows supplied by the words of his opponent.

he'll be destroyed by my notions
as if he were stung on his whole face
and on both eyes by hornets!
    CHORUS [*song*].
Now let the two, trusting   [*Strophe.*]
in their very shrewd   950
speeches and thoughts and
notion-coining ponderings,
show which of them will be
manifestly better as they speak.
For now the whole hazard   955
of wisdom is being risked here,
and about it there is a very great contest
among my friends.
[*The leading Cloud addresses Just Speech.*]
But you who crowned the elders with many upright habits,
utter forth your voice however you delight, and tell us your own
      nature.   960
    JUST. I will speak then of the ancient education as it was
      established
when I was flourishing, speaking the just things, and when mod-
      eration was believed in.
First, it was needful that no one hear a boy muttering a sound;
next, that those from the same neighborhood walk on the streets
      here in good order
to the cithara teacher's, lightly clad, in a group, even if the snow
      came down like barley-meal.   965
Next, again, he used to teach them to learn a song by heart (stand-
      ing with their thighs apart),[157]
"Pallas, Terrible Sacker of Cities" or "A Far-Reaching Shout,"[158]
pitched to the harmony that their fathers handed down.
If anyone was ribald or added any modulation
of the sort they use nowadays   970
(those difficult modulations of Phrynis),[159]
he would be thrashed and beaten with many blows, as one who
      would efface the Muses.
It was needful for the boys to keep their thighs covered while
      sitting at the gymnastic trainer's,

---

[157]Holding the thighs together was apparently regarded as an unseemly or girlish posture.
[158]These are probably the first words of ancient Athenian patriotic and warlike songs.
[159]Phrynis was a musician whose musical innovations were already introduced before Aristophanes was born.

so as to show nothing cruel to those outside.[160]
Next, again, when they stood up, they had to smooth the sand
    back again and be mindful   975
not to leave behind an image of puberty for their lovers.
At that time no boy would anoint himself below the navel,
so that dew and down bloomed on their private parts as on fruit.
Nor would he make up a soft voice and go to his lover,
he himself pandering himself with his eyes.   980
Nor was it allowed him at dinner to help himself to the radishes,
nor to snatch dill or parsley from his elders,
nor to eat relishes, nor to giggle, nor to cross his legs.

    UNJUST. Yes, ancient and Dipolia-like and full of grasshoppers
and of Cecides and of the Buphonia![161]

    JUST.   Yes, but these are the things   985
from which my education nurtured the men who fought at
    Marathon.[162]
But *you* teach them now to bundle themselves up in their cloaks
    right away,[163]
so that I'm ready to choke whenever someone at the Panathenaea
    who ought to be dancing
holds his shield in front of his haunch, having no care for
    Tritogeneia.[164]
[*To Pheidippides.*] In view of these things, lad, be bold and choose
    me, the stronger speech,   990
and you'll have knowledge of how to hate the marketplace and
    keep away from the baths;
and to be ashamed at shameful things and to be inflamed if anyone
    mocks you;

[160]I.e., the sight of a boy's nakedness is a torment to his older male lovers, with whom Just Speech expresses a certain sympathy by using the word "cruel."

[161]The Dipolia was a festival honoring Zeus Polieus ("City-Guardian"), probably full of old-fashioned ritual. "Grasshoppers" was the name given to golden brooches used by Athenian men of the Marathon period to fasten up their long hair (Thucydides I.6.3). Cecides was an early dithyrambic poet. The Buphonia ("ox-slaying") was probably a part of the festival Dipolia.

[162]Marathon, twenty-six miles from Athens, was the site of the famous battle at which the Athenians defeated the invading Persian army (490 B.C.). This victory was traditionally regarded as the peak of ancient Athenian valor.

[163]I.e., they are unable to endure cold even for a moment.

[164]"At the Panathenaic festival young men danced the famous Pyrrhic war dance, naked and armed only with helmet and shield. But the youth who had always been 'coddled' in cloaks found his shield more useful to keep his abdomen warm than to brandish in warrior-fashion. [It also required a strong arm to hold the shield out from the body during the vigorous dance.] This was neglectful of the honor of Athena the war-goddess, Tritogeneia." Quoted from Lewis L. Forman's edition of the *Clouds* (New York: American Book, 1915), p. 179.

and to stand up from your seat for your elders when they
      approach,
and not to misbehave toward your own parents; and not to do
anything shameful that would tarnish the statue of Awe;[165]   995
and not to dart into a dancing girl's house, lest you be broken off
      from your good fame
by being hit with a fruit by a whore[166] while gaping at the things
      there;
and not to talk back to your father at all, and not maliciously to
      remind him,
by calling him "Iapetus,"[167] of the age when he nourished you as a
      nestling.

   UNJUST. If you obey him in these things, lad, by Dionysus,   1000
You'll be like the sons of Hippocrates and they'll call you "honey-
      mama"![168]

   JUST. Yes, but you'll pass your time in the gymnasium, sleek and
      flourishing,
not mouthing prickly perversities in the marketplace as they do
      nowadays,
and you won't be dragged into court over a greedy, contradicting,
      shystering, petty affair.
Rather, you'll go down to the Academy[169] and run under the sa-
      cred olive trees   1005
with a moderate youth of your own age; you'll be crowned with a
      wreath of white reed,
smelling of yew and of leisure and of the white poplar shedding its
      leaves,
and in the season of spring you'll delight whenever the plane tree
      whispers to the elm.
If you do these things that I tell you
and pay mind to them,   1010
you will always have
a sleek chest, bright complexion,
large shoulders, slender tongue,

---

[165]I.e., do not disgrace the goddess Awe (*Aidōs*), mentioned in Hesiod, *Works and Days* 200,
and probably frequently represented as a statue.

[166]It is thought that girls sometimes indicated their willingness to be seduced by tossing a
man a piece of fruit.

[167]Iapetus, the brother of Kronos, is another name for "old fogy."

[168]The sons of Hippocrates were apparently regarded as simpletons. The expression "hon-
ey-mama" alludes to a child's begging for sweets.

[169]The Academy was a public park and gymnasium located outside the city walls, later
famous as the location of Plato's school.

large buttocks, small penis.
But if you pursue what they do nowadays,   1015
first you will have
a pale complexion, small shoulders,
narrow chest, big tongue,
small buttocks, big haunch, long decree.
[*Pointing to Unjust Speech.*]
And he will persuade you to believe everything shameful   1020
is noble, and the noble is shameful.
And besides this, he will fill you up
with the pederasty of Antimachus![170]
    CHORUS [*song by the Clouds*].
[*To Just Speech.*]
O you who toil at nobly towering   [*Antistrophe.*[171]]
wisdom most glorious,   1025
what a pleasantly moderate bloom
is upon your speeches!
They were happy who lived
back then with former men.
[*To Unjust Speech.*]
In view of these things, you who possess   1030
a conspicuously elegant Muse,
you must say something novel,
since that man is so well-reputed.
[*The leading Cloud addresses Unjust Speech.*]
You are likely to need terrific counsels against him
if you are going to overthrow the man and not bring laughter onto
       yourself.   1035
    UNJUST. In fact I have long been choking in my innards, and I've
      been desiring
to confound all these things of his with opposing notions.
For I've been called the weaker speech among the thinkers here
because of this very thing: that I was the first to have it in mind
to speak things opposed to these laws and to justice.   1040
And it is worth more than ten thousand staters[172]
to choose the weaker speeches and then to win.
[*To Pheidippides.*]
But consider how I'll refute the education he trusts in.

---

[170]Antimachus: apparently a well-known homosexual; his name literally means "Against
Battle" (i.e., "Pacifist").
[171]Antistrophe: corresponding to the strophe preceding Just Speech's oration.
[172]A stater is a coin of substantial value.

He says, first, that he won't let you wash in warm water.
[*To Just Speech.*]
Yet by means of what notion do you blame warm baths?   1045
    JUST. That they are most evil and make a man cowardly.
    UNJUST. Hold on! I've got you by the waist right away, with no
        escape.
Tell me this too. Which of the children of Zeus do you believe is
        best
in soul, tell me, and has performed the most labors?
    JUST. I judge no man to be better than Heracles.   1050
    UNJUST. Where indeed have you ever seen *cold* baths of
        Heracles?[173]
And yet who was more courageous?
    JUST.   These things, these are
what make the bath-house full of youngsters chattering all day,
but the wrestling schools empty!
    UNJUST. Next, you blame spending time in the marketplace, but I
        praise it.   1055
If it was villainous, Homer would never have made
Nestor an orator,[174] and all his wise men.
[*To Pheidippides.*]
From here I go back to the tongue, which *he*
says the young should not practice, while *I* say they should.
Again, he also says they should be moderate. These are two of the
        greatest evils.   1060
[*To Just Speech.*]
For whom have you ever seen anything good happen to
because of being moderate? Speak up, and refute me by telling
        whom.
    JUST. There are many. Peleus, at any rate, got his sword because
        of this.[175]
    UNJUST. A sword? A pretty gain the miserably unhappy man got!

---

[173]Heracles was traditionally "a benefactor of mankind, a slayer of monsters, and the ideal of male courage, strength, and endurance" (Dover, p. 224). Natural hot springs were called "baths of Heracles." They were held to have been given to him as a gift from the gods.

[174]"Orator" is *agorētēs*, a word closely related to *agora*, which can mean not only "marketplace" but also "assembly." Nestor, a venerable old man, is called *agorētēs* in *Iliad* I.248 and IV.293.

[175]Peleus once was a guest of Acastus. When Peleus repelled the advances of Acastus' wife, she accused him of trying to seduce her. Acastus thereupon contrived that Peleus would be left defenseless in a wilderness of wild beasts. But the god Hephaestus brought Peleus a sword, enabling him to escape the danger.

[176]Hyperbolus, the demagogue mentioned at line 551, was originally in the business of manufacturing or selling lamps.

Hyperbolus of the lamp-market[176] got very many talents   1065
because of villainy—but no, by Zeus, no sword!

JUST. Yes, and Peleus also married Thetis because of his
    moderation.[177]

UNJUST. Yes, and then she went off and abandoned him, for he
    wasn't hubristic

or pleasant to spend all night with in the bedclothes.

A woman delights in being treated wantonly. But *you* are a big
    Kronos.   1070

[*To Pheidippides.*]

For consider, lad, all that moderation involves,

and how many pleasures you're going to be deprived of:

boys, women, cottabus,[178] relishes, drinking, boisterous laughter.

Yet what is living worth to you if you're deprived of these things?

Well, then. From here I go on to the necessities of nature.   1075

You've done wrong, fallen in love, committed some adultery, and
    then you've been caught.

You're ruined, for you're unable to speak. But if you consort with
    me,

then use your nature, leap, laugh, believe that nothing is shameful!

For if you happen to be caught as an adulterer, you'll reply to
    him[179]

that you've done him no injustice. Then you'll refer him to Zeus,   1080

how "even he was worsted by love and women;

yet how could you, a mortal, be greater than a god?"

JUST [*to Unjust Speech*].

But what if he has a radish stuck up his rear end and has his hair
    plucked out with hot ash because he obeys you?[180]

By what argument will he be able to say that he's not buggered?[181]

UNJUST. And if he's buggered, what evil will he suffer?   1085

JUST. What evil could he ever suffer still greater than this?

[177]The sea goddess Thetis was given by the gods as a wife to Peleus because of his virtues, according to Pindar, *Isthmian Ode* VIII. Peleus is particularly praised there for his reverence, but moderation is also mentioned (lines 27, 40). Their son was Achilles. There are several traditions about why Thetis deserted him, none having to do with sexual disappointment.

[178]Cottabus was a popular game at Athenian banquets, requiring each person to toss the last drops of wine in his cup into a central basin without spilling any.

[179]Him: i.e., the husband. The following three lines allude to the frequent stories in Greek poetry of Zeus's affairs with mortal and immortal women.

[180]Such punishments were sometimes visited upon adulterers caught in the act.

[181]"Buggered" (*euryprōktos:* literally, "wide-anus") is literally descriptive of the punishment here described, but the term was commonly applied to passive homosexuals, who habitually submitted to buggery. Just Speech's point is that Pheidippides will be infamous if he follows Unjust's advice. Unjust refutes this in the lines following by showing him that all the famous men, in fact almost all Athenians, are infamous: "infamy" is perfectly compatible with a good reputation.

UNJUST. What will you say if you're defeated by me on this point?

JUST. I'll be silent. What else could I say?

UNJUST.   Come now, tell me,
from what group come the public advocates?

JUST. From the buggered.

UNJUST.   I'm persuaded.   1090
What then? From what group come the tragedians?

JUST. From the buggered.

UNJUST.   You speak well.
But from what group come the popular orators?

JUST. From the buggered.

UNJUST.   Then surely
you recognize that you're speaking nonsense?   1095
And among the spectators, consider which are the greater number.

JUST [*peering at the audience*].
I *am* considering.

UNJUST.   What do you see, then?

JUST. Many more, by the gods, who are buggered!
[*Pointing to particular men in the audience.*]
Him, at any rate, *I* know, and that one,
and him, with the long hair.   1100

UNJUST. Then what will you say?

JUST. We've been worsted!
[*Flinging his cloak into the audience, he addresses the spectators.*]
                    You debauchees!
Before the gods, receive my cloak,[182] since
I'm deserting to you!
[*He runs back into the thinkery, followed by Unjust Speech. Socrates
comes out and addresses Strepsiades.*]

SOC.[183] What now? Do you wish to take your son here   1105
and lead him away, or shall I teach him to speak for you?

STREP. Teach and punish him and remember to
sharpen him up well for me: on the one side,
sharpen his jaw for petty lawsuits,
and on the other, for the greater matters.   1110

SOC. Have no care, you'll take him back as a shrewd sophist.

PHEID. No, but pale, I think, and miserably unhappy.

SOC. Let's go now.

---

[182]A soldier intending to desert to the enemy would discard his cloak, which may have served as a uniform or as identification.

[183]Contrary to the manuscripts, Dover assigns lines 1105–6 and 1111 to Unjust Speech, and lines 1113–14 to the Chorus.

PHEID.   I think that
you'll regret these things.

[*Socrates retires into the thinkery with Pheidippides for his further instruction; Strepsiades goes into his house. The Chorus comes forward for its second parabasis, delivered to the audience by the leading Cloud.*]

What the judges[184] will gain if they justly grant this Chorus   1115
a certain benefit, we wish to tell.
First, if you wish to plow your fields in season,
we will rain for you first, for the others later.
Next, we will guard the vines when they are bearing fruit,
so that neither drought nor too much rain will weigh them down.   1120
But if someone who is mortal dishonors us who are goddesses,
let him apply his mind to the sorts of evils he will suffer from us.
He will get neither wine nor anything else from his land,
for whenever his olives and grapes are budding,
they will be knocked off. With such slings we will strike.   1125
If we see him making bricks, we will rain,[185] and
we will shatter the tile of his roof with round hailstones.
And if he himself or any of his kinsmen or friends ever get married,
we will rain all night,[186] so that he will perhaps wish
that he happened to be even in Egypt[187] rather than to judge
        badly.   1130

[*The Chorus now retires from center stage. In this interlude an indefinite length of time has passed, during which Pheidippides has been receiving instruction indoors. Strepsiades comes out of his house and approaches the thinkery to call for his newly educated son. He is carrying a gift of some sort for Socrates, perhaps a sack of meal.*]

STREP. Fifth, fourth, third, after this the second,
then that day of all days which
I have dreaded and shuddered at and loathed the most:
right after this is the old and new.[188]

---

[184]A panel of judges ranked the comedies performed at a given festival in the order of their merit. The Clouds are demanding the first prize.

[185]Bricks were made by drying blocks of mud in the sun.

[186]Much of the ceremony at Greek weddings was conducted outdoors, particularly the torchlight procession which accompanied the bride to her husband's house and the dancing that followed.

[187]Although Egypt is remote and its customs outlandish ("the country of the most ancient antiquity and of excessive piety": Strauss, p. 35), at least it hardly ever rains there.

[188]Strepsiades is counting off the last days of the month, the "twenties" (line 17), which were reckoned backwards. The penultimate day was the "second"; the last day was called the "old and new," and it was on this day that interest fell due. It was perhaps so called because during part of the day the moon was old and for the remaining part new.

For everyone whom I happen to owe says on oath   1135
that he will ruin and destroy me by putting down a deposit[189]
    against me.
While I am begging for due measure and just things
("You daimonic man, don't take this just now";
"Please postpone that"; "Let me off from the other"), they say
they will never get it back this way: they rail at me   1140
for being unjust, and they say they will bring lawsuits against me.
So now let them bring their lawsuits! Little do I care,
if Pheidippides has in fact learned to speak well.
But I'll soon know by knocking at the thinkery.
[*He knocks.*]
Boy, I say, boy! Boy!
    SOC. [*opening the door*]. I greet Strepsiades.   1145
    STREP. And I you. But take this first.
[*He hands him the gift, which Socrates sets down inside.*]
For one should show admiration in some way for the teacher.
And my son—tell me if he has learned that speech
which you introduced just now.
    SOC. He has learned it.
    STREP.   Well done, O Fraud, queen of all!   1150
    SOC. So you may be acquitted of any lawsuit you wish.
    STREP. Even if witnesses were present when I took the loans?
    SOC. So much the better, even if a thousand were present.
    STREP. Then I will shout an overstrained shout!
Ho, weep, you moneylenders—   1155
you yourselves, and your principal, and interest on interest![190]
For you won't do me any more dirt.
Such a boy is nurtured for me
in these halls here,
brilliant with two-edged tongue,   1160
my bulwark, savior to our halls, to enemies a harm,
surceaser of a father's great evils!
[*To Socrates.*]
Run and call him
to me from within!
[*Socrates goes inside to fetch Pheidippides; Strepsiades calls after him.*]

---

[189]A "deposit" was a sum of money paid to the city by the prosecutor on the first day of the new month to initiate a lawsuit; the deposit was forfeited if the suit was lost.
[190]The words for "principal" (*archaia*) and "interest" (*tokoi*) may also mean "ancestors" and "offspring."

My child, my boy, come out of the house!   1165
Hear your father![191]
[*Socrates and Pheidippides enter.*]
   soc. Here is the man.
   strep. [*embracing him*]. My dear, my dear!
   soc. Take him and depart. [*He returns into the thinkery.*]
   strep. Ho, ho, my child! Oh, oh!   1170
How pleased I am, first, to see your complexion!
Now you have, first, a negating and
contradicting look, and the local color
is simply blooming on you: the "what do you mean?"[192] and the
     reputation
for suffering injustice when (I know!) you are doing injustice and
     working evil.   1175
And on your face is an Attic visage.
So save me, now that you have ruined me.
   pheid. What are you afraid of, then?
   strep.   The old and new.
   pheid. Is "old and new" a certain day?
   strep. Yes, it's the one on which they say they'll put down their
     deposits against me.   1180
   pheid. Then those who put them down will lose them again. For
     there is no way that
one day could turn out to be two days.
   strep. It couldn't?
   pheid.   How could it, unless, of course, the same woman
could turn out to be old and young at once?
   strep. And yet that is the law.
   pheid.   That's because, I suppose,   1185
they don't know correctly what the law has in mind.
   strep.   What does it have in mind?
   pheid. Solon[193] of long ago was a friend to the people in his
     nature—
   strep. Surely that has nothing to do with the old and new.

---

[191]These two lines parody Euripides, *Hecuba* 171–173. Hecuba is calling to her daughter Polyxena so she can announce to her that the Greeks, who have conquered Troy, have decreed that Polyxena must die as a sacrifice to the dead Achilles.

[192]"What do you mean?" (literally, "what are you saying?"): uttered contentiously, the question challenges and disputes anything said by anyone. The "local color" of the previous line probably refers to a pale complexion from time spent studying indoors.

[193]Solon was a famous Athenian statesman of the late sixth century B.C. He reformed the constitution by abolishing serfdom, by dividing the citizenry into four classes based on wealth rather than descent, and by granting to the common people some political authority.

PHEID. —so he put the summons into two days,
into the old and into the new   1190
so that the deposits would occur at the new moon.
　　STREP. Then why did he add the old?
　　PHEID.　　　　　　　　So that the defendants, my dear man,
by being present one day beforehand,
might be voluntarily released. Or if not,
so that they might be distressed on the morning of the new
　　　　moon.[194]   1195
　　STREP. Then why don't the officials receive the deposits
at the new moon instead of on the old and new?[195]
　　PHEID. The same thing happens to them, it seems to me, as to the
　　　　Foretasters:[196]
they do their tasting one day earlier
so that the deposits may be filched as quickly as possible.   1200
　　STREP. [to Pheidippides].
Well done!
[To the spectators]
　　　　　　You wretchedly unhappy ones, why do you sit there
　　　　stupidly?
You are the booty of us wise men, since you are stones,
number, mere sheep, stacked-up jars.[197]
Therefore I must sing an encomium to myself
and to my son here upon our good fortune.   1205
[Sings.]
"O blessed Strepsiades.
your own nature—how wise!
And such a son you are nurturing!"
That's what my friends and demesmen will say
in their envy when you win   1210
our lawsuits by your speaking!
But I will take you inside,
for I wish first to feast you.

---

[194]Pheidippides is saying that the "old," the last day of the old month, must be different from the "new," the first day of the new month. By scheduling the summons one day before the suit could begin, Solon intended to encourage out-of-court settlements ("voluntarily released").

[195]I.e., why do the officials take the deposits one day earlier than Solon's law intended?

[196]Foretasters: public officials responsible for seeing to it that the food prepared for public festivals was satisfactory. Apparently they exercised their office on the day preceding the festival (Dover, p. 236).

[197]The spectators, sitting in rows, one above another, must have looked like stacked jars from the stage.

[*Father and son retire into the house for their feast. While they are dining, one of Strepsiades' creditors approaches, a fat man, bringing a witness with him, with whom he is conversing.*]

CREDITOR.[198] What? Should a man give up any of his own
    belongings?
Never! It would have been better to blush at once   1215
back then, than to have troubles now,
when for the sake of my own money
I am dragging you as a witness to my summons.[199] Besides, I'll
    also become
an enemy to a man who is a fellow demesman.
But never will I shame my fatherland[200]   1220
while I live.
[*In a loud voice.*] I summon Strepsiades—
    STREP. [*opening the door and coming out*]. Who's there?
    CRED. —to the old and new.
    STREP. [*to the audience*].   I call to witness
that he said two days.
[*To the creditor.*]
                        What's the matter?
    CRED. It's about the twelve minae you got when you bought the
dappled horse.
    STREP. [*to the audience*].
                        A horse? Don't you hear?   1225
All of you know I hate horsemanship!
    CRED. And by Zeus, you swore by the gods that you would give
        it back.
    STREP. No, by Zeus, for then my Pheidippides hadn't yet
gained knowledge of the unassailable speech.
    CRED. Do you have in mind to deny it now because of this?   1230
    STREP. Yes, for what else would I get out of his learning?
    CRED. And will you be willing to deny it on an oath by the gods
wherever I bid you?[201]
    STREP.   What gods indeed!
    CRED. Zeus, Hermes, Poseidon.[202]

---

[198]Some manuscripts identify this first creditor as Pasias (line 21).

[199]In other words, "I should have suffered the shame of refusing him the loan in the first place, in order to spare myself the trouble I will now incur by bringing a lawsuit against a neighbor."

[200]He alludes to the Athenian addiction to litigation.

[201]Oaths were felt to be more binding when sworn at an altar or sanctuary of the god in question.

[202]Probably Zeus as the chief god, Hermes as the god of commerce, and Poseidon as the god of horses.

STREP.   Yes, by Zeus,
and I'd even put down a three-obol piece besides, just to swear!   1235
   CRED. May you perish someday, then, for your lack of awe!
   STREP. [*to the audience*].
This man would profit from being rubbed down with salt.[203]
   CRED. Oh me! How you're ridiculing me!
   STREP. [*pointing to the belly*].
                             There'll be room for six gallons.
   CRED. By great Zeus and the gods,
you won't get away with this!
   STREP. [*laughing*].   I'm wondrously pleased by gods,   1240
and swearing by Zeus is laughable to those who know.
   CRED. Verily, in time you will pay the penalty for this!
But before you send me away, answer me
whether you will give me back my money or not.
   STREP.   Keep quiet now,
for I'll give you a plain answer immediately.   1245
[*He goes into his house.*]
   CRED. [*to the witness*].
What does it seem to you he'll do? Does it seem to you that he'll
     give it back?
[*Before the witness can reply, Strepsiades comes out of the house with a
kneading pan.*]
   STREP. Where's the one who's asking for his money?
Tell me, what is this?
   CRED.   What's this? a pan.
   STREP. And then you ask for money, being such as you are?
I wouldn't give back even an obol to anyone   1250
who would call a panette a "pan."
   CRED. So you won't give it back?
   STREP.   Not so far as I know.
So won't you hurry up and quickly pack yourself off
from my door? ·
   CRED.   I'm going. And know this:
I'll put down a deposit, or may I live no longer!   1255
[*Creditor and witness stalk toward the exit. Strepsiades calls after them.*]
   STREP. Then you'll throw that away too, in addition to the twelve
     minae!
[*Pretending condolence.*]

---

[203]Strepsiades is saying that he could make a good wineskin out of the creditor's belly; hides in tanning were thoroughly rubbed with salt.

Yet I don't wish for you to suffer this
just because you foolishly called it "pan."
[*Creditor and witness depart. Strepsiades goes back into the house with his
kneading pan. A second creditor enters limping.*]

2ND CRED. Oh me! Me!

STREP. [*coming out*].   Ho!
Who ever is this who is lamenting? Surely it's not   1260
one of the daimons of Carcinus[204] that gave utterance?

2ND CRED. What? Do you wish to know who I am?
A miserably unhappy man.

STREP.   Then follow your path by yourself.

2ND CRED. O harsh daimon! O fortune, smashing the wheels
of my horses! O Pallas, how you have ruined me!   1265

STREP. But what evil has Tlepolemus[205] ever done you?

2ND CRED. Do not mock me, sir, but bid your son
to give me back the money he got,
especially since I've fared so badly.

STREP. What money is this?

2ND CRED.   That which he borrowed.   1270

STREP. Then you really *are* badly off, at least as it seems to me.

2ND CRED. Yes, I fell out of a chariot while I was driving horses,
    by the gods!

STREP. Why are you babbling, as if you had fallen off an ass?[206]

2ND CRED. Am I babbling if I wish to get my money back?

STREP. There's no way you yourself[207] could be in health.

2ND CRED.   Why?   1275

STREP. You seem to me like one whose brain has been shaken.

2ND CRED. And *you* seem to *me*, by Hermes, about to receive a
    summons
if you won't give back the money.

STREP.   Tell me now,
do you believe that Zeus always rains fresh
water on each occasion, or does the sun   1280
draw the same water back up from below?

[204]Strepsiades perhaps refers to a lamenting god in one of the tragedies of the poet Carcinus, none of whose works has survived.

[205]Xenocles, one of the sons of Carcinus, was also a tragic poet, and his lost *Licymnius* is thought to be the source of the creditor's lines 1264–1265. The tragic persona adopted by the creditor is Licymnius, an old man who was killed by his nephew Tlepolemus, a son of Heracles. The story is told in outline in *Iliad* II.653–670.

[206]A man who was *apo nou* (out of his mind) was said by the Greeks to have had a fall *ap' onou* (off an ass).

[207]I.e., you yourself in your mind (as opposed to your bodily injuries).

2ND CRED. I don't know which, nor do I care.

STREP. How then is it just for you to get your money back
if you know nothing of the matters aloft?

2ND CRED. Well, if you're short, give me the interest on the
money.   1285

STREP. Interest? What beast is that?

2ND CRED. What else but that the money always
becomes more and more by month and by day
as time flows along?

STREP.   Beautifully spoken.
What then? Do you believe that there is more sea   1290
now than before?

2ND CRED.   No, by Zeus, but equal,
for it's not just for there to be more.[208]

STREP.   Then how,
you miserably unhappy man, does *it* become no
more, though rivers flow into it, while *you*
seek to make your money more?   1295
Won't you prosecute yourself away from my house?
[*Calling into the house.*]
Bring me the goad!
[*A servant enters with an animal prod, then exits.*]

2ND CRED. [*in a loud voice*].
                    I call for witnesses to this!

STREP. [*prodding him with the goad*].
Move on! What are you waiting for? Won't you ride on, you
thoroughbred?

2ND CRED. Is this not hubris indeed?

STREP. [*goading him across the stage*].
                                   Will you pull? I'll prod
and goad you in the ass, you tracehorse!   1300
[*Exit second creditor, at a run.*]
Do you flee? I was bound to get you moving
with those wheels of yours and chariots!
[*Strepsiades returns to his house. While he finishes his interrupted feast,
the Chorus comes forward and sings.*]

CHORUS.
Such a thing it is to be in love with low matters!   [*Strophe.*]
For this old man, having fallen passionately in love,
wishes to cheat them   1305

---

[208]I.e., it is not the appropriate or normal conduct for the sea to increase its size.

of the money he borrowed.
And it must be
that some matter will come upon
this sophist today which will make him
suddenly come upon some evil for the knaveries he has begun.   1310
For I suppose he will presently find just what   [*Antistrophe.*]
he was seeking long ago:
that his son is clever
at speaking notions opposed
to the just things, so as   1315
to defeat everyone, whomever he
associates with, even when he speaks
all-villainous things. But perhaps, perhaps
he will even wish
him to be voiceless.   1320
[*Strepsiades bursts out of the house, still carrying his tall drinking mug,
which he drops outside the door.*]
STREP. Oh! Oh!
O neighbors and kinsmen and demesmen!
Defend me with every art: I'm being beaten!
Oh me, miserably unhappy! My head and jaw!
[*Pheidippides enters.*]
Wretch, do you beat your father?
PHEID.   Yes, father.   1325
STREP. [*to the audience*].
Do you see him agreeing that he beats me?[209]
PHEID.   Certainly I do.
STREP. Wretch! Parricide! Housebreaker!
PHEID. Say again that I am these same things and more.
Do you know that I delight in being called many bad things?
STREP. You're hyper-buggered!
PHEID.   Sprinkle me with many roses!   1330
STREP.
Do you beat your father?
PHEID.   Yes, and I will make it clearly apparent, by Zeus,
that I was beating you with justice.
STREP.   Most wretched one,
how could beating a father be with justice?
PHEID. I will demonstrate it and defeat you by speaking.

---

[209]Father-beating was a serious crime, and Strepsiades calls on witnesses as though under-
taking the first step of a lawsuit against his son.

STREP. You will defeat me in *this?*

PHEID.   Yes, greatly and easily.   1335
But choose which of the two speeches you wish to be spoken.

STREP. What two speeches indeed!

PHEID.   The stronger or the weaker.

STREP. I *did* teach you, by Zeus, my dear,
how to speak against the just things, if you *are*
going to persuade me that it is just and noble   1340
for a father to be beaten by his sons.

PHEID. I do suppose that I will persuade you, so that
when you have heard it, not even you yourself will say anything against it.

STREP. In fact, I do wish to hear what you will say.

CHORUS [*song, addressing Strepsiades*].

Your work, elderly one, is to give thought to how   [*Strophe.*]   1345
you will overcome this man,
since he would not be so unrestrained unless
he were confident in something.
But there is something by which he is emboldened:
the audacity of the man is clear.   1350

[*The leading Cloud, to Strepsiades.*]

But you must now tell the Chorus out of what the fight first
began to arise. (You will do this anyway.)

STREP. All right, then, from where we first began to rail at each
other,
I will tell you. We were feasting, as you know,
and first I bade him to take the lyre   1355
and sing a song of Simonides: "The Ram, How He Was Shorn."[210]
Right away he said that it was old-fashioned to play the lyre
and sing while drinking, just like a woman grinding barley.[211]

PHEID. Yes, shouldn't you have been struck and trampled on
right away back then
when you bade me to sing, as if you were providing a feast for
grasshoppers?[212]   1360

---

[210]The traditional lyric poet Simonides, a contemporary of Pindar and Aeschylus, lived during the Persian Wars. "The Ram, How He Was Shorn" apparently told of the defeat of a mighty wrestler called Crius ("Ram"). It was customary at old-fashioned Athenian banquets for a guest to accompany himself at singing one of the good old songs.

[211]Women often sing simple songs as they perform monotonous manual work.

[212]Grasshoppers, according to legend, spend all their time singing and do not need to eat or drink (*Phaedrus* 259c). Perhaps there is an allusion to the old-fashioned "grasshoppers" of line 984.

STREP. Such are the things he was also saying then inside, just as
    he is now.
He also declared that Simonides is a bad poet.
And at first I put up with him—with difficulty, but nevertheless I
    did.
Well, then I bade him to take a sprig of myrtle
and recite some verses from Aeschylus for me.[213] And then right
    away he said,   1365
"*I* believe Aeschylus is first among poets:
full of noise, incoherent, wordy, bombastic."
And then how do you suppose my heart swelled up!
Nevertheless I bit my spirit and said, "Well, recite something
from one of these newer ones, whatever wise things are there."   1370
Right away he sang some passages from Euripides, how
(defend us from evil!) a brother had intercourse with his sister from
    the same mother.[214]
And I no longer put up with him, but right away I struck out at him
with many bad and shameful names. And from there, as was
    likely,
we hurled word upon word at each other. Then he leaps on me,   1375
and then he was pounding and crushing and choking and batter-
    ing me!
    PHEID. Wasn't it just, since you don't praise most wise
    Euripides?
    STREP. *Him* most wise? You—what shall I call you?
But again, I'll be beaten again!
    PHEID.   Yes, by Zeus, and it would be with justice.
    STREP. How could it be just? For I'm the one who nurtured you,
    O shameless one,   1380
perceiving what you had in mind when you used to lisp
    everything.
If you'd say "bryn," I'd recognize it and offer you something to
    drink.

[213]Apparently it was traditional for those who sang at banquets to do so with a branch of myrtle in the hand. Aeschylus was *the* old-fashioned tragedian. It was not usual to recite tragic poetry at banquets, but Strepsiades is compromising: Pheidippides does not have to sing lyric poetry if only he will recite good old Aeschylus.

[214]The tragedy is *Aeolus*, of which only fragments survive. The incest was committed by Aeolus' children, Macareus and Canace. Strepsiades emphasizes "from the same mother" because Athenian law permitted marriage between children of the same father but different mothers. Euripides was regarded as a daring, unconventional, even atheistic poet (cf. Aristophanes' *Frogs* and *Thesmophoriazusae* 450–451).

And when you'd ask for "mamman," I'd come and bring bread to
    you.
No sooner would you say "ca-ca" than I would take you through
    the door
and carry you outside, holding you out in front of me. But now
    you, strangling me   1385
as I was shouting and crying out that
I needed to crap, didn't have the decency
to carry me outside, you wretch,
through the door. Instead, while I was being choked,
I made "ca-ca" right there!   1390
    CHORUS [*song*].
I suppose that the hearts of the youths   [*Antistrophe.*[215]]
are leaping at what he will say.
For if, having done such deeds as these,
he persuades him by his chatter,
I wouldn't even give a chick-pea for the   1395
skin of old men.
[*The leading Cloud addresses Pheidippides.*]
Your work, you mover and heaver of novel words,
is to seek some way of persuasion so that you will seem to speak
    just things.
    PHEID. How pleasant it is to consort with novel and shrewd
      matters
and to be able to look down on the established laws!   1400
For *I*, when I was applying my mind to horsemanship alone,
couldn't even say three phrases before I went wrong.
But now that he himself has made me stop these things
[*indicating the thinkery*]
and I am associating with subtle notions and speeches and
    ponderings,
I do suppose that I will teach him that it is just to punish one's
    father.   1405
    STREP. Then keep on with your horses, by Zeus, since it is better
      for me
to nurture a four-horse team than to be beaten and battered!
    PHEID. I'll pursue that point of my speech where you interrupted
      me,
and first I will ask you this: did you beat me when I was a boy?

---

[215]This antistrophe, introducing Pheidippides' rebuttal, corresponds to the strophe preceding Strepsiades' statement (1345–1350).

STREP. Yes, I did; I was well-intentioned and concerned for you.

PHEID.   Then tell me,   1410
isn't it also just for me likewise to be well-intentioned toward you
and to beat you, since in fact to be well-intentioned is to beat?
For why should *your* body be unchastised by blows,
but not mine? And in fact I too was born free.[216]
Children weep: does it seem fit to you that a father not weep?[217]   1415
You will say that it is the law that this is a boy's work,
but *I* would say in return, "Old men are children twice."
And it's more appropriate for the old to weep than the young,
inasmuch as it's less just for them to do wrong.

STREP. But nowhere is it the law that the father suffer this.   1420

PHEID. Wasn't he who first set down this law a man
like you and me, and didn't he persuade those of long ago by
      speaking?
Is it any less allowable for me too, then, to set down in turn
for the future a novel law for sons to beat their fathers in return?
As for the blows that we got before the law is set down,   1425
we dismiss them, and we give them our past thrashings gratis.
Consider the chickens and the other beasts:
they defend themselves against their fathers. Yet how do they
      differ
from us, except that they do not write decrees?

STREP. What then? Since you imitate the chickens in all things,   1430
won't you eat dung and sleep on a perch?

PHEID. It's not the same, sir, and it wouldn't seem so to Socrates,
      either.

STREP. In view of this, don't beat me. Otherwise you'll only have
      yourself to blame someday.

PHEID. How so?

STREP.   Because it's just for me to punish you
and for you to punish your son, if you have one.

PHEID.   But if I don't have one,   1435
I'll have wept in vain, and you'll have died with the laugh on me.

STREP. [*to the old men in the audience*].
To me, O men of my age, he seems to speak just things,

---

[216]A free man was permitted to strike his children, but it was forbidden for them to strike
him (cf. n. 209). "Born" is *phyein*, related to *physis*, "nature."

[217]This line is an adaptation of Euripides, *Alcestis* 691, where Pheres indignantly refuses to
die in the place of his son Admetus, saying: "You delight in seeing the light: does it seem to
you that a father does not delight?"

and to me at least, it also seems fitting to concede to them[218] what
    is fair.
For it's proper for us to weep if we do things that aren't just.
    PHEID. Consider yet another notion.
    STREP.   No, for I'll be ruined!   1440
    PHEID. And yet perhaps you won't be annoyed at suffering what
    you've just suffered.
    STREP. How so? Teach me how you'll benefit me from this.
    PHEID. I'll beat my mother too, just as I did you.
    STREP.   What are you saying? What are you saying?
This other one is a still greater evil!
    PHEID.   But what if I defeat you
by means of the weaker speech, saying   1445
that one *should* beat one's mother?
    STREP. If you do this, then nothing
will prevent you from throwing yourself
into the Pit[219]
along with Socrates   1450
and the weaker speech!
[*To the Chorus.*]
I have suffered these things because of you, O Clouds,
from referring all my affairs to you.
    CHORUS [*the leading Cloud speaking*].
No, you yourself are responsible for these things by yourself,
because you twisted yourself into villainous affairs.   1455
    STREP. Then why didn't you tell me this back then
instead of stirring up an old and rustic man?
    CHORUS. We do this on each occasion to whomever
we recognize as being a lover of villainous affairs,
until we throw him into evil   1460
so that he may know dread of the gods.
    STREP. Oh me! This is villainous, O Clouds, but just.
For I shouldn't have deprived them of the money
I borrowed.
[*To Pheidippides.*]
          So now, dearest one, come with me
and destroy the wretch Chaerephon and Socrates,   1465
who have deceived you and me!
    PHEID. But I wouldn't do injustice to my teachers.

---

[218]Them: the youth.

[219]The bodies of executed criminals were thrown into "the Pit," a place just outside the
walls of Athens.

STREP. Yes, yes! Have awe before ancestral Zeus!

PHEID. See! "Ancestral Zeus"! How ancient you are!
Is there any Zeus?

STREP.   There is!

PHEID.   No, there isn't, since   1470
Vortex is king, having driven out Zeus.

STREP. He has *not* driven him out, but I supposed he had
[*pointing to the drinking goblet lying on the ground*]
because of this "vortex" here.[220] Ah me, what a wretch I am
for holding that *you*, earthenware, were a god!

PHEID.
Be deranged and babble here by yourself!   1475
[*Exit.*]

STREP. Oh me! What derangement! How mad I was,
when I even threw out the gods because of Socrates!
But dear Hermes,[221] in no way be angry with me
and don't batter me, but forgive me
for being out of my mind with prating.   1480
And become my fellow counselor: should I prosecute them
with an indictment, or what seems fitting to you?
[*Pause.*]
You advise me correctly in not letting me stitch up a lawsuit,
but rather to set the house of the praters on fire
as quickly as possible.
[*Calling to a slave inside the house.*]
                            Come here, come here, Xanthias!   1485
Come outside with a ladder and bring a hoe!
[*Xanthias enters with this equipment.*]
Next go up onto the thinkery and
tear off the roof (if you love your master)
until you throw the house down upon them!

---

[220]The word *dinos* may mean either "vortex" or "goblet." Apparently Strepsiades misunderstood Socrates' assertion (that vortex [*dinos*] replaces Zeus, who does not even exist) to mean that the statue of Zeus was replaced by a goblet (*dinos*).

There is controversy over what Strepsiades points to on the stage. Our stage directions at 1320 and here indicate that he refers to a goblet that he himself dropped on the ground when he came out of the house. Another opinion, widely accepted by modern scholars, proposes that Strepsiades points to a large goblet (symbolizing Vortex) which stands next to the door of the thinkery, occupying the place of the statue of Hermes which regularly stood by the entrance of Athenian homes.

[221]It is not clear whether Strepsiades addresses a bust of Hermes outside his door or whether he simply looks off into the distance. Strepsiades certainly thinks or pretends that he hears Hermes at 1483.

[*Xanthias climbs up the ladder and begins to hack off the roof tiles with the hoe. Strepsiades again shouts into his house.*]

Someone bring me a lighted torch!   1490

[*Another slave enters with a torch, hands it to Strepsiades, and exits.*]

I too will make one of them pay the penalty today

to me, even if they are such great boasters!

[*Strepsiades ascends the ladder with the torch and begins to set fire to the rafters exposed where the tiles are being hacked away by Xanthias.*]

STUDENT [*within*]. Oh! Oh!

STREP. Your work, torch, is to send forth much flame!

STUDENT [*rushing out of the smoke-filled thinkery and seeing Strepsiades on the roof*].

You, fellow, what are you doing?

STREP.   What am I doing? What else but   1495
holding subtle conversation with the beams of the house?

2ND STUDENT [*comes out; the remaining students emerge over the next several lines*].

Oh me! Who's burning down our house?

STREP. The one whose cloak you took.

2ND STUDENT. You'll destroy us, you'll destroy us!

STREP.   Yes, that's the very thing I do wish for,
unless my hoe betrays my hopes   1500
or I first fall somehow and break my neck.

SOC. [*coming out*].

You there on the roof! Really, what are you doing?

STREP. "I tread on air and contemplate the sun."

SOC. Oh me, alas! Wretched me, I'll be choked!

2ND STUDENT. And I, miserably unhappy me, will be burned up!   1505

STREP. Yes, for why is it that you were hubristic toward the gods
and were looking into the seat of the Moon?

HERMES[222] [*the god himself appears*].

After them! Strike! Hit them because of many things,
but most of all since I know that they were doing injustice to the
        gods!

[*The thinkery is in flames. Climbing down the ladder, Strepsiades and his slave pursue Socrates and the students out of the theater.*]

CHORUS. Lead the way out, for we have chorused   1510
in due measure today.

[*The Clouds retire and exit.*]

---

[222]Some manuscripts and most modern scholars deny that Hermes appears at all. They attribute Hermes' lines to Strepsiades. The reading of Strauss, *Socrates and Aristophanes*, p. 46, is followed here.

Selected Bibliography

The items listed here are a small portion of a massive literature on Socrates and on the four works in this collection. The selections here include the best published writings in English on the dialogues and play, along with other items included as representative of current trends.

Readers should be aware that the assessments of these works are based on the understanding of Plato and Aristophanes that informs the Introduction.

The Bibliography is arranged under the following topics:

—Writings on Plato's *Apology of Socrates* (and on Plato or Socrates generally)
—Writings on Plato's *Euthyphro*
—Writings on Plato's *Crito*
—Writings on Aristophanes' *Clouds*
—Greek Texts: Plato
—Greek Texts: Aristophanes

Writings on Plato's *Apology of Socrates* (and on Plato or Socrates generally)

Alfarabi's Philosophy of Plato and Aristotle. Ed. and trans. Muhsin Mahdi. Rev. ed. Ithaca: Cornell University Press, 1969. Alfarabi, a ninth-century Islamic philosopher, presents a thoughtful overview of Plato's writings that is playful, elusive, and profound. The focus is on the political aspects of the thought of Plato and Socrates.

Allen, R. E. "The Trial of Socrates: A Study in the Morality of the Criminal Process." In *Socrates: Critical Assessments*, vol. 2. Ed. William J. Prior. New York: Routledge, 1996. Pp. 1–17. Repr. from *Courts and Trials: A Multi-disciplinary Approach*. Toronto: University of Toronto Press, 1975. Pp. 3–21. Allen criticizes the Athenians for supposedly denying Socrates a lawful trial. See also Allen's book listed under *Crito* below.

Anastaplo, George. *Human Being and Citizen: Essays on Virtue, Freedom, and the Common Good.* Chicago: Swallow Press, 1975. Ch. 2, "Human Being and

Citizen: A Beginning to the Study of the *Apology of Socrates*," contains useful observations about the dialogue.

Beckman, James. *The Religious Dimension of Socrates' Thought*. Waterloo, Ontario: Wilfred Laurier University Press, 1979. There are chapters on the *Apology* and *Crito*. Beckman takes Socrates' religious professions in the *Apology* seriously, but he makes it clear that Socrates' religion has little in common with that of the Athenians. Whatever the validity of its overall thesis, this book is useful.

Brann, Eva. *The Past-Present*. Annapolis, Md.: St. John's College Press, 1997. Pp. 81–98. "The Offense of Socrates: A Re-Reading of Plato's *Apology*," is a perceptive account of the *Apology* that emphasizes Socrates' guilt and his deliberate affront to Athenian customs and orthodoxy. Repr. from *Interpretation* 7 (1978), 1–21.

Brickhouse, Thomas C., and Nicholas D. Smith. *Socrates on Trial*. Princeton: Princeton University Press, 1989. An examination of the *Apology* that is easily satisfied with the surface of what Socrates says. The authors see in Socrates' speech nothing but a sincere effort to defend himself while telling the truth. The idea that Socrates might willingly have offended the jury, or made an argument that he knew was weak, is dismissed out of hand. That Socrates might actually have been guilty is inconceivable. For these reasons, Brickhouse and Smith barely mention the line of interpretation presented in the Introduction to *Four Texts* and in West's book on the *Apology*.

Clay, Diskin. "Socrates' Mulishness and Heroism." *Phronesis* 17 (1972), 53–60. This witty article makes sense of some of the peculiarities of Socrates' speech in the *Apology*, especially concerning his *daimonion* and his implicit claim to heroism.

Cropsey, Joseph. *Plato's World: Man's Place in the Cosmos*. Chicago: University of Chicago Press, 1995. This is an account by a leading scholar of his generation of the *Euthyphro, Apology, Crito,* and five other dialogues. At first it reads like a series of unremarkable plot summaries, but on closer attention it discloses many sage and sensible observations marshalled to yield a coherent and controversial account of "Plato's world."

Feaver, Douglas D., and John E. Hare. "The *Apology* as an Inverted Parody of Rhetoric." *Arethusa* 14 (1981), 205–216. The authors maintain that "every section of Socrates' main speech is in fact a parody, using the traditional [rhetorical] form with the reverse of the function traditionally associated with it." Their argument is persuasive.

Fox, Marvin. "The Trials of Socrates: An Interpretation of the First Tetralogy." *Archiv für Philosophie* 6 (1956), 226–261. Argues plausibly that the "*Apology*, *Crito*, and *Phaedo* may be fruitfully understood as three versions of the trial of Socrates." A useful discussion.

Friedländer, Paul. *Plato*. Vol. 2, *The Dialogues: First Period*. Translated by Hans Meyerhoff. New York: Pantheon, 1964. Although Friedländer pays some attention to the dramatic features of the dialogues and their bearing on the arguments, his approach remains mostly "conventional" (see Guthrie for explanation). There are separate chapters on the *Euthyphro, Apology,* and *Crito.* The author was a well-known classicist, and his work is still widely read.

Fustel de Coulanges, Numa Denis. *The Ancient City: A Classic Study of the Religious and Civil Institutions of Ancient Greece and Rome.* Translated by Arnaldo Momigliano and S. C. Humphreys. Baltimore: Johns Hopkins University Press, 1980. First published in 1864, this study illuminates the nature of the prephilosophic self-understanding of the ancients. Fustel conveys a vivid sense of the lingering traditions of Greek piety that Socrates opposed in his thought.

Guthrie, W. K. C. *Socrates.* Cambridge: Cambridge University Press, 1971. This book competently presents the generally accepted contemporary view of the life and thought of Socrates. Those who favor this view try to understand Socrates by gathering together his statements on various topics from different dialogues, rather than by first studying each dialogue by itself to discover the underlying thought informing Socrates' remarks on each occasion. Guthrie's book and other "conventional" interpretations tend to accept Socrates' statements at face value and to underestimate the philosophical import of the dramatic settings and features of the Platonic dialogues.

Hathaway, Ronald. "Law and the Moral Paradox in Plato's *Apology.*" *Journal of the History of Philosophy* 8 (1970), 127–142. A sensible consideration of the dialogue, concentrating on the deliberately paradoxical stance adopted by Socrates in his examination of Meletus.

Havelock, Eric. "Why Was Socrates Tried?" In *Studies in Honour of Gilbert Norwood,* edited by Mary E. White. *Phoenix* suppl. vol. 1. Toronto: University of Toronto Press, 1952. Pp. 95–109. Argues that Socrates was prosecuted because he challenged the traditional Athenian education of young men, conducted informally by the old families and prominent citizens.

Hegel, Georg W. F. *Lectures on the History of Philosophy.* Vol. 1, *Greek Philosophy to Plato.* Translated by E. S. Haldane. 1892; repr. Lincoln, Neb.: University of Nebraska Press, 1995. Hegel presents in his account of Socrates' trial and death (pp. 426–448) his famous thesis that it was a genuine tragedy, in which both sides were right: Athens' "abstractly objective freedom," which expressed itself in its conviction that it possessed divine right, opposed Socrates' "subjective freedom," which expressed itself in philosophy. Hegel discusses the *Clouds* on pp. 426–430.

Kendall, Willmoore. *Willmoore Kendall Contra Mundum.* Ed. Nellie D. Kendall. 1971; repr. Lanham, Md.: University Press of America, 1994. "The People versus Socrates Revisited" (pp. 149–167) is a cogent defense of the Athenian jury that condemned Socrates to death.

Klein, Jacob. *A Commentary on Plato's Meno.* Chapel Hill: University of North Carolina Press, 1965. The "Introductory Remarks" (pp. 3–31) provide a fine discussion of how to read Plato, with emphasis on Plato's use of the dialogue form.

MacDowell, Douglas M. *The Law in Classical Athens.* Ithaca: Cornell University Press, 1978. A competent historical summary of the Athenian judicial system, this book contains reliable information on indictment and trial procedures, prosecutions for impiety, homicide, and so on.

Neumann, Harry. "Plato's *Defense of Socrates*: An Interpretation of Ancient and Modern Sophistry." *Liberal Education* 56 (1970), 458–475. Argues that the contemporary belief that Socrates was innocent is an instance of "modern sophistry," which wrongly transforms philosophy into ideology, i.e., passionate moral convictions that should not be questioned. Socratic philosophy questions above all those moral authorities closest to one's heart, but in order to appear respectable before political men it pretends, as Plato does, to be moralistic and "tragic." A thoughtful article.

Nietzsche, Friedrich. *The Birth of Tragedy*. Translated by Walter Kaufmann. New York: Random House (Vintage), 1967. Originally published 1872. This and other writings of Nietzsche, one of the greatest philosophers of the past two centuries, offer a brilliant analysis and critique of Socrates. Here Socrates is presented as the incarnation of the scientific spirit. Along with Euripides, he successfully supplanted the pessimistic "Dionysian" wisdom of Greek tragedy.

Nietzsche, Friedrich. "The Problem of Socrates." In *Twilight of the Idols*. In *The Portable Nietzsche*, edited by Walter Kaufmann. 1954; repr. New York: Penguin, 1977. This is Nietzsche's pithy restatement of his case against Socrates, who is presented in this late work (1889) as the man who out of weakness and perhaps desperation taught the decadent Greeks to believe in the healing power of reason.

Redfield, James. "A Lecture on Plato's *Apology*." *Journal of General Education* 15 (1963), 93–108. A sound overview of the dialogue, considerably superior to the usual treatments, but somewhat lacking in the detail of its argument.

Reeve, C. D. C. *Socrates in the Apology: An Essay on Plato's Apology of Socrates*. Indianapolis: Hackett, 1989. A conventional, earnest treatment that gives a learned defense of the surface meaning of what Socrates says. Reeve has little patience for the view of Socrates presented in the Introduction to this volume.

Sallis, John. *Being and Logos: The Way of Platonic Dialogue*. Pittsburgh: Duquesne University Press, 1975. Contains analyses of the *Apology* and several other dialogues. The author appears to be a phenomenologist influenced by Husserl and Heidegger, as well as by the Platonic studies of Leo Strauss and Jacob Klein.

Santas, Gerasimos X. *Socrates: Philosophy in Plato's Early Dialogues*. Boston: Routledge & Kegan Paul, 1979. Chapter 2 discusses the apparent conflict between the *Apology* and *Crito*. The approach is "analytical" (see Vlastos entry below).

Schaefer, David L. "Was Socrates a Corrupter? A Study of Plato's *Apology of Socrates*" in *Law and Philosophy: The Practice of Theory: Essays in Honor of George Anastaplo*. Vol. I. Ed. John Murley et al. Athens: Ohio University Press, 1992. Pp. 73–83. Schaefer argues that Socrates recognizes a tension between philosophy and the city, but that Socrates has a coherent argument showing that philosophy is beneficial to the city.

Sesonske, Alexander. "To Make the Weaker Argument Defeat the Stronger." *Journal of the History of Philosophy* 6 (1968), 217–231, In the *Apology* Socrates reports that he was accused of "making the weaker speech the stronger." Sesonske points out that Socrates not only never responds to this charge but also commits the wrong in question in the course of his defense speech.

Stone, I. F. *The Trial of Socrates*. New York: Doubleday, 1988. This book, by a retired journalist who became an ardent classical scholar, was a best seller. The author is a liberal upset by Socrates' trial and death. He interprets the trial in that light.

Strauss, Leo. *The City and Man*. Chicago: Rand McNally, 1964. The beginning of the chapter on Plato's *Republic* (pp. 50–62) is an excellent general discussion of how to read a Platonic dialogue.

Strauss, Leo. *Studies in Platonic Political Philosophy*. Chicago: University of Chicago Press, 1984. Ch. 2, "On Plato's *Apology of Socrates* and *Crito*," is the most thoughtful available account of the two dialogues, but it is written in the elusive manner of Strauss's late works.

Strycker, Emile de. *Plato's Apology of Socrates: A Literary and Philosophical Study with a Running Commentary*. Ed. and completed by S. R. Slings. New York: E. J. Brill, 1994. The treatment of the *Apology* here is mostly conventional. There is an extensive commentary on individual Greek phrases that supplements Burnet's commentary on the Greek text, listed at the end of the Bibliography below.

Taylor, A. E. *Socrates: The Man and His Thought*. Garden City: Doubleday Anchor, 1953. A good summary of the generally accepted view of Socrates that has prevailed for a century or more.

Umphrey, Stewart. "*Eros* and *Thumos*." *Interpretation* 10 (1982), 353–422. Contains a sharp critique of West's *Apology* book. This essay defends the view that Socrates was innocent of the charges for which he was tried. Umphrey suggests that Socratic philosophizing is based on an illusion, since Socrates acts upon the conviction that the philosophical way of life is good although he admits that he does not know the good.

Vlastos, Gregory, ed. *The Philosophy of Socrates: A Collection of Critical Essays*. Garden City: Doubleday Anchor, 1971. Contains fourteen essays on various topics mostly authored by those who favor Vlastos' "analytical" approach to Plato. This approach typically subjects a particular argument from a dialogue to close logical analysis. The argument is often (and rightly) found wanting. The disadvantage of this approach is that it tends not to consider the place of the argument within the dialogue from which it is taken. For example, in many cases Socrates deliberately employs a bad argument as part of his larger rhetorical or philosophical strategy. The first two essays (by Vlastos and A. R. Lacey) present a general account of Socrates' thought.

West, Thomas G. "Defending Socrates and Defending Politics." In *Natural Right and Political Right: Essays in Honor of Harry V. Jaffa*. Ed. Thomas B. Silver and Peter W. Schramm. Durham: Carolina Academic Press, 1984. Pp. 235–249. Also in *Interpretation* 11 (1983), 383–397. Responds to Stewart Umphrey's "*Eros* and *Thumos*" (see above).

West, Thomas G. *Plato's Apology of Socrates: An Interpretation, with a New Trans-lation*. Ithaca: Cornell University Press, 1979. Contains a section-by-section analysis of the argument of the dialogue. This is the account of the *Apology of Socrates* that is summarized in the Introduction above, pp. 16–24.

Xenophon. *Apology of Socrates to the Jury*. Several translations are available. Xenophon, a student of Socrates, presents in his *Apology* a version of Socra-tes' trial somewhat different from Plato's. Socrates' trial and the charge against him are also discussed in Xenophon's *Memorabilia*, trans. Amy L. Bonnette (Ithaca: Cornell University Press, 1994), bk. 1, chs. 1–2 and bk. 4, ch. 8.

Zuckert, Michael. "Rationalism and Political Responsibility: Just Speech and Just Deed in the *Clouds* and the *Apology of Socrates*." *Polity* 17 (1984), 271–297. Explores two themes: "the *Apology* as a response to Aristophanes' cri-tique of Socrates in the *Clouds*"; and "Plato, art imitating art, has taken the most significant structural feature of the *Apology* from the *Clouds*." Zuckert develops a critique of both Allen (below, under *Crito*) and West's book on the *Apology*. He thinks Socrates' defense speech is rhetorically effective for its true purpose: "Socrates chooses to die that philosophy may live."

Writings on Plato's *Euthyphro*

See the chapters on, or discussions of, the *Euthyphro* in the writings by the following authors, listed under *Apology of Socrates* above: Alfarabi, Beck-man, Cropsey, Friedländer.

Allen, R. E. *Plato's Euthyphro and the Earlier Theory of Forms*. New York: Hu-manities Press, 1970. The dialogue is examined with a view to Plato's sup-posed philosophical development; the teaching of the *Euthyphro* on piety is of secondary interest to the author.

Anastaplo, George. "Rome, Piety, and Law: Explorations." *Loyola Law Review* 39 (1993), 873–882. In the context of an examination of famous "trials," Anastaplo argues that Socrates benefited the city and Euthyphro's family by attempting to restrain the pious excesses of Euthyphro.

Blits, Jan H. "The Holy and the Human: An Interpretation of Plato's *Euthy-phro*." *Apeiron* 14 (1980), 19–40. This fine essay presents a detailed and persuasive reading of the entire dialogue. Socrates' implicit reduction of the pious to the realm of the human is the main theme.

Garrett, Roland. "The Structure of Plato's *Euthyphro*." *Southern Journal of Phi-losophy* 12 (1974), 165–183. Garrett makes some interesting suggestions about the role of motion and rest in the dialogue. Socrates seeks to move Euthyphro from being in constant motion to a position of stability, from the realm of shifting opinion and particularity to the firm ground of knowledge and universality.

Geach, P. T. "*Euthyphro*: An Analysis and Commentary." In *Socrates: Critical Assessments*. Vol. 3. Ed. William J. Prior. New York: Routledge, 1996. Pp. 152–162. Repr. from *The Monist* 50 (1966), 369–382. A brief evaluation of the logical validity of the several arguments advanced by Socrates and Euthyphro in the course of the dialogue. Geach concludes that both men argue badly for the most part. However, unlike many contemporary scholars, Geach does defend the argument that Socrates makes against Euthyphro's claim that piety is "what is dear to the gods."

Hoerber, Robert G. "Plato's *Euthyphro*." *Phronesis* 3 (1958), 95–107. A decent presentation of some leading features of the dialogue.

Lewis, Marlo. "An Interpretation of the *Euthyphro*." Part 1 is in *Interpretation* 12 (1984), 225–259; part 2 in *Interpretation* 13 (1985), 33–65. A thorough and thoughtful interpretation which takes into account not only the argument but also the dramatic setting of the *Euthyphro*.

McPherran, M. L. "Socratic Piety in the *Euthyphro*" and "Socratic Reason and Socratic Revelation." In *Socrates: Critical Assessments*. Vol. 2. Ed. William J. Prior. New York: Routledge, 1996. Pp. 118–143, 167–194. Repr. from *Journal of the History of Philosophy* 23 (1985), 283–309, and 29 (1991), 345–73. Two articles using the "analytic" approach (see Vlastos above). "Socratic Piety" is also reprinted as ch. 13 of *Essays on the Philosophy of Socrates*, ed. Hugh H. Benson. New York: Oxford University Press, 1992.

Neumann, Harry. "The Problem of Piety in Plato's *Euthyphro*." *The Modern Schoolman* 43 (1966), 265–272. An excellent essay that relates Euthyphro's character to his belief in personal deities and contrasts his self-oriented piety with Socrates' impersonal, rational approach.

Rabinowitz, W. Gerson. "Platonic Piety: An Essay toward the Solution of an Enigma." *Phronesis* 3 (1958), 108–120. Argues that the *Euthyphro* identifies the gods with mind or thought (*nous*). An interesting essay but not fully persuasive.

Rosen, Frederick. "Piety and Justice: Plato's *Euthyphro*." *Philosophy* 42 (1968), 105–115. A sensible essay, although not as thorough and convincing as Blits's, Lewis's, or Strauss's, with which it may be compared. Rosen argues that according to Socrates "justice, not piety, connects the human and the divine."

Strauss, Leo. *The Rebirth of Classical Political Rationalism*. Ed. Thomas Pangle. Chicago: University of Chicago, 1989. "On the *Euthyphron*," pp. 187–206, is a very close reading which focuses on the Socratic investigation of piety and its relationship to the question of reason and revelation in general. Probably the best interpretation available.

Versenyi, Laszlo. *Holiness and Justice: An Interpretation of Plato's Euthyphro*. Washington: University Press of America, 1982. Contains a number of helpful suggestions for interpretation. Versenyi interprets the difference between Euthyphro and Socrates in light of the conflict between traditional orthodoxy and the life of autonomous reason.

Vlastos, Gregory. *Socrates: Ironist and Moral Philosopher*. Ithaca: Cornell University Press, 1991. Ch. 6, "Socratic Piety," is helpful insofar as it looks at statements of Socrates from many dialogues touching on the subject of piety, but also somewhat questionable insofar as it abstracts from the dramatic setting of all the dialogues mentioned. Vlastos is a leading analytic philosopher (see Vlastos entry under *Apology* above).

Weiss, Roslyn. "Virtue Without Knowledge: Socrates' Conception of Holiness in Plato's *Euthyphro*." In *Socrates: Critical Assessments*. Vol. 2. Ed. William J. Prior. New York: Routledge, 1996. Pp. 195–216. Weiss argues that, for Socrates, piety is the virtue that does not require knowledge. An interesting article.

West, Elinor J. M. "An Ironic Dilemma, or Incompatible Interpretations of *Euthyphro* 5a–b." In *Plato's Dialogues: New Studies and Interpretations*. Ed. Gerald A. Press. Lanham, Md.: Rowman and Littlefield, 1993. Pp. 147–167. An examination of the issues of irony and the spoken word in the context of the opening scenes of the *Euthyphro*.

Writings on Plato's *Crito*

See the chapters on, or discussions of, the *Crito* in the writings by the following authors, listed under *Apology of Socrates* above: Alfarabi, Cropsey, Friedländer, Fox, Santas, Strauss.

Allen, R. E. *Socrates and Legal Obligation*. Minneapolis: University of Minnesota Press, 1980. Although the author repeats several conventional theses about the *Crito* (with which he is mostly concerned) and the *Apology*, he honestly attempts to rethink the argument of both dialogues, with some success.

Anastaplo, George. *Human Being and Citizen: Essays on Virtue, Freedom, and the Common Good*. Chicago: Swallow Press, 1975. Ch. 16, "Citizen and Human Being: Thoreau, Socrates, and Civil Disobedience," presents a brief but useful comparison of Thoreau and the Socrates of Plato's *Crito*.

Brown, Hunter. "The Structure of Plato's *Crito*." *Apeiron* 25 (1992), 67–82. Argues that Crito never really accepts Socrates' argument that one should never do harm in retaliation for a harm; Socrates therefore shifts the ground of the conversation to a ground that Crito accepts, namely, that the harm to the city's laws *in this case* is not justified. This analysis is helpful in understanding Socrates' rhetorical strategy with Crito.

Coby, Patrick. "The Philosopher Outside the City." In *Law and Philosophy: The Practice of Theory: Essays in Honor of George Anastaplo*. Vol. I. Ed. John Murley et al. Athens: Ohio University Press, 1992. Pp. 84–110. This essay is one of the best available on the *Crito*. It takes a strong stance against the Kraut book (below), arguing that Socrates' apparent patriotism and respect for law are not his real position. Coby discusses the *apolitical* Socrates of the *Crito* in this article; for his discussion of the *political* Socrates of the *Crito*, see his *Socrates and the Sophistic Enlightenment: A Commentary on Plato's Protagoras* (Lewisburg, Pa.: Bucknell University Press, 1987), pp. 183–187.

Colson, Darrel D. "*Crito* 51A–C: to what does Socrates owe obedience?" *Phronesis* 34 (1989), 27–55. Colson examines the apparent contradiction between Socrates' claim that he will never stop philosophizing in the *Apology* and his argument for obedience to the laws in the *Crito*. Colson argues that there is no real contradiction between the two.

Herrera, C. D. "Civil Disobedience and Plato's *Crito*." *The Southern Journal of Philosophy* 33 (1995), 39–55. A reading of the *Crito* that focuses on what links the dialogue might have to contemporary questions concerning civil disobedience. Herrera concludes that the *Crito* has little if anything to do with it.

Hyland, Drew A. "Why Plato Wrote Dialogues." *Philosophy and Rhetoric* 1 (1968), 38–50. Contains a sound discussion (at pp. 44–49) of the dramatic situation facing Socrates in the *Crito,* namely, the need to persuade a non-philosopher to approve the actions of a philosopher.

Kahn, Charles. "Problems in the Argument of Plato's *Crito*." *Apeiron* 22 (1989), 29–43. Another example of the "analytical" approach by a prominent classicist.

Kraut, Richard. *Socrates and the State.* Princeton: Princeton University Press, 1984. Kraut argues that the speech of the laws presented by Socrates in the *Crito* (calling on Socrates either "to persuade us" or "obey") is compatible with Socrates' statement in the *Apology* that he will never stop philosophizing, even if the Athenian people order him not to. Kraut's argument rests on his strange claim that when the laws say "persuade," they mean "try to persuade." That is, as long as one openly confesses and justifies one's disobedience, the laws will not object. Clifford Orwin presents a brief but powerful critique of Kraut, to which Kraut responds, in *Platonic Writings, Platonic Readings,* ed. Charles L. Griswold. New York: Routledge, 1988. Pp. 171–182. See also Coby's critique in the article listed above.

Martin, Rex. "Socrates on Disobeying the Law." *Review of Metaphysics* 24 (1970), 21–36. Maintains that Socrates in the *Crito* argues that all laws must unqualifiedly be obeyed, whether just or unjust. Martin presents some reasonable criticisms of this argument—criticisms with which Socrates probably agrees to a greater extent than Martin suspects.

McNeal, Richard A. *Law and Rhetoric in the Crito.* New York: Peter Lang, 1992. This is an unusual book whose approach the author calls "Neoplatonic" or "Plotinian." Seeing "mysticism" in the *Crito,* McNeal's focus is on the speech of the laws, which is said to contain a natural law doctrine, as well as evidence of Plato's "religious belief in the reality of god."

Miller, Mitchell. "'The Arguments I Seem to Hear': Argument and Irony in the *Crito*." *Phronesis* 41 (1996), 121–137. Miller here makes the case that there is an ironic element in the argument that the laws proffer. There are some good observations here, but the article is not of the same rank as Strauss and Coby.

Panagiotou, Spiro. "Socrates and Civil Disobedience." In *Socratic Questions: New Essays on the Philosophy of Socrates and Its Significance.* Ed. Barry S. Gower and Michael C. Stokes. London: Routledge, 1992. Pp. 93–121. An examination of the arguments of Crito, Socrates, and the laws in the *Crito*. In typical "analytic" fashion, it takes Socrates at face value.

Payne, Thomas. "The *Crito* as a Mythological Mime." *Interpretation* 11 (1983), 1–23. Argues persuasively that the *Crito* reenacts in important respects the embassy scene in Homer's *Iliad*, Book IX, in which Odysseus and others try to persuade Achilles to rejoin the Achaean army.

Penner, Terry. "Two Notes on the *Crito*: The Impotence of the Many, and 'Persuade or Obey.'" *Classical Quarterly* 47 (1997), 153–166. Penner takes issue with the common interpretation of the intention of the many in offering harm (Burnet, Allen) and Kraut's liberalization of the argument of the laws in the *Crito*.

Rosen, Frederick. "Obligation and Friendship in Plato's *Crito*." *Political Theory* 1 (1973), 307–316. A good treatment that examines the links between dramatic detail and explicit argument in the *Crito*.

Vlastos, Gregory. *Studies in Greek Philosophy Volume II: Socrates, Plato, and Their Tradition*. Princeton: Princeton University Press, 1995. "Socrates on Political Obedience and Disobedience," pp. 30–42, is an attempt, using the techniques of analytic philosophy, to reconcile the seemingly contradictory claims of Socrates that he will never stop philosophizing (*Apology*) and that one must obey the law (*Crito*). Repr. from *Yale Review* 63 (1974), 517–534.

Weinrib, Ernest J. "Obedience to the Law in Plato's *Crito*." *American Journal of Jurisprudence* 27 (1982), 85–108. "The speeches of the Laws, with which Socrates closes, are not intended to be philosophically cogent, since they are inconsistent with the principles laid out in the preceding conversation between Socrates and Crito. The arguments of the Laws are rather directed towards Crito, Socrates' decent and unphilosophic friend."

Weiss, Roslyn. *Socrates Dissatisfied: An Analysis of Plato's Crito*. New York: Oxford University Press, 1998. A detailed examination of the *Crito*. An intelligent and helpful work.

White, James Boyd. "Plato's *Crito*: The Authority of Law and Philosophy." In *The Greeks and Us: Essays in Honor of Arthur W. H. Adkins*. Ed. Robert B. Louden and Paul Schollmeier. Chicago: University of Chicago Press, 1996. Pp. 97–133. A sensible account of the dialogue.

Woozley, A. D. *Law and Obedience: The Arguments of Plato's Crito*. Chapel Hill: University of North Carolina Press, 1979. Presents a straightforward but not very penetrating analysis of the leading arguments of the *Crito*. Vlastos's *The Philosophy of Socrates* (listed above under *Apology*) also contains an essay by Woozley on the *Crito*.

Yaffe, Martin D. "Civil Disobedience and the Opinion of the Many: Plato's *Crito*." *The Modern Schoolman* 54 (1977), 123–136. A helpful overview of the argument for obeying the laws.

Young, Gary. "Socrates and Obedience." *Phronesis* 19 (1974), 1–29. Presents a logical analysis of the arguments in the *Crito* (and *Apology of Socrates*) for obedience to the laws. Young argues that the defect of the arguments used by Socrates in the *Crito* may be traced to his speaking *ad hominem* to Crito, a non-philosopher.

Writings on Aristophanes' *Clouds*

See the chapters on, or discussions of, the Clouds in the writings by the following authors, listed under *Apology of Socrates* above: Alfarabi, Friedländer, Hegel, Zuckert.

Adkins, A. W. H. "Clouds, Mysteries, Socrates, and Plato." *Antichthon* 4
(1970), 13–24. Argues that by making Socrates abuse the language of religious initiation in the *Clouds,* Aristophanes deliberately arouses in the
Athenian audience "a response of pious fear, detestation and execration of
Socrates and all his works."

Bowie, A. M. *Aristophanes: Myth, Ritual, and Comedy.* Cambridge: Cambridge
University Press, 1993. The plays of Aristophanes are explained in light of
Greek customs and attitudes (Athenian in particular) that would have af-
fected how the audience reacted to the plays. There is a chapter on the
Clouds.

Dover, K. J. *Aristophanic Comedy.* Berkeley: University of California Press,
1972. Discusses all of the surviving plays, including such matters as staging
production techniques, literary structure, and plots. A good presentation of
the prevailing conventional view of Aristophanes. The chapter on the
Clouds presents the play as a condemnation of the new scientific attitudes
about nature and society that were being discussed in Aristophanes'
Athens.

Dover, K. J. "Socrates in the *Clouds.*" In *The Philosophy of Socrates: A Collection
of Critical Essays.* Edited by Gregory Vlastos. Garden City: Doubleday Anchor, 1971. Pp. 50–78. (Reprinted from Dover's edition of the *Clouds;* see
"Greek Texts" below.) This essay presents the prevailing view of the *Clouds:*
"Aristophanes attaches to Socrates the characteristics that belonged to the
sophists in general but did not belong to Socrates."

Edmunds, Lowell. "Aristophanes' Socrates." *Proceedings of the Boston Area Col-
loquium in Ancient Philosophy* 1 (1985), 209–230. A helpful introduction.

Harriot, Rosemary. *Aristophanes: Poet and Dramatist.* Baltimore: Johns Hopkins
University Press, 1986. A book that focuses on the dramatic aspects of Aristophanes' work. Includes a chapter on the *Clouds.*

Havelock, Eric A. "The Socratic Self as It Is Parodied in Aristophanes'
Clouds." *Yale Classical Studies* 22: *Studies in Fifth-Century Thought and Litera-
ture.* Edited by Adam Parry. Cambridge: Cambridge University Press, 1972.
Pp. 1–18. Contains several observations (especially concerning common vo-
cabulary) that suggest a close connection between the Aristophanic and
Platonic Socrates.

Kleve, Knut. "Anti-Dover or Socrates in the Clouds." *Symbolae Osloenses* 58
(1983), 23–37. In a light tone, this article shows numerous parallels between
the Socrates of the *Clouds* and the Socrates of Plato and Xenophon.

MacDowell, Douglas M. *Aristophanes and Athens: An Introduction to the Plays.*
New York: Oxford University Press, 1995. Ch. 6 is a very readable introduction to the *Clouds* for students. It presents the "conventional" view of the
play (see Dover above).

Marianetti, Marie C. *Religion and Politics in Aristophanes' Clouds*. Hildesheim 1992.

Neumann, Harry. "Civic Piety and Socratic Atheism: An Interpretation of Strauss' *Socrates and Aristophanes*." *Independent Journal of Philosophy* 2 (1978), 33–37. Proposes a radical reading of Strauss's difficult book. Provocative and persuasive, this essay should be read along with *Socrates and Aristophanes* to appreciate the scope of Aristophanes' thought and claim to godhood.

Neumann, Harry. "Socrates in Plato and Aristophanes." *American Journal of Philology* 90 (1969), 201–214. A thoughtful contrast of the Socrates of Plato's *Republic,* who refuses to criticize the traditional religious convictions of old Cephalus as long as Cephalus is present, with the Socrates of the *Clouds,* who openly attacks Strepsiades' belief in Zeus.

Nichols, Mary P. *Socrates and the Political Community: An Ancient Debate*. Albany: State University of New York Press, 1987. Part I, pp. 7–28, is an intelligent and helpful treatment of the *Clouds.*

Nussbaum, Martha. "Aristophanes and Socrates on Learning Practical Wisdom" in *Socrates: Critical Assessments*. Vol. 1. Ed. William J. Prior. New York: Routledge, 1996. Pp. 74–118. Takes the *Clouds* seriously as a presentation of Aristophanes' understanding of morality and education. Repr. from *Yale Classical Studies* 26: *Aristophanes: Essays in Interpretation*. Ed. Jeffrey Henderson. Cambridge: Cambridge University Press, 1980. Pp. 43–97.

O'Regan, Daphne Elizabeth. *Rhetoric, Comedy, and the Violence of Language in Aristophanes' Clouds*. New York: Oxford University Press, 1992. The play is interpreted as a drama revealing the weakness of speech and logic in comparison with nature and the body. There are many helpful observations here.

Plato. *Symposium*. Many translations available. Aristophanes' speech at this famous fictional banquet is a profound Platonic commentary on the poet's project in his comedies.

Rosen, Stanley. *Plato's Symposium*. Ch. 5, "Aristophanes," has an intelligent discussion of the *Clouds*; it also shows how Aristophanes' speech in the *Symposium* casts light on the meaning of the play.

Segal, Eric, ed. *Oxford Readings in Aristophanes*. Oxford: Oxford University Press, 1996. Contains essays on Aristophanes' politics, the nature of comedy, various Aristophanic plays, and a chapter by Charles Segal on the cloud-chorus in the *Clouds.*

Strauss, Leo. *The Rebirth of Classical Political Rationalism*. Ed. Thomas Pangle. Chicago: Chicago University Press, 1989. "The Problem of Socrates: Five Lectures." Pp. 103–183. The first two of these lectures deal with the problem of Socrates as presented by Aristophanes. A transcript of public lectures, it is easier to understand than Strauss's book, *Socrates and Aristophanes.*

Strauss, Leo. *Socrates and Aristophanes*. New York: Basic Books, 1966. Discussion of *Clouds,* pp. 9–53. This is the best available account of the *Clouds,* and

Strauss is one of the few who regard Aristophanes as a serious thinker of the rank of Socrates himself.

Vander Waerdt, Paul A. "Socrates in the Clouds." In *The Socratic Movement.* Ed. Paul A. Vander Waerdt. Ithaca: Cornell University Press, 1994. Pp. 48– 86. The author argues against Dover that the Socrates of the *Clouds* is a comically exaggerated version of the real Socrates. He presents evidence that the young Socrates was a student of Diogenes of Apollonia, a Greek physicist.

Whitman, Cedric H. *Aristophanes and the Comic Hero.* Cambridge: Harvard University Press, 1964. A conventional account by a well known classical scholar. In his chapter on the *Clouds* Whitman calls the play an "unsatisfy- ing" portrayal of the "war between the generations" that arose because of the new sophistical education in Athens.

Greek Texts: Plato

Burnet, John, ed. *Plato's Euthyphro, Apology of Socrates, and Crito.* Oxford: Clarendon Press, 1924. Contains the standard Greek text of all three dia- logues along with many detailed historical and philological notes. The grammatical notes are supplemented by Strycker, *Plato's Apology of Socrates,* listed above.

Hare, John E., ed. *Plato's Euthyphro.* Bryn Mawr Commentaries. Bryn Mawr: Department of Greek, Bryn Mawr College, 1981. Reprints Burnet's Oxford text with grammatical notes useful for those who wish to read the work in the original Greek.

Helm, James J., ed. Plato. *Apology.* Chicago: Bolchazy-Carducci Publishers, 1981. Reprints Burnet's Oxford text with the grammatical notes useful for those who wish to read the work in the original Greek.

Rose, Gilbert P., ed. *Plato's Crito.* Bryn Mawr Commentaries. Bryn Mawr: De- partment of Greek, Bryn Mawr College, 1980. Reprints Burnet's Oxford text with grammatical notes useful for those who wish to read the work in the original Greek.

Greek Texts: Aristophanes

Aristophanes, *Clouds: Text.* Bryn Mawr: Bryn Mawr Greek Commentaries, 1987. The companion volume to Barnard, below.

Barnard, Laura Stone. *Aristophanes' Clouds: Commentary.* Bryn Mawr: Bryn Mawr Greek Commentaries, 1987. Contains grammatical and other notes helpful to students reading the Greek text.

Dover, K. J., ed. Aristophanes. *Clouds.* Oxford: Clarendon Press, 1968. The best available Greek text of the *Clouds,* with thorough historical and philological notes.

Sommerstein, Alan H., ed. *The Comedies of Aristophanes,* vol. 3, *Clouds.* War- minster, Wilts., England: Aris and Phillips, 1982. Contains a Greek text and a good prose translation with explanatory notes like ours. Sommerstein's editions of Aristophanes' other plays also contain prose translations, which are among the most accurate available.

Starkie, W. J. M., ed. Aristophanes. *Clouds*. 1911; repr. Amsterdam: Hakkert, 1966. This edition, containing the Greek text and copious notes, was considered the best until Dover's appeared.